TEST ITEM FILE

PAUL KALDJIAN
University of Wisconsin–Eau Claire

PAUL L. KNOX   SALLIE A. MARSTON

Prentice
Hall

Upper Saddle River, NJ 07458

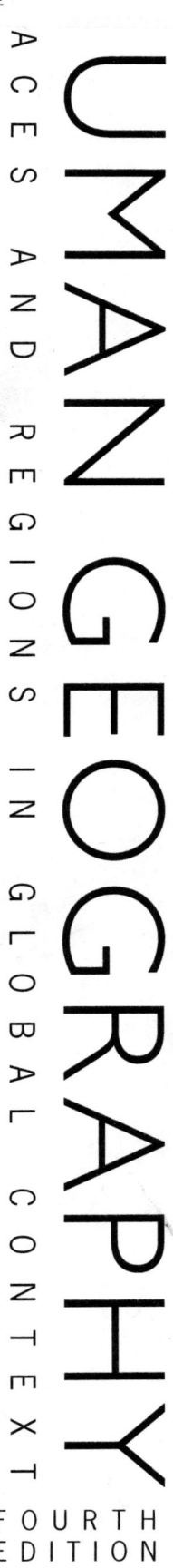

UMAN GEOGRAPHY

ACES AND REGIONS IN GLOBAL CONTEXT

FOURTH
EDITION

Editor-in-Chief, Science: Dan Kaveney
Acquisitions Editor, Geography: Jeff Howard
Associate Editor, Geography: Amanda Brown
Executive Managing Editor: Kathleen Schiaparelli
Senior Managing Editor: Nicole M. Jackson
Assistant Managing Editor: Karen Bosch
Production Editor: Gina M. Cheselka
Supplement Cover Manager: Paul Gourhan
Supplement Cover Designer: Christopher Kossa
Manufacturing Buyer: Ilene Kahn
Manufacturing Manager: Alexis Heydt-Long

© 2007 Pearson Education, Inc.

Pearson Prentice Hall

Pearson Education, Inc.

Upper Saddle River, NJ 07458

Printed in the United States of America

10 9 8 7 6 5 4 3 2 1

ISBN 0-13-154779-8

Pearson Education Ltd., *London*
Pearson Education Australia Pty. Ltd., *Sydney*
Pearson Education Singapore, Pte. Ltd.
Pearson Education North Asia Ltd., *Hong Kong*
Pearson Education Canada, Inc., *Toronto*
Pearson Educación de Mexico, S.A. de C.V.
Pearson Education—Japan, *Tokyo*
Pearson Education Malaysia, Pte. Ltd.

Contents

Places and Regions in Global Context: Human Geography
4th Edition

Dear Colleague and Test-Bank User,

Let me welcome you to this revised collection of test questions by explaining what has been done to provide a meaningful pool of questions around which to construct exams. The questions are designed for readers of the latest edition of Knox and Marston's *Places and Regions in Global Context: Human Geography*—one of the most widely used textbooks in the United States for undergraduate-level, introductory human/culture geography courses.

For the first time, images are incorporated into test bank questions. As in typical test banks, this edition has a wide selection of multiple choice, true/false (T/F) questions, and matching questions. Now, some questions in the multiple choice and matching sections include maps, graphs and other images used in the text. Highly appropriate for geography, these range from technical questions—about map types for example—to questions of interpretation and understanding.

Also new to this test bank is a set of "minimal choice" questions for each chapter. Something of a hybrid between multiple choice and T/F, these test questions require the student to choose from only a pair of answer choices. In contrast to T/F, students are not required to consider the world of correct and incorrect possibilities. "Minimal choice" questions are like multiple choice questions in which the student has narrowed the choice down to two answers. They provide a sometimes-needed variety to scan-form questions and are especially easy for the instructor to alter and adapt to specific style and content.

A third new feature of this test bank edition is a country identification section for each chapter. The Knox and Marston textbook is bursting with place-specific examples from across the globe. While place identification is usually the domain of regional geography classes, I find that many of my human/cultural geography students have no idea where on earth places are—they attempt to understand case studies, issues and examples in isolation, without knowing their location and spatial context. Every world map might as well be a *Rorschach* projection!!

In response, I have begun to require that my students be able to identify on a map those countries (and know their capitals) to which we refer in class. Initial indications are that learning the location of a handful of countries for each chapter has helped students improve their understanding of course content. By improving their global mental maps, they are improving the spatial framework into which to put new geographical knowledge. In turn, they are more receptive to following and caring about those global events and forces introduced in our courses.

Thus, for each chapter, the test bank provides a set of country identification questions based on the place-specific examples used in that chapter. With six or seven countries to learn for each chapter, a student will cover approximately 70 countries and their capitals by the end of the semester. Because all the country identification questions reference a single test map, questions from numerous chapters can be combined. Table 1 lists the countries that students need to know for each chapter; Table 2 is the key for the map used in the country identification questions. Figures 1a (world) and 1b (Europe) are the maps to which the country identification questions refer. In addition, these figures can be used by students for studying. Numerous other blank maps and a variety of place identification resources are available on the Companion Website. Table 3 shows the countries in the country identification by world region.

Finally, a note on the level of difficulty assigned to each question. While somewhat subjective, attempts have been made to base levels of difficulty on the nature of the understanding needed to answer correctly. Generally, levels of difficulty are as follows:

> **1 – conceptually simplest**, these questions require rote memorization of facts as presented in the text, including definitions, examples, figures, dates and values. These range from the prominent to the obscure;

> **2 – conceptually more complicated**, these can include relations and comparisons, and generally require a broad understanding of the concept;

> **3 – conceptually most involved,** these questions require a comprehension sufficient to apply learned concepts and principals to new examples and situations. Answers to these are not explicitly presented in the textbook, but can be determined with proper understanding. These questions can also combine concepts from throughout the chapter, or incorporate the text's overriding themes.

Whether you use the questions in the test bank as they are, or use them around which to develop your own, personalized exams, I hope that you find the questions useful. Ultimately, the goal is to save you time in ways that are meaningful to you and your students, and to allow you to concentrate your efforts on the other, more rewarding elements of teaching and learning. If you have any questions or suggestions for this test bank, please contact me or the editors at Prentice Hall.

Thank you,

Paul Kaldjian
Department of Geography & Anthropology
University of Wisconsin at Eau Claire

TABLE 1: COUNTRIES IN COUNTRY IDENTIFICATION QUESTIONS

Places and Regions in Global Context: Human Geography, 4th Edition

	Chapter 1	Chapter 2	Chapter 3	Chapter 4	Chapter 5	Chapter 6
1	Canada	Argentina	Bangladesh	Australia	Iran	Cuba
2	China	Ghana	Brazil	Bolivia	Iraq	England
3	Ethiopia	Japan	Cote D'Ivoire	Somalia	Mongolia	Indonesia
4	France	Kenya	Egypt	Dominican Rep.	Nigeria	Mali
5	India	USA	Germany	Haiti	Pakistan	Romania
6	Mexico	Portugal	Netherlands	Peru	Saudi Arabia	Sudan
7	Russia	Spain	S. Africa	Uganda	Sri Lanka	Venezuela
8	Kazakhstan	Morocco				

	Chapter 7	Chapter 8	Chapter 9	Chapter 10	Chapter 11	Chapter 12
1	Angola	Chile	Afghanistan	Belgium	Colombia	Botswana
2	Cambodia	Niger	Algeria	Turkey	Croatia	Bulgaria
3	Finland	Myanmar	Estonia	Guatemala	Ecuador	Dem. Rep. of the Congo
4	Namibia	New Zealand	Israel	Philippines	Hungary	Jamaica
5	Norway	Nicaragua	Latvia	Poland	Kazakhstan	Mozambique
6	Taiwan	Thailand	Lithuania	S. Korea	Libya	Ukraine
7	Yemen	Vietnam	Syria	Sweden	Morocco	Zambia
8			Azerbaijan			

TABLE 2: KEY TO MAPS

Places and Regions in Global Context: Human Geography, 4th Edition

World Map

1	Iraq	21	Angola	41	Indonesia	59	Afghanistan
2	Cote D'Ivoire	22	DRC	42	Philippines	60	Mongolia
3	Thailand	23	Sudan	43	Taiwan	62	S. Korea
4	Cambodia	24	Nigeria	44	Nicaragua	63	New Zealand
5	Vietnam	25	Mali	45	Guatemala	64	Australia
6	Syria	26	Algeria	46	Ecuador	65	Morocco
7	Myanmar (Burma)	27	Libya	47	Pakistan	66	China
8	Ghana	28	Egypt	48	Bangladesh	67	Japan
9	Uganda	29	Ethiopia	49	Sri Lanka	68	Niger
10	Russia	30	Colombia	50	Kenya		
11	Kazakhstan	32	Argentina	51	Israel		
12	Iran	33	Chile	52	Botswana		
13	Saudi Arabia	34	Bolivia	53	Zambia		
14	Yemen	35	Brazil	54	Venezuela		
15	Turkey	36	Peru	55	Cuba		
16	Romania	37	Mexico	56	Dominican Rep.		
17	Somalia	38	USA	56	Haiti		
19	S. Africa	39	Canada	57	Jamaica		
20	Namibia	40	Mozambique	58	India		

Map of Europe

1	Bulgaria
6	Croatia
7	Hungary
9	Poland
10	Russia
11	Latvia
12	Estonia
14	Ukraine
21	Germany
23	Norway
24	Sweden
25	Finland
26	Netherlands
27	Belgium
28	France
29	Spain
30	Portugal
31	England
34	Lithuania

TABLE 3: COUNTRIES FOR COUNTRY IDENTIFICATION, DISTRIBUTION BY WORLD REGION

Places and Regions in Global Context: Human Geography, 4th Edition

Middle East & North Africa	Other Core	Latin America	Europe
Afghanistan	Australia	Argentina	Azerbaijan
Algeria	Canada	Bolivia	Belgium
Egypt	New Zealand	Brazil	Bulgaria
Iran	USA	Chile	Croatia
Iraq		Colombia	England
Israel		Cuba	Estonia
Libya		Dominican Rep.	Finland
Morocco		Ecuador	France
Saudi Arabia		Guatemala	Germany
Syria		Haiti	Hungary
Turkey		Jamaica	Latvia
Yemen		Mexico	Lithuania
		Nicaragua	Netherlands
		Peru	Norway
		Venezuela	Poland
			Portugal
			Romania
			Russia
			Spain
			Sweden
			Ukraine

Sub-Saharan Africa	Central & East Asia	South Asia	Southeast Asia
Angola	China	Bangladesh	Cambodia
Botswana	Japan	India	Indonesia
Cote D'Ivoire	Kazakhstan	Myanmar	Philippines
Congo, Dem. Rep. of	Mongolia	Pakistan	Thailand
Ethiopia	S. Korea	Sri Lanka	Vietnam
Ghana	Taiwan		
Kenya			
Mali			
Mozambique			
Namibia			
Niger			
Nigeria			
S. Africa			
Somalia			
Sudan			
Uganda			
Zambia			

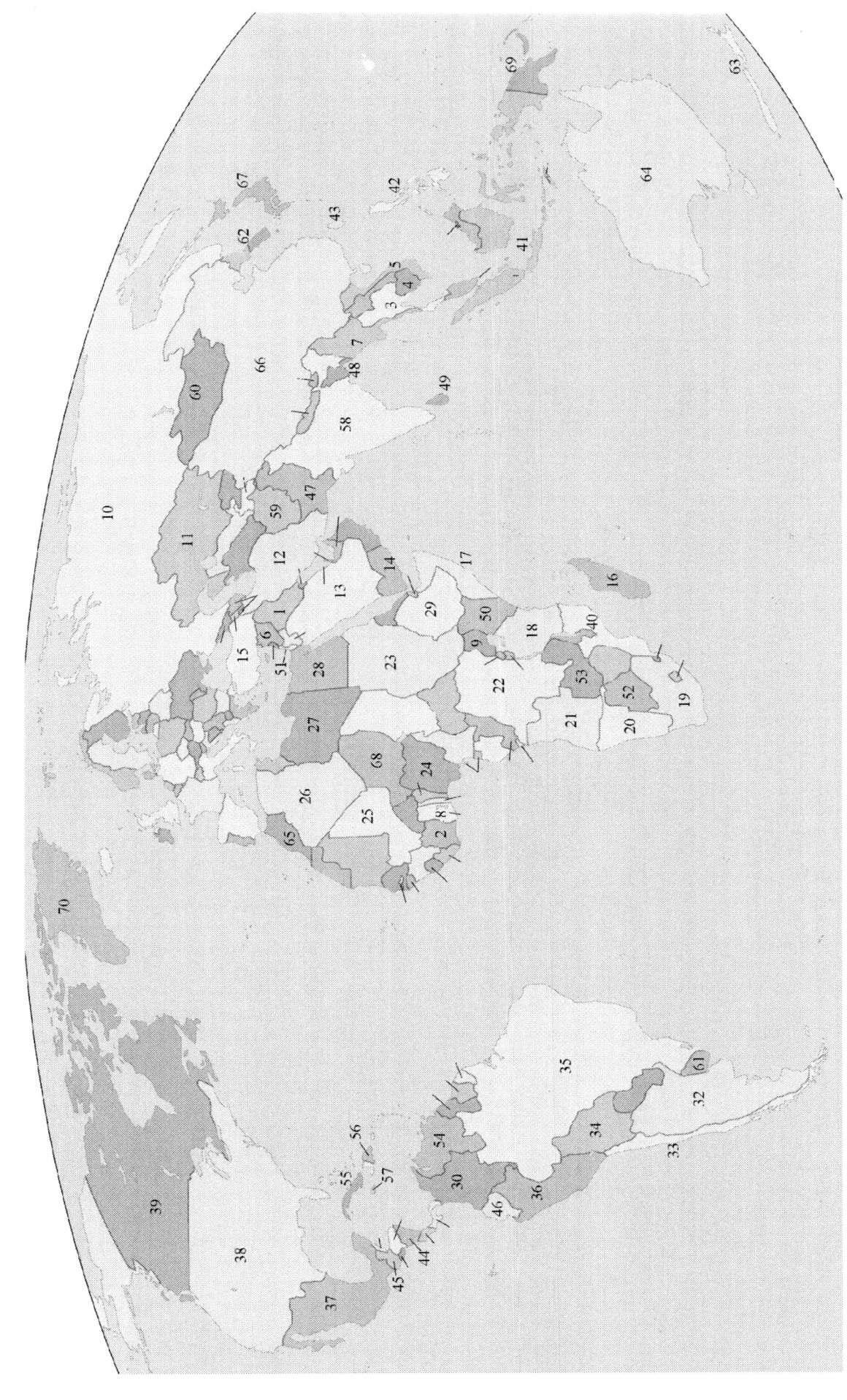

FIGURE 1b (Europe)
Places and Regions in Global Context: Human Geography, 4th Edition

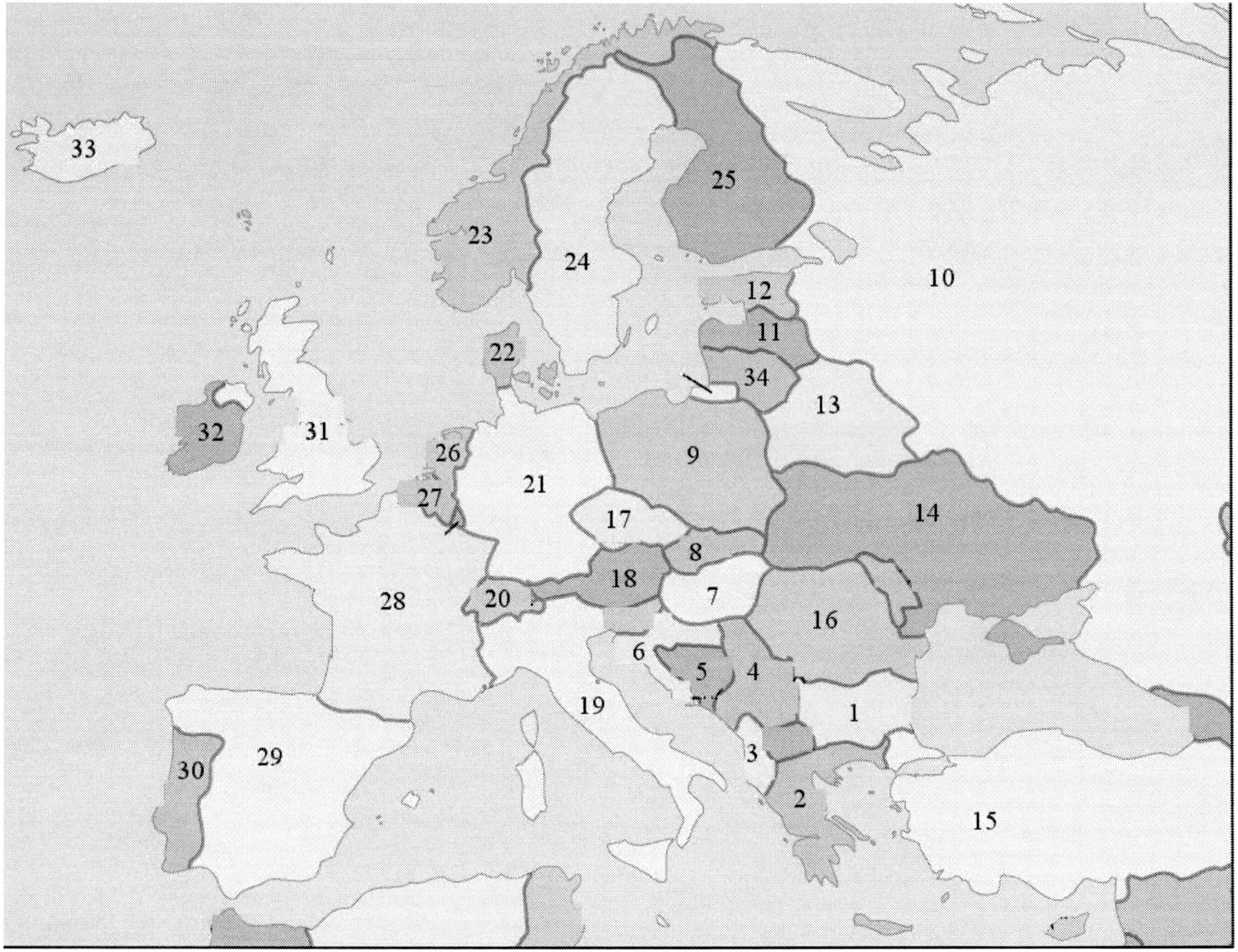

Chapter 1 Geography Matters

1.1 Minimal Choice

1) Given the convergence of time and space over the last century, our grandparents' general sense of the cognitive distance between places was most likely _____ than ours.

    A) greater   B) less

Answer: A
Diff: 3

2) Of the world's labor force, _____% are industrial workers in high–income countries.

    A) 40   B) 4

Answer: B
Diff: 2

3) Physical geographers study things like weather, soil formation and animal ecology. Human geographers are more likely to study

    A) landscapes.   B) landforms.

Answer: A
Diff: 1

4) People's relationships with their environments are more likely to be studied by

    A) physical geographers.   B) human geographers.

Answer: B
Diff: 3

5) In contemporary globalization debates, the decline of nations and states and the rise of free trade and economic integration across the world is most likely held by those with the

    A) the skeptical view.   B) hyperglobalist view.

Answer: B
Diff: 1

6) According to our text, the new mobility of money, labor, products and ideas _____ the significance of place.

    A) increases   B) decreases

Answer: A
Diff: 2

7) Agricultural production, resource management, population change, ecology of human disease and the symbolism of place and landscape are studied by

    A) human geographers.   B) physical geographers.

Answer: A
Diff: 2

8) The shared meanings that come from the lived experiences of daily life -- those common & routine interactions that allow us to become familiar with one another's vocabulary, humor, dress codes, gestures, etc. -- is known as

    A) intersubjectivity.   B) spatial interaction.

Answer: A
Diff: 1

9) The scale of social interaction -- of personal relationships and daily routine -- for most people is the scale of the.

    A) community.   B) national state.

Answer: A
Diff: 2

10) The prime meridian cuts through

    A) Greenwich, England.   B) Quito, Ecuador.

Answer: A
Diff: 1

11) On a marshy delta, at and below sea level, in a hurricane region -- all of these are characteristics that describe New Orleans'

    A) site.   B) situation.

Answer: A
Diff: 2

12) On the Canadian border across the river from Detroit, Windsor, Ontario's _____ provides ideal access to the American automotive industry.

    A) site   B) situation

Answer: B
Diff: 2

13) The spread of gossip among students seated in a classroom would best be characterized as _____ diffusion.

    A) expansion   B) heirarchical

Answer: A
Diff: 2

14) In contrast to regions defined by some common or homogenous feature(s), metropolitan areas like the Twin Cities (Minneapolis & St. Paul, MN) are best described as _____ regions.

    A) formal   B) functional

    Answer: B
    Diff: 2

15) The landscape(s) you pass every day on the way to school, the ones you do not give much thought to, are known as

    A) vernacular landscapes.   B) *de jure* landscapes.

    Answer: A
    Diff: 1

16) Extreme devotion of people with different cultural backgrounds to regional interests and customs is known as

    A) sectionalism.   B) irredentism.

    Answer: A
    Diff: 1

1.2 Multiple Choice

1) That places are interdependent means that individual places are

    A) connected to events and processes around them.

    B) separated from the world around them.

    C) independent of the world around them.

    D) not unique, but just like the places around them.

    Answer: A
    Diff: 2

2) The dependence of Minneapolis on vegetables from Florida, New York City on energy from Quebec, California on immigrant labor from Mexico, and Colorado on tourists from New York city demonstrate the interdependence of

    A) latitude.

    B) projection.

    C) place.

    D) situation.

    E) site.

    Answer: C
    Diff: 3

3) A rise in international oil prices associated with an outbreak of war in an oil producing country demonstrates the interdependence of geographic

    A) scale.

    B) situation.

    C) site.

    D) projection.

    E) longitude.

Answer: A
Diff: 3

4) The declining fortunes of a potato farmer in Idaho due to a decline in North American cultural preferences for French fries demonstrates interdependence of

    A) scale.   B) place.   C) situation.   D) site.   E) region.

Answer: A
Diff: 3

5) Changes in and around Russia's Lake Baykal over the last few decades exemplify the ability of globalization to

    A) distribute resources.   B) degrade environments.

    C) improve environments.   D) change political systems.

Answer: B
Diff: 2

6) The study of natural events such as tornadoes, forest fires or landslides are explored within the _____ branch of geography.

    A) physical   B) human   C) regional   D) spatial   E) natural

Answer: A
Diff: 1

7) Human Geography is best described as the

    A) study of how human activity is organized in space.

    B) relationship between people and their environment(s).

    C) location of places (capitals, rivers, countries, etc.) around the earth.

    D) description of the world's environments in terms of its landforms.

    E) both A and B

Answer: E
Diff: 2

8) Which of the following is a tool or technique of the contemporary geographer?

   A) GPS

   B) GIS

   C) remote sensing

   D) maps

   E) All of the above are used by contemporary geographers.

   Answer: E
   Diff: 1

9) Which of the following is *not* among the critiques of GIS as an effective geographic tool?

   A) GIS adds little to our understanding of people and places.

   B) GIS increases the opportunity to judge people by where they live.

   C) GIS increases the level of surveillance by those in positions of power.

   D) GIS is economically impractical.

   E) All of the above are ongoing critiques of GIS.

   Answer: D
   Diff: 2

10) Reference to "Greenwich Village" as a neighborhood in New York City or "the Loop" business region in Chicago identifies these places in terms of their _____ location.

   A) absolute   B) cognitive   C) nominal   D) spatial   E) relative

   Answer: C
   Diff: 3

11) Global Positioning Systems (GPS) rely upon satellites orbiting the Earth to help us accurately identify the _____ location of a place on earth.

   A) absolute   B) cognitive   C) nominal   D) spatial   E) relative

   Answer: A
   Diff: 3

12) In the grid of coordinates that cover the earth, lines of _____ intersect at the North and South Poles.

   A) latitude   B) longitude

   C) prime meridians   D) parallel

   Answer: B
   Diff: 2

13) When driving from Chicago to Minneapolis–St. Paul, the absolute distance between them is measured in terms of the number of

    A) cups of coffee one might drink between them.

    B) music compact disks one will listen to.

    C) hours and minutes it takes to make the drive.

    D) potty stops the children will require.

    E) miles or kilometers between them.

Answer: E
Diff: 2

14) When one expresses the distance between home and her favorite restaurant as "a $6.00 cab ride," she is referring to the _____ distance between them.

    A) absolute

    B) cognitive

    C) relative

    D) spatial

    E) situational

Answer: C
Diff: 3

15) Hawaii's tropical location, sandy beaches, volcanoes, volcanic soils, and plentiful moisture play an important role in its economic activities. In terms of its relative location, these characteristics refer to Hawaii's

    A) site.   B) situation.   C) place.   D) space.   E) distance.

Answer: A
Diff: 3

16) The statement, "Mexico's location next to the United States has had a great impact on its economic development," suggests that Mexico's economic development is related to its

    A) site.

    B) situation.

    C) spatial interaction.

    D) cognitive distance.

    E) sense of place.

Answer: B
Diff: 3

17) For each person who makes the 250-mile trip from Saint Louis to Kansas City, which of the following varies the least from person to person?

    A) absolute distance

    B) relative distance

    C) cognitive distance

    D) All of the above will vary significantly from person to person.

Answer: A
Diff: 3

18) In contrast to the suburbs on the far outskirts of a city, the location of a neighborhood next to a downtown university has high _____ to the students.

    A) utility

    B) distance decay function

    C) situation

    D) cognitive space

    E) time-space convergence

Answer: A
Diff: 3

19) The utility of a specific place to live is generally measured in terms of

    A) access to things like work, school and leisure.

    B) housing costs.

    C) quality of life.

    D) cost of living.

    E) all of the above

Answer: E
Diff: 2

20) The concept of _____ suggests that the farther one has to travel to Green Bay, WI, the less likely he or she is to attend a Green Bay Packers football game.

    A) friction of distance.   B) distance decay.

    C) cognitive distance.   D) absolute distance.

Answer: A
Diff: 3

21) A transportation map, such as a bus or subway map showing the routes and connections between places, is a representation of

    A) relative space.

    B) cognitive space.

    C) topological space.

    D) outer space.

    E) none of the above

Answer: C
Diff: 3

22) Topological space is best represented by a

    A) topographic map.

    B) metro (subway) system map.

    C) page from a road atlas.

    D) weather map.

    E) map of the trails and features in a state park.

Answer: B
Diff: 2

23) Geographers characterize accessibility in terms of

    A) absolute distance.   B) relative distance.

    C) cognitive distance.   D) all of the above

Answer: B
Diff: 2

24) For there to be interdependence between Detroit and Toronto, all of the following are necessary *except*

    A) complementarity between Detroit and Toronto.

    B) transferability between Detroit and Toronto.

    C) the lack of intervening opportunities between Detroit and Toronto.

    D) spatial diffusion.

Answer: D
Diff: 3

25) Which of the following best demonstrates complementarity?

    A) U.S. demand for coffee & Nicaragua's ability to supply it effectively

    B) the ability to easily ship coffee beans from Nicaragua to the U.S.

    C) the fact that Vietnam and Indonesia (big coffee producers) are so much further away than Central American countries

    D) All of the above explain the coffee complementarity between the U.S. & Central America.

Answer: A
Diff: 2

26) Despite great demand for fresh water in Saudi Arabia and the great availability of fresh water in Canada, spatial interdependence between the two countries is limited due to

    A) high complementarity.   B) low complementarity.

    C) high transferability.   D) low transferability.

Answer: D
Diff: 3

27) The transferability of a good is most likely to change over time with changes in

    A) technology.

    B) cultural preferences.

    C) demand.

    D) supply.

    E) all of the above

Answer: A
Diff: 3

28) The critical factor of location for a grocery store is its

    A) access to material inputs.

    B) proximity to consumer markets.

    C) the availability of specialized labor.

    D) processing costs.

    E) government policies.

Answer: B
Diff: 2

29) For a car parts company that is considering closing its factory in Milwaukee to reopen production in Indonesia, the critical factor of location is

A) access to material inputs.   B) proximity to consumer markets.

C) processing costs.   D) government policies.

Answer: C
Diff: 2

30) The concentration of the United States auto industry in and around Detroit, MI is an example of a(n)

A) localization economy.   B) external economy.

C) ancillary activity.   D) regional economy.

Answer: A
Diff: 2

31) Localization economies are cost savings that a firm achieves by

A) using local rather imported than labor.

B) clustering with other similar firms.

C) locating in rural areas.

D) locating in multiple areas.

E) avoiding globalization.

Answer: B
Diff: 2

32) External economies (typically achieved in urban areas) result from all of the following except

A) shared ancillary activities.

B) shared information and innovation.

C) shared infrastructure.

D) shared fixed social capital.

E) shared profits.

Answer: E
Diff: 3

33) A formal region is defined

A) in terms of the uniformity or homogeneity of certain characteristics.

B) in terms of its interdependent parts, typically tied to a central node.

C) conceptually, typically in terms of feelings, attitudes and images.

D) by the National Geographic.

Answer: A
Diff: 2

34) The best example of cascade (or hierarchal) diffusion is the spread of

A) HIV/AIDS across the world's major urban centers.

B) an agricultural innovation across a farming region.

C) a disease from one side of a country to the other.

D) a rumor across campus.

Answer: A
Diff: 2

35) Landscapes that represent the aspirations and/or values of the people that created them (such as the Capital, White House and other Federal buildings in the center of Washington, DC) are referred to as _____ landscapes.

A) ordinary   B) vernacular   C) symbolic   D) patriotic

Answer: C
Diff: 1

36) Of the following, which is *least* likely to increase time–space convergence?

A) increasing the speed limits between two cities

B) building a bridge across a river dividing two halves of a city

C) replacing a bicycle with a motorcycle

D) participating in the World Wide Web

E) traveling around the world and crossing the international date line

Answer: E
Diff: 2

37) The way that things spread through space and over time is known to geographers as

    A) time–space convergence.

    B) spatial diffusion.

    C) globalization.

    D) irredentism.

    E) transferability.

Answer: B
Diff: 1

38) Based on all the songs and stories written about it, the Mississippi River carries a strong _____ for both those who have lived on it and those who have not.

    A) sense of place   B) geographical imagination

    C) mental map   D) social construction

Answer: A
Diff: 2

39) The realm of experience for most people is the scale of

    A) world economy.

    B) world regions.

    C) national states.

    D) human settlements.

    E) the periphery.

Answer: D
Diff: 1

40) The increasing connectedness of different parts of the world through common processes of economic, environmental, political, and cultural change is what we mean by

    A) world regions.

    B) globalization.

    C) spatial diffusion.

    D) distance–decay.

    E) time–space convergence.

Answer: B
Diff: 1

41) Though we don't generally think of it when we talk about globalization, a world economy has been in existence for

    A) millions of years.

    B) thousands of years.

    C) centuries.

    D) decades.

    E) years.

Answer: C
Diff: 2

42) To help understand and visualize the extent and intensity of the human impact on the earth, some scientists use the concept of the human (also known as the ecological)

    A) analysis.

    B) convergence.

    C) footprint.

    D) region.

    E) settlement.

Answer: C
Diff: 1

43) The prime meridian is also known as (the)

    A) international date line

    B) 0 (zero) degrees longitude

    C) 0 (zero) degrees latitude

    D) equator

    E) North Pole

Answer: B
Diff: 2

44) Places are *socially constructed*. This refers to the

    A) buildings & monuments humans have built in places.

    B) meanings different groups give to different places.

    C) relationships between the different social groups of a place.

    D) interrelationships between places.

    E) way cartographers organize places when making maps.

Answer: B
Diff: 2

45) A helpful way of understanding geographic scale is to think of it as

    A) the balance between physical and human geography.

    B) how human impacts to the environment are measured.

    C) the delicate balance between nature and society in the protection of the environment.

    D) the partitioning of space within which different processes are played out.

Answer: D
Diff: 2

46) As presented in your text, which of the following best describes the relationship between Ethiopia and Switzerland?

    A) They are both Sub-Saharan African countries.

    B) They are the world's poorest and richest countries, respectively.

    C) They are both considered neutral countries in the world system.

    D) Their combined traditions have given the world a unique form of "world beat" music.

    E) They exemplify the best and worst of globalization.

Answer: B
Diff: 2

47) According to your text, in debates over globalization, those that believe the world will increasingly consist of a three-tiered system -- elites, the embattled and the marginalized -- are most likely

    A) skeptics.

    B) hyperglobalists.

    C) transformationalists.

    D) neoliberals.

    E) interdependents.

Answer: C
Diff: 2

48) Of the world's globalized labor force, most (40%) work

    A) in the formal sector in low- and middle-income countries.

    B) on family farms in low- and middle income countries.

    C) as service workers high-income countries.

    D) in industry in high-income countries.

    E) in the tourism industry.

Answer: B
Diff: 2

49) One sign of the environmental mismanagement of Russia's Lake Baykal in Siberia -- the world's deepest and largest (by volume) lake -- was the 1997 death of thousands of

A) Siberian black bears.

B) migratory cranes.

C) tourists from western Russia.

D) freshwater seals.

E) the world's largest salmon.

Answer: D
Diff: 1

50) Medical geographers have observed that the world-wide spread of HIV/AIDS from its hearth in Central Africa is best explained by a(n) _____ diffusion pattern.

A) expansion   B) heirarchical   C) relocation   D) contagious

Answer: B
Diff: 2

51) The heirarchical (also known as cascade) diffusion pattern by which HIV/AIDS spread across the world is characterized by moving first across the world's

A) lowest income countries.

B) major urban areas.

C) most popular tourist areas.

D) island countries.

E) tropical regions.

Answer: B
Diff: 2

52) The world region with the highest HIV/AIDS infection rate -- 8 times the world average -- is

A) North America.

B) Sub-Saharan Africa.

C) Southeast Asia.

D) the Caribbean.

E) Europe.

Answer: B
Diff: 1

53) According to our course text, the leading cause of death in Africa is

   A) war.

   B) HIV/AIDS.

   C) famine.

   D) malaria.

   E) SARS.

Answer: B
Diff: 1

54) Among today's geographer's numerous tools is remote sensing. Fundamental to remote sensing are

   A) aerial photographs and satellite imagery.

   B) binoculars.

   C) mental maps.

   D) computerized library archives.

   E) Global positioning systems.

Answer: A
Diff: 1

55) Regional geography

   A) is the theoretical side of cartography.

   B) is the part of human geography that emphasizes landscapes.

   C) combines elements of both human and physical geography.

   D) is pure physical geography.

   E) is the geological side of geography.

Answer: C
Diff: 1

56) Of the following, which would probably be the most helpful in evaluating the loss of farmland to urban growth around the edges of Chicago over a 20 year period?

   A) geodemographic research

   B) global positioning systems

   C) remote sensing

   D) mental maps

   E) spatial diffusion

Answer: C
Diff: 3

57) Which of the following helps describe New Orleans' situation?

    A) It lies at or below sea level.

    B) It is in hurricane alley.

    C) It is on the coast.

    D) It has a subtropical climate.

    E) It is at the mouth of the Mississippi transportation waterway.

Answer: E
Diff: 3

58) Which of the following is most likely to be found around the outer parts of a culture region as modeled by geographer Donald Meinig?

    A) Core

    B) Sphere

    C) Domain

    D) Cultural hearth

    E) Symbolic landscapes

Answer: B
Diff: 2

59) _____ are interdependent.

    A) Places

    B) Regions

    C) Spaces

    D) People

    E) All of the above

Answer: E
Diff: 1

60) Of the following, the best example of a *de jure* space is

    A) the Corn Belt.

    B) the West Coast.

    C) the Mississippi Delta.

    D) Michigan.

    E) North America.

Answer: D
Diff: 3

61) The European Union and the North American Free Trade Association are both

    A) lifeworlds.

    B) world regions.

    C) supranational organizations.

    D) ordinary landscapes.

    E) geographic information systems.

Answer: C
Diff: 1

62) As explained in our text, as we have moved from traditional societies to our global society, the risks we face as individuals and groups have

    A) declined.

    B) become more manageable.

    C) shifted to the world's poor regions.

    D) become more catastrophic.

    E) mostly been the result of natural events.

Answer: D
Diff: 2

63) In the context of human geography, places

    A) have changing properties.   B) have fixed boundaries.

    C) are static.   D) all of the above

Answer: A
Diff: 1

64) Compared to a young woman living in a suburb of an Iranian city, a young woman who grew up in a small, American city in the Midwest would be more likely to

    A) place more importance on the family.

    B) care what her neighbors thought of her actions.

    C) have a stronger sense of individualism.

    D) choose a husband that pleased her family.

Answer: C
Diff: 2

65) Places can best be thought of as

    A) independent.   B) interdependent.

    C) co-dependent.   D) dependent.

Answer: B
Diff: 1

66) The first people significantly to develop geographic knowledge were the

    A) Chinese.

    B) Romans.

    C) Mayans.

    D) Europeans.

    E) Greeks.

Answer: E
Diff: 1

67) The European Age of Discovery is most strongly tied to this country:

    A) Britain   B) France   C) Germany   D) Italy   E) Portugal

Answer: E
Diff: 1

68) In the Middle Ages, between the fifth and sixteenth centuries, geographic knowledge was preserved and expanded by

    A) Greek and Latin scholars.

    B) Middle Eastern and Chinese scholars.

    C) Scandinavian scholars.

    D) French and German scholars.

    E) English scholars.

Answer: B
Diff: 1

69) The most important reason for European voyages of discovery was the desire

    A) for economic gain.

    B) to spread Christianity.

    C) to gain geographic knowledge and make better maps.

    D) to spread European social and cultural values to the New World.

Answer: A
Diff: 1

70) Advances in cartography were dependent upon

    A) mathematics.   B) astronomy.

    C) geography.   D) all of the above

Answer: D
Diff: 1

71) Strabo's approach to geography

    A) built upon the work of Ptolemy.

    B) helped the Romans overthrow the Greeks in the Mediterranean.

    C) emphasized regions and places.

    D) laid the groundwork for geographic information systems.

Answer: C
Diff: 2

72) Ptolemy's map of the world

    A) was based on the assumption that the earth was flat.

    B) was strongly influenced by the findings of Chinese geographers.

    C) was the first precise estimate of the size of the earth.

    D) represented to the basic world maps up until the time of Columbus.

Answer: C
Diff: 2

73) _____ produced the most influential geographers of the nineteenth century.

    A) Germany

    B) United States

    C) China

    D) Britain

    E) Italy

Answer: A
Diff: 1

74) Positivism

    A) was part of the quantitative revolution in social sciences.

    B) sought to bring metaphysics and religion into the scientific method.

    C) had been discredited by the middle of the twentieth century.

    D) was developed by Carl Sauer.

Answer: A
Diff: 2

75) The study of geography in the late nineteenth-century was least influenced by

    A) ethnocentrism.   B) imperialism.

    C) environmental determinism.   D) feminism.

Answer: D
Diff: 1

76) The global scope and activity of the global financial system has been made possible in large part by

    A) policies of the World Bank.   B) new information technologies.

    C) the global decline of communism.   D) the strength of the U.S. dollar.

Answer: B
Diff: 2

77) The success of Geographic Information Systems is primarily due to the use of this technology:

    A) shipping   B) the world wide web

    C) computers   D) global satellites

Answer: C
Diff: 1

78) Geographic Information Systems (GIS) has been used for

    A) urban planning.

    B) monitoring the spread of disease.

    C) targeting potential customers for businesses.

    D) land use planning.

    E) all of the above

Answer: E
Diff: 1

79) The most important data requirement for Geographic Information Systems is

    A) where.   B) when.   C) why.   D) how.

Answer: A
Diff: 2

80) Physical geography focuses the least on

  A) landforms.

  B) animal ecology.

  C) culture.

  D) soil formation.

  E) climate.

Answer: C
Diff: 1

81) At the heart of geographic research is

  A) getting published in *National Geographic*.

  B) analysis of data.

  C) collection of facts.

  D) getting government grants.

  E) learning place names.

Answer: B
Diff: 1

82) Of the following tools of the geographer, which is most commonly used?

  A) computer simulations   B) surveys

  C) lab experiments   D) maps

Answer: D
Diff: 1

83) The Prime Meridian

  A) is essentially a latitude line.

  B) passes through Greenwich, England.

  C) forms an angle of 0 degrees with the earth's equator.

  D) was established by the Greeks.

Answer: B
Diff: 1

84) Cognitive images (mental maps) can be based on

   A) visual representations of actual locations.

   B) direct experiences.

   C) people's imaginations.

   D) all of the above

   E) none of the above

Answer: D
Diff: 1

85) Denver is now one of the world's most important centers of cable television in large part because

   A) its location is ideal for satellite transmission around the world.

   B) it has a well-educated work force.

   C) the Federal Communications Commission is headquartered there.

   D) it offers tax incentives to cable television corporations.

Answer: A
Diff: 2

86) Friction of distance

   A) is usually negligible over distances of less than ten miles.

   B) is dependent in part upon an individual's cognitive distance.

   C) is now considered an outdated concept with little current utility.

   D) is another term for the distance-decay function.

   E) all of the above

Answer: B
Diff: 2

87) The utility of a specific place

   A) varies directly with its distance from a person's primary place of residence.

   B) is unaffected by the friction of distance.

   C) is the same for all people.

   D) is a measure of usefulness of that place for a certain person or group.

Answer: D
Diff: 2

88) Absolute space is

    A) socioeconomic space.   B) behavioral space.

    C) mathematical space.   D) experiential/cultural space.

Answer: C
Diff: 2

89) A point in mathematical space corresponds to this in behavioral space:

    A) landmark   B) distribution   C) territory   D) configuration

Answer: A
Diff: 2

90) Which of the following is NOT one of the basic concepts of spatial interaction?

    A) transferability

    B) complementarity

    C) concentration

    D) diffusion

    E) intervening opportunity

Answer: C
Diff: 2

91) Time-space convergence

    A) has been hampered by the computer revolution.

    B) increases as the friction of distance decreases.

    C) has severely hindered the ability of companies to take advantage of economies of scale.

    D) all of the above

Answer: B
Diff: 2

92) The major increase in fifteenth-century exploration was initiated by this country:

    A) Portugal   B) Spain

    C) England   D) the Netherlands

Answer: A
Diff: 1

93) Human geographers, like most social scientists, begin with

    A) model formation.   B) observation.

    C) statistical analysis.   D) data visualization.

Answer: B
Diff: 1

94) This is NOT one of the fundamental concepts of spatial analysis:

    A) location   B) distance   C) value   D) accessibility

Answer: C
Diff: 2

95) The Prime Meridian

    A) always crosses the equator at an angle of less than 90 degrees.

    B) goes through Paris and New York.

    C) is the main reference point for determining latitude.

    D) runs through both poles.

Answer: D
Diff: 2

1.3 True or False

1) The most detailed scale with which geographers work is the body and the self.

Answer: TRUE
Diff: 2

2) According to your text, globalization will eventually make geography obsolete through destruction and homogenization.

Answer: FALSE
Diff: 1

3) As explained in the course text, all the world's people and places benefit equally from globalization.

Answer: FALSE
Diff: 1

4) The prime meridian and the equator are both lines of latitude.

Answer: FALSE
Diff: 1

5) One can not have a cognitive image (nor draw a mental map) of a place to which he or she has not been.

Answer: FALSE
Diff: 3

6) Complementarity emerges from the ability of two places to understand and appreciate each other.

Answer: FALSE
Diff: 2

7) Cost savings from high volumes of production are known as external economies.

Answer: FALSE
Diff: 2

8) Small family farms are unable to compete with large factory farms because they are unable to operate at similar economies of scale.

Answer: TRUE
Diff: 1

9) For a family from Saint Louis considering a drive to Las Vegas, the Ozark entertainment center of Branson, Missouri presents an intervening opportunity.

Answer: TRUE
Diff: 3

10) Geographers understand that just because a place is near by does not mean that it is accessible.

Answer: TRUE
Diff: 2

11) Climatic complementarity helps explain why a retiree spends summers in the north and winters in the south.

Answer: TRUE
Diff: 2

12) Complementarity is sufficient to explain the interdependence between places.

Answer: FALSE
Diff: 2

13) Car tires have higher transferability than Swiss watches.

Answer: FALSE
Diff: 2

14) Time-space convergence refers to the shrinking relative distances between places.

Answer: TRUE
Diff: 1

15) All the mental maps of people from the same home town will be identical.

Answer: FALSE
Diff: 1

16) Regions come in many scales.

Answer: TRUE
Diff: 1

17) The more universal the diffusion of material culture and lifestyle, the more valuable regional and ethnic identifies become.

Answer: TRUE
Diff: 2

18) Though globalization is increasingly making geography obsolete, it is still important to study place names.

Answer: FALSE
Diff: 2

19) Geographic Information Systems (GIS) are used mostly by physical geographers, rarely by human geographers.

Answer: FALSE
Diff: 1

20) Insiders and outsiders tend to construct a given place differently.

Answer: TRUE
Diff: 1

21) The pattern by which AIDS first spread across the United States was by expansion diffusion.

Answer: TRUE
Diff: 1

22) People's relationships with their environments is a central theme of human geography.

Answer: TRUE
Diff: 1

23) Geographic scales are typically interdependent.

Answer: TRUE
Diff: 1

24) The term "geography" means the study of maps and cartography.

Answer: FALSE
Diff: 1

25) Human geography is about cartography, map–making and clearly portraying where things are.

Answer: FALSE
Diff: 2

26) Globalization increases as the interdependence of people in different places increases.

Answer: TRUE
Diff: 2

27) Geography is a theoretical science with few practical applications to real world problems and issues.

Answer: FALSE
Diff: 1

28) Regional geography is still very relevant in today's hyper–globalized world.

Answer: TRUE
Diff: 1

29) Geographical research attempts to formulate hypotheses and create models.

Answer: TRUE
Diff: 2

30) GIS is the one analytical tool used by all geographers.

Answer: FALSE
Diff: 2

31) The geographical term "situation" refers to a place's location relative to other places and human activities.

Answer: TRUE
Diff: 1

32) Generally, the greater the absolute distance, the lesser the cognitive distance.

Answer: FALSE
Diff: 2

33) Advances in telecommunications and transportation technologies have reduced cognitive distances.

Answer: TRUE
Diff: 2

34) Generally, people try to maximize the overall utility of a location.

Answer: TRUE
Diff: 2

35) For two places to be interdependent, there must be a demand for something in one place and an accessible supply of it in the other place.

Answer: TRUE
Diff: 2

36) Economic specialization is an obstacle to achieving economies of scale.

Answer: FALSE
Diff: 2

37) There is rarely any significant interdependence between geographic scales.

Answer: FALSE
Diff: 1

38) Human geography includes the study of human interactions with the natural environment.

Answer: TRUE
Diff: 1

39) Cognitive images are mental maps that precisely portray real life.

Answer: FALSE
Diff: 2

40) The friction of distance refers to the inhibiting effect of distance on human activity.

Answer: TRUE
Diff: 2

1.4 Matching

SPACE: Match the example to the type of space.

1) Absolute space
   Diff: 3

2) Relative space
   (socioeconomic)
   Diff: 3

3) Relative space
   (experiential/cultural)
   Diff: 3

4) Cognitive space
   Diff: 3

A) sacred spaces of holy cities

B) U.S. cities as sprawling with strip
   malls

C) coastal regions

D) 100 square mile area

1) D   2) C   3) A   4) B

REGIONS: Match the type of region to the example.

5) Wisconsin as a place of cheese
   heads
   Diff: 2

6) Nashville as the buckle of the
   Bible Belt
   Diff: 2

7) Chicago as the region from
   which people commute to
   Chicago
   Diff: 2

8) Corn Belt as those counties in
   which corn is the dominant
   crop
   Diff: 2

9) Rocky Mountain West as
   those states with Rocky
   Mountains
   Diff: 2

A) formal region

B) functional region

C) perceptual region

5) C   6) C   7) B   8) A   9) A

Latitude & longitude: Match the line to its correct name

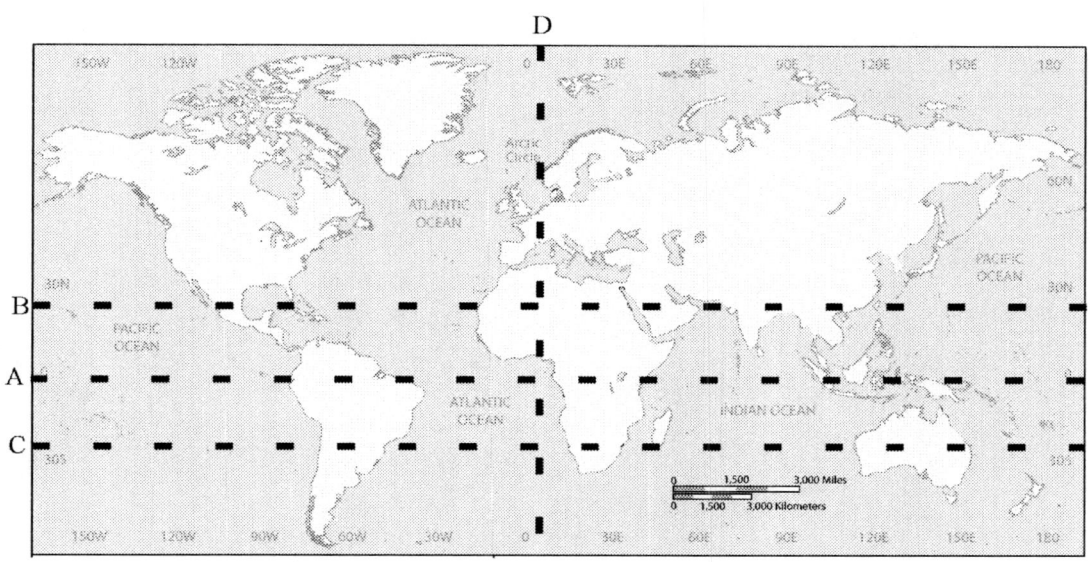

10) The prime meridian   A) A
    Diff: 1
                                B) B
11) the equator
    Diff: 1   C) C

12) a line of longitude   D) D
    Diff: 1

13) Tropic of Capricorn
    Diff: 2

14) Tropic of Cancer
    Diff: 2

10) D   11) A   12) D   13) C   14) B

1.5 Map Identification

World Map

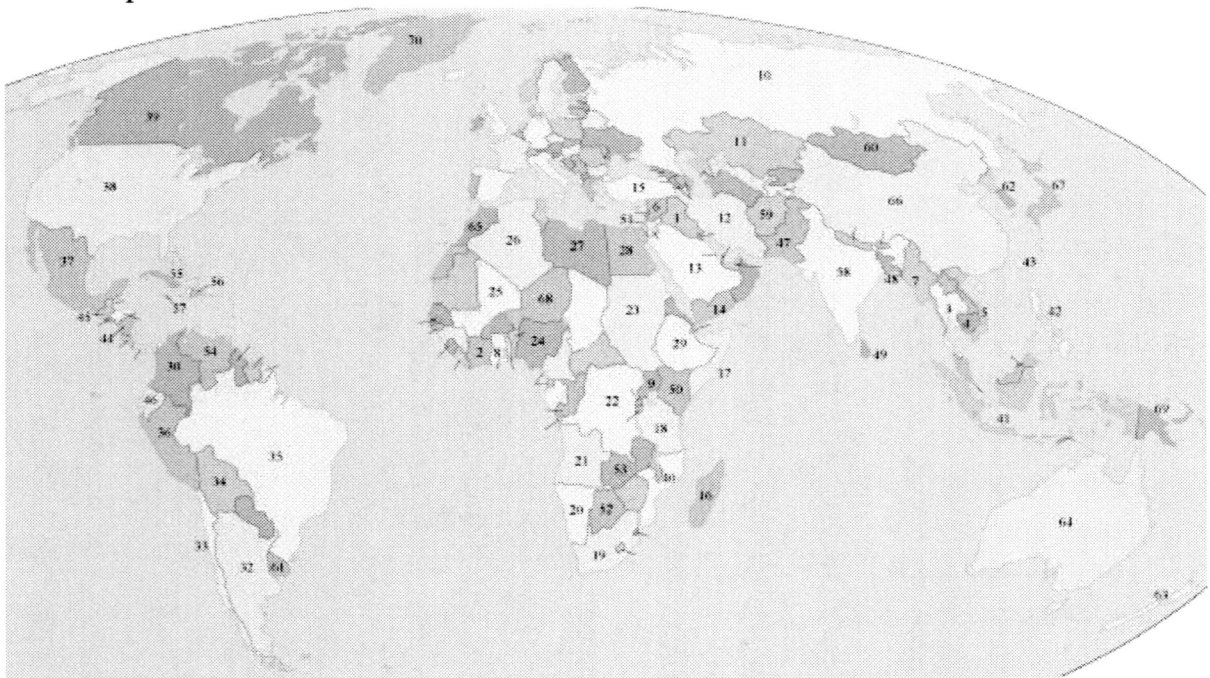

1) China shares a border with which of the following countries:

    A) Russia

    B) India

    C) France

    D) Canada

    E) Both Russia and India

Answer: E
Diff: 1

2) The country of Ethiopia is identified by the number

    A) 25.   B) 29.   C) 34.   D) 59.   E) 60.

Answer: D
Diff: 1

3) Ankara is the capital of

    A) Turkey.

    B) Iran.

    C) Jamaica.

    D) Botswana.

    E) Kazakhstan.

Answer: A
Diff: 1

4) Ottawa is the capital of

    A) Canada.   B) France.   C) Iran.   D) Mexico.   E) India.

Answer: A
Diff: 1

5) The capital of country #10 is .

    A) Moscow

    B) Ottawa

    C) Beijing

    D) Cairo

    E) Adis Ababa

Answer: A
Diff: 1

6) The capital of country #11 is

    A) Moscow

    B) Ottawa

    C) Paris

    D) Astana

    E) Adis Ababa

Answer: D
Diff: 2

7) The country situated between countries 37 and 39 is

   A) Canada.

   B) China.

   C) Mexico.

   D) Russia.

   E) the United States of America.

Answer: E
Diff: 1

8) Mexico City is the capital of which country?

   A) 34   B) 35   C) 36   D) 37   E) 38

Answer: D
Diff: 1

9) Countries 20, 21 and 22 are all part of

   A) North Africa.

   B) Sub–Saharan Africa.

   C) Southeast Asia.

   D) the Middle East.

   E) North America.

Answer: B
Diff: 2

10) Which pair of countries share a border?

   A) Russia & Kazahkstan

   B) Canada & Mexico

   C) Ethiopia & Kazakhstan

   D) Canada & France

   E) India & Mexico

Answer: A
Diff: 2

11) Of the following, which is farthest from the prime meridian?

   A) 5   B) 15   C) 20   D) 25   E) 50

Answer: C
Diff: 2

12) Of the following, which is closest to the prime meridian?

A) 5   B) 15   C) 20   D) 25   E) 50

Answer: D
Diff: 2

1.6 Chapter 1 Questions with images

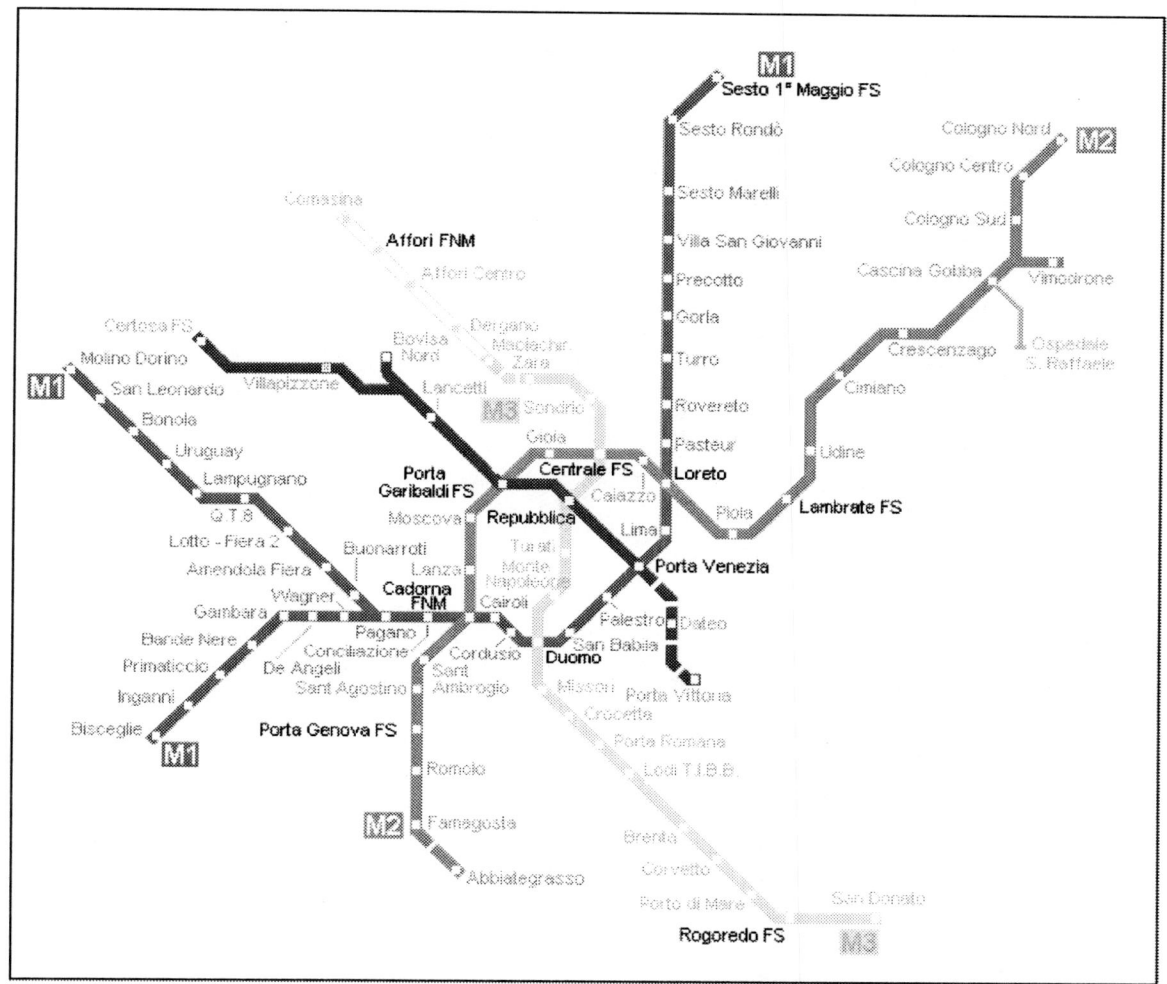

1) The map of Milan, Italy's metrorail transportation system in the figure above is an example of a

A) mental map.

B) topological map.

C) isoline map.

D) topographical map.

E) culture region.

Answer: B
Diff: 2

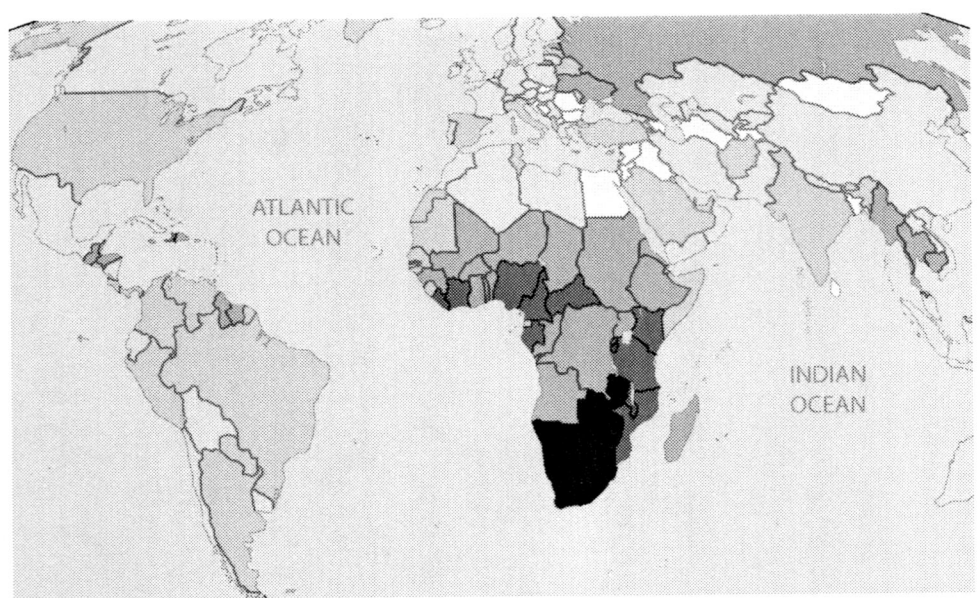

2) The above map shows the worldwide distribution of what phenomena (darker colors indicate more of it)?

    A) HIV/AIDS

    B) Human Footprint

    C) SARS

    D) wealth

    E) fresh water

Answer: A
Diff: 3

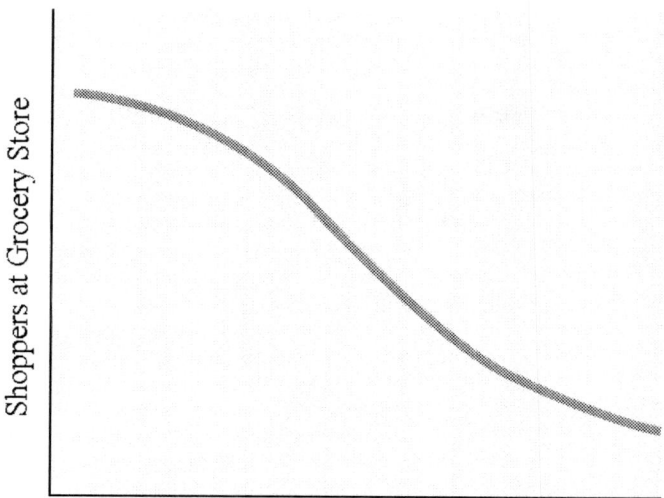

Distance of Residence from Grocery Store

3) The above graph shows that the farther people have to travel, the less likely they are to do so. The inhibiting effect of distance is ascribed to

A) the friction of distance.

B) the problem of space.

C) time–space convergence.

D) cognitive distance.

E) irredentism.

Answer: A
Diff: 3

4) As conceptualized in the above graph, the farther people have to travel, the less likely they are to do so. This is best captured in the geographic concept of

A) distance decay

B) friction of distance

C) spatial analysis

D) complementarity

E) transferability

Answer: B
Diff: 3

Chapter 2   Changing Global Context

2.1 Minimal Choice

1) The first agricultural revolution introduced

   A) hunting & gathering.   B) agricultural production.

   Answer: A
   Diff: 1

2) The first agricultural revolution lasted

   A) millenia.   B) centuries.

   Answer: A
   Diff: 1

3) A few, remnant _____ still remain at the start of the twenty-first century.

   A) minisystems   B) external arenas

   Answer: A
   Diff: 2

4) In a sense, globalization has been around for a long time. For example, trade routes have connected the Europeans with _____ for over a thousand years.

   A) China   B) the Americas

   Answer: A
   Diff: 1

5) He introduced the concept of "world-system."

   A) Immanuel Wallerstein   B) Alexander von Humboldt

   Answer: A
   Diff: 1

6) In the seventeenth and eighteenth centuries, the Cassinis were multiple generations of

   A) map makers.   B) explorers.

   Answer: A
   Diff: 1

7) The first to appreciate the practical importance and usefulness of geography were the

   A) Greeks.   B) Germans.

   Answer: A
   Diff: 1

8) Between about A.D. 500 and A.D. 1400, geographic knowledge was preserved and expanded by _____ scholars.

    A) Islamic and Chinese   B) European and North American

Answer: A
Diff: 1

9) European economic growth benefited greatly from the transportation network of rivers and _____ that first integrated Europe's industrial regions.

    A) canals   B) railroads

Answer: A
Diff: 1

10) The fundamental logic or driving force behind colonization of the late nineteenth century was

    A) economic.   B) cultural.

Answer: A
Diff: 1

11) In the international division labor, the world's periphery provides

    A) raw materials.   B) manufactured goods.

Answer: A
Diff: 2

12) One example that old colonial patterns persist comes from the fact that 48 of the 55 sub–Saharan countries earn more than half of their export earnings from

    A) coffee, tea and cocoa.   B) clothing, textiles and shoes.

Answer: A
Diff: 2

13) The system of practical and theoretical knowledge about making distinctive visual representations of Earth's surface in the form of maps is known as

    A) cartography.   B) projection science.

Answer: A
Diff: 1

14) The simplistic idea that peoples' social and economic development and behavior are fundamentally shaped by their physical environment is known as

    A) environmental determinism.   B) ecocentrism.

Answer: A
Diff: 2

15) The early twentieth century geographers Ratzel, Semple and Huntington are known for their use of _____ to explain the differences between peoples of different places.

   A) environmental determinism   B) postmodernism

   Answer: A
   Diff: 2

16) The influential nineteenth century geographers von Humboldt and Ritter saw geography as an integrative science showing the interdependencies between

   A) people and nature.   B) places.

   Answer: A
   Diff: 2

17) River steamboats had their greatest utility from

   A) 1830 to 1850.   B) 1920 to 1940.

   Answer: A
   Diff: 1

18) The early–twentieth century increase in agricultural productivity was primarily due to

   A) tractors with combustion engines.   B) synthetic fertilizers.

   Answer: A
   Diff: 2

2.2 Multiple Choice

1) According to your text, which country has *not* been hegemonic over the world economy at some time in the last 500 years?

   A) Spain

   B) Holland

   C) England

   D) the United States of America

   E) Japan

   Answer: E
   Diff: 2

2) According to Knox and Marston, globalization of the last 25 years is linked to all of the following except

   A) new international division of labor.

   B) internationalization of finance.

   C) growth of new technology systems.

   D) end of neocolonialism.

   E) growth of consumer markets.

   Answer: D
   Diff: 2

3) Which of the following was NOT among the important geographical phenomena introduced by world empires?

   A) urbanization   B) colonization

   C) religion   D) inter regional trade

   Answer: C
   Diff: 2

4) The first agricultural revolution set the preconditions for early world empires by

   A) enabling an increase in population densities & trade between minisystems.

   B) eliminating the need for hunting and gathering.

   C) introducing colonialism and imperialism.

   D) highlighting the benefits of import substitution and comparative advantage.

   E) all of the above

   Answer: A
   Diff: 2

5) Slash–and–burn –– the name given to an early innovation that enabled the growth of minisystems into early world empires –– refers to an innovation in

   A) agriculture.

   B) warfare.

   C) metal–working.

   D) urbanization.

   E) colonization.

   Answer: A
   Diff: 1

6) World empires are organized around a

A) reciprocal social economy.

B) subsistence production economy.

C) redistributive–tributary social economy.

D) capitalist social economy.

E) all of the above

Answer: C
Diff: 2

7) The first agricultural revolution was characterized by all of the following *except*

A) domestication of animals such as sheep and cattle.

B) new methods to process, prepare and store foods.

C) sedentary agriculture based on burning plant matter as a way of returning nutrients to the soil.

D) uprising of rural populations against urban landholders.

E) occurred in Fertile Crescent, South Asia, East Asia, Mesoamerica and the Andes.

Answer: D
Diff: 2

8) Faced with problems associated with law of diminishing returns, world empires characteristically _____ in order to feed and provide for their populations.

A) colonized nearby lands

B) imported slave labor

C) regularly invented new technologies

D) promoted import substitution

E) established trade relations with countries having comparative advantages

Answer: A
Diff: 2

9) World–empires introduced _____ to enlarge their resource base in the face of rising populations

A) colonization

B) the law of diminishing returns

C) urbanization

D) import substitution

E) mini–systems

Answer: A
Diff: 2

10) Strabo and Ptolemy were

    A) Greek geographers interested in the relationships between people, places and environments.

    B) Greek explorers responsible for gathering information about resources for Greek generals.

    C) Roman generals that expanded the Roman Empire into Europe.

    D) Portuguese cartographers responsible for the first maps of the Roman Empire.

Answer: A
Diff: 2

11) The sphere of economic influence around cities -- from which products for export and taxes are collected and to which imports are distributed -- is known as the city's

    A) external arena.

    B) hinterland.

    C) hearth area.

    D) peripheral region.

    E) Any of the above because they are synonymous.

Answer: B
Diff: 2

12) By the fifteenth century, centers of capitalism in the developing world system included all but

    A) New York.

    B) Cairo.

    C) Stockholm.

    D) London.

    E) southeast China.

Answer: A
Diff: 3

13) Which of the following centers of early global civilization was not linked by the Silk Road?

    A) Eastern Mediterranean

    B) China

    C) northern India

    D) Central Andes and MesoAmerica

    E) All of the above were linked by the Silk Road.

Answer: D
Diff: 2

14) Motivations for sixteenth-century European overseas exploration and expansion included all but which of the following?

   A) Europe's growing population and limited agricultural resource base

   B) competition among numerous small monarchies in Europe

   C) declining wealth and land holdings of the European aristocracy

   D) boredom with European food, culture and ways of doing things

   E) search for commercial advantage and economic gain

Answer: D
Diff: 2

15) Until the Industrial Revolution of the late 1700s, the volume and velocity of world trade were constrained by technologies limited to those based on

   A) wood, wind and water.   B) coal, steel and rail.

   C) oil, plastics and roads.   D) human labor and animal power.

Answer: A
Diff: 3

16) Whereas the Europeans created plantations around the world to exploit resources and labor to produce high-value crops for the core, crops such as _____ changed European agriculture and ways of life profoundly.

   A) corn and potatoes

   B) sugar and teas

   C) coffee and cocoa

   D) cotton and hemp

   E) all of the above

Answer: A
Diff: 3

17) The concept of import substitution is best characterized as

   A) purchasing imported goods to replace locally produced goods.

   B) manufacturing goods that had previously been imported.

   C) exporting and importing the same type of product.

   D) changing suppliers of imported goods.

Answer: A
Diff: 3

18) Production of sugar from sugar beets, as an alternative to trading for sugar made from sugar cane in a foreign, tropical country, is an example of

A) import substitution.

B) comparative advantage.

C) spatial justice.

D) division of labor.

E) the law of diminishing returns.

Answer: A
Diff: 3

19) The specialization of peripheral countries in raw materials and foodstuffs, the decentralization of manufacturing to areas of low labor costs, and the emphasis of core regions on high–tech manufacturing and services describes

A) the digital divide.

B) the international division of labor.

C) comparative advantage.

D) import substitution.

E) initial advantage.

Answer: B
Diff: 3

20) Plantations established to exploit labor and resources in the periphery are geared toward

A) high value luxury items like sugar and cocoa.

B) mixed fruits and vegetables like tomatoes and apples.

C) staple crops like corn and potatoes.

D) industrial crops like cotton, flax and sunflowers.

E) any and all of the above

Answer: A
Diff: 3

21) The core–periphery framework for explaining the world system is based on geographic divisions that have emerged as a result of

A) private economic competition.

B) competition between countries.

C) competition between religious groups.

D) competition between political perspectives.

E) both A and B

Answer: A
Diff: 2

22) Colonialism always results in _____ exploitation of a foreign society by the colonizing power.

A) political

B) legal

C) economic

D) cultural

E) both A and B

Answer: A
Diff: 2

23) While people and societies do, indeed, respond to the opportunities and constraints of their physical environments, _____ takes this to a simplistic, and often racist, extreme by claiming that people's social and economic development and behavior are fundamentally the result of their physical environments.

A) ecological determinism

B) ethnocentrism

C) egocentrism

D) masculinism

E) environmental determinism

Answer: E
Diff: 3

24) Over the last 200 hundred years, clusters of improved technological innovations seem to have come in waves of industrialization every half–century or so. With each successive wave, the world–system

A) core expanded.

B) periphery expanded.

C) core and periphery remained unchanged.

D) core and periphery both expanded.

E) core and periphery both shrank.

Answer: A
Diff: 2

25) According to Knox and Marston, the current technology system is built around a cluster of technological innovations with _____ as its energy source.

A) water power and steam engines

B) coal and coal–powered steam engines

C) oil and the internal combustion engine

D) nuclear power

E) solar power

Answer: C
Diff: 1

26) Since the Industrial Revolution, changes in the geography of the world's core have been the result most directly of technological innovations in

A) transportation.   B) communications.

C) energy production.   D) manufacturing.

Answer: A
Diff: 2

27) While exploitation of the tropical world for such things as minerals and plantation products had been underway for centuries, industrialization in the core led to an increase in

A) the number of colonies exploited by the core.

B) the number of people under colonial rule.

C) interest in the periphery's grasslands for food (grain and livestock).

D) all of the above

E) both A and B

Answer: D
Diff: 2

28) In a surge of European imperialism to protect established interests, expand territory and compete for world influence (at the end of the nineteenth century), European core countries carved almost the entire _____ into a collection of colonies.

    A) continent of Africa

    B) continent of South America

    C) country of India

    D) country of Brazil

    E) world

Answer: A
Diff: 1

29) After WWII, the world system periphery was referred to as the

    A) First World.   B) Second World.   C) Third World.   D) Last World.

Answer: C
Diff: 1

30) Because of their ability and willingness to exercise power and influence in peripheral states, giant, transnational corporations have been referred to as commercial

    A) colonialists.   B) neocolonialists.

    C) imperialists.   D) determinists.

Answer: C
Diff: 2

31) The new international division of labor is characterized by

    A) decentralization of manufacturing from the core.

    B) increase of the United States as an industrial producer.

    C) new high tech manufacturing and producer service specializations in the periphery.

    D) all of the above

    E) both A and B

Answer: A
Diff: 1

32) In the context of the new international division of labor, producer services refer to

A) consulting services, insurance and market research designed to help specialized firms maintain a competitive edge.

B) high tech, scientific and engineering innovations designed to improve production efficiencies in manufacturing plants.

C) fast food restaurants, cleaning and other convenience services.

D) shopping malls, mail order and other modern retail operation.

E) all of the above

Answer: A
Diff: 2

33) Globalization of the last 3 decades or so is characterized by a significant increase in

A) the transnational scope of global economic and cultural activities.

B) the expansion and intensification of linkages and flows of capital, people, goods, ideas and cultures across national borders.

C) the influence of transnational rules and organizations.

D) all of the above

E) both A and B

Answer: D
Diff: 2

34) Awareness of the _____ linking overseas production with U.S. consumption has led some to be concerned with the working conditions in the Asian factories in which their clothing is made.

A) commodity chains

B) transnational corporations

C) division of labor

D) producer services

E) comparative advantage

Answer: A
Diff: 2

35) An important factor in the recent intensification of globalization has been the growth of consumer markets, characterized by

A) materialism and consumption.

B) global marketing of world products and popular culture.

C) growing dominance of Mexican products.

D) all of the above

E) both A and B

Answer: E
Diff: 1

36) Which of the following is *not* considered part of the slow world?

A) the vast majority (85%) of the world's people

B) the countries of subsaharan African

C) residents of urban slums and neglected ural regions in core countries

D) residents of elite neighborhoods in the world's periphery with computers and Internet access

E) All of the above are part of the slow world.

Answer: E
Diff: 3

37) A global commodity chain is the network of linkages describing

A) international loans -- from initial application to final project.

B) products -- from its production origins to final consumption.

C) manufacturing plants -- from shutting down in the core to opening in the periphery.

D) transnational companies -- the links between headquarters and their retail outlets.

E) cultural trends -- from its origins in the periphery to diffusion to the core.

Answer: B
Diff: 1

38) The phrase "Jihad vs. McWorld" is intended to symbolize the struggle and tensions between

A) nutritious/traditional food and unhealthy/processed food.

B) religious fundamentalists and secular capitalists.

C) traditionally based cultural values and pop culture/shallow materialism.

D) the local and the global.

E) the North and the South.

Answer: C
Diff: 3

39) The digital divide separates

    A) the core from the periphery.

    B) the fast from the slow world.

    C) Europe from North America.

    D) the World's North from its South.

    E) the Internet era from earlier times before the Internet became widespread.

Answer: B
Diff: 3

40) With the increase in globalization since 1960, the gap between the poorest one-fifth (20%) and the richest one-fifth of the world's people has

    A) remained constant.

    B) narrowed a little.

    C) narrowed a lot.

    D) widened a little.

    E) widened a lot.

Answer: E
Diff: 1

41) The Berlin Conference of 1885-1886 is notable for

    A) the founding of Imperialism and the establishment of the world into cores and peripheries.

    B) giving independence to African colonies, but moving them into neocolonial positions within the world system.

    C) bringing Africa into the world system as a carved up collection of European colonies.

    D) signifying the end of the Cold War, symbolized by tearing down the Berlin Wall.

    E) bringing an end to the Ottoman Empire, the last of the world's great world empires.

Answer: C
Diff: 3

42) The world's agricultural hearth areas are those regions

    A) from where the core gets most of its food.

    B) where an agricultural surplus is produced.

    C) where plants and animals were domesticated

    D) where swidden cultivation is practiced.

    E) where industrial agriculture is most prominent.

Answer: C
Diff: 2

43) Which of the following is not among the the world's main agricultural hearth areas?

    A) North America's Mississippi and St. Lawrence Rivers

    B) Middle East's Tigris and Euphrates Rivers

    C) South Asia's Indus, Ganges and Brahmaputra Rivers

    D) South America's Andes Mountains

    E) Central America's Tamaulipas and Tehuacan Valley

Answer: A
Diff: 3

44) The first agricultural revolution and the subsequent transition to food-producing minisystems resulted in all of the following *except*

    A) more settlements.

    B) higher population densities.

    C) industrialization.

    D) non-agricultural specializations.

    E) barter and trade between communities.

Answer: C
Diff: 2

45) The modern world system had its origins in late fifteenth-century Europe, and was especially associated with a rise in

    A) consumer demand for imported products.

    B) art.

    C) food production.

    D) manufacturing.

    E) exploration.

Answer: E
Diff: 2

46) With the emergence of the world-system, European _____ reshaped the world.

    A) merchant capitalism

    B) languages

    C) sports

    D) transnational corporations

    E) comparative advantages

Answer: A
Diff: 2

47) Satin, muslin, damask and calico are all named after Asian

   A) animals.   B) cities.   C) fabrics.   D) foods.   E) people.

   Answer: B
   Diff: 2

48) The first core regions of the world-system were the trading hubs of

   A) Italy, Greece and Spain

   B) Portugal, Spain and North Africa

   C) Austria, Hungary and Germany

   D) Holland, England and France

   E) Japan, Korea and China

   Answer: D
   Diff: 2

49) Which of the following entered the core after having been in the periphery?

   A) United States

   B) Mexico

   C) Brazil

   D) Portugal

   E) Taiwan

   Answer: A
   Diff: 1

50) The United States entered the world-system core on the strength of

   A) its vast resource base.

   B) large labor force.

   C) large population to buy manufactured goods.

   D) access to British capital.

   E) all of the above.

   Answer: E
   Diff: 2

51) Japan joined the world-system core in the early twentieth century through industrial development built around

    A) textiles and shipbuilding.

    B) rice and soybeans.

    C) electronics and cameras.

    D) glass and plastics.

    E) automobiles and computers.

Answer: A
Diff: 2

52) Of the following, which was not important to internal development and integration within the world's core during industrialization?

    A) barges

    B) trains

    C) trucks

    D) containerization

    E) all of the above

Answer: A
Diff: 2

53) With the introduction of _____ in the first part of the twentieth century, manufacturing could decentralize from urban, industrial cores.

    A) airplanes

    B) barges

    C) trucks

    D) trains

    E) steamships

Answer: C
Diff: 1

54) The two most important innovations stimulating the international division of labor in the early twentieth century were the metal–hulled, ocean–going steamship and

   A) an international telegraph network.

   B) the airplane.

   C) the semi–automatic rifle.

   D) the World Trade Organization.

   E) the division of the world into time zones.

Answer: A
Diff: 2

55) The system of practical and theoretical knowledge about making distinctive visual representations of Earth's surface in the form of maps is known as

   A) cartography.

   B) map science.

   C) projection science.

   D) mapology.

   E) choroplethography.

Answer: A
Diff: 3

56) The beginning of the modern world–system generally coincides with the

   A) fall of the Roman Empire.

   B) arrival of Europeans in the Americas.

   C) Industrial Revolution.

   D) colonization of Africa.

   E) dropping of the nuclear bomb on Japan.

Answer: B
Diff: 2

57) The core regions of the modern world–system

   A) dominate world trade.

   B) are primarily in the southern hemisphere.

   C) tend to have low per–capita incomes.

   D) became core regions by refusing to engage in colonialism.

   E) all of the above

Answer: A
Diff: 1

58) Semiperepheral regions

A) currently include Japan and Scandinavia.

B) often exploit peripheral regions.

C) will eventually evolve to become core regions.

D) are geographically located between core regions and peripheral regions.

Answer: B
Diff: 3

59) Of the following, the most important determinant of a state's classification within the world-system is its

A) military power.

B) population size.

C) ability to keep out foreign goods and run a positive trade balance.

D) ability to ensure international economic competitiveness of its domestic companies.

Answer: D
Diff: 3

60) Which of the following is NOT a characteristic of the early world empires?

A) colonialization

B) agriculturally based economy

C) use of religion and/or the military to control subjects

D) distribution of wealth from the upper classes to the lower classes

Answer: D
Diff: 2

61) In 1400 A.D., the dry steppes and desert margins that ranged from the western Sahara to Mongolia were populated by

A) tribal pastoral systems.   B) land speculators.

C) newly evangelized Christians.   D) European immigrants.

Answer: A
Diff: 2

62) Hadrian's Wall, the defensive structure stretching across northern Britain, was built by the

A) Vandals.   B) Romans.   C) Greeks.   D) Vikings.   E) Packers.

Answer: B
Diff: 2

63) The formation of the modern world-system was driven primarily by

    A) colonial missionaries.   B) racially-motivated Europeans.

    C) enlightened monarchs.   D) European merchant capitalists.

Answer: D
Diff: 1

64) In 1750 the core of the world-system was located in

    A) North America.

    B) Japan.

    C) western Europe.

    D) the countries surrounding the Mediterranean.

    E) China.

Answer: C
Diff: 1

65) In order to establish hegemony in the world-system, a state needed this most of all:

    A) economic strength and competitiveness   B) a big navy

    C) a large and efficient bureaucracy   D) the blessing of the Pope

Answer: A
Diff: 2

66) European industrialization began in the _____ century.

    A) fourteenth

    B) fifteenth

    C) sixteenth

    D) seventeenth

    E) eighteenth

Answer: E
Diff: 1

67) European industrialization got its start in

    A) France.   B) Sweden.   C) Italy.   D) Spain.   E) Britain.

Answer: E
Diff: 1

68) Which sequence matches the order in which the countries were world-system hegemons?

A) British, Dutch, Portuguese

B) Dutch, British, Portuguese

C) Portuguese, Dutch, British

D) Dutch, Portuguese, British

Answer: C
Diff: 1

69) Britain's dominance of the world-system in the eighteenth and nineteenth centuries was helped most by which of the following?

A) naval power

B) the fall of Napoleon

C) decline of the Roman Empire

D) British prowess in land battles

Answer: A
Diff: 2

70) The United States became a part of the world-system core

A) in the 1600s.

B) in the 1700s.

C) in the 1800s.

D) at the end of World War I.

E) at the end of World War II.

Answer: C
Diff: 2

71) In 1920 the United States' Manufacturing Belt stretched from

A) Miami to New Orleans.

B) San Diego to Seattle.

C) Minneapolis to Kansas City.

D) Baltimore to Milwaukee.

E) Chicago to Minneapolis/St. Paul.

Answer: D
Diff: 1

72) Which form of transportation developed first?

    A) steamboat

    B) railroad

    C) canal barge

    D) truck

    E) cargo container shipping

Answer: C
Diff: 1

73) In 1790, which state had the most miles of canals and canalized rivers?

    A) Britain

    B) France

    C) United States

    D) Holland

    E) Sweden

Answer: A
Diff: 2

74) Railroads originated in this country:

    A) United States

    B) Canada

    C) Britain

    D) France

    E) Germany

Answer: C
Diff: 1

75) Nineteenth–century railroad development in the United States

    A) was paltry compared to that of France.

    B) helped consolidate the Manufacturing Belt.

    C) was slowed by the Napoleonic wars in Europe.

    D) made the California Gold Rush possible.

Answer: B
Diff: 2

76) Which technological development was most closely linked to the emergence of an international division of labor?

A) radio communication

B) hydroelectric power

C) the telegraph

D) the metal–hulled steamship

Answer: D
Diff: 2

77) In the early 1900s, peripheral countries

A) were well on their way to becoming core countries.

B) imported most of their manufactured goods from core countries.

C) diversified their economies.

D) in Africa and Asia achieved their independence.

Answer: B
Diff: 2

78) The great scramble for African colonies occurred

A) just after the Napoleonic wars.

B) during Portugal's domination of the world–system.

C) in the three decades preceding World War I.

D) in the two decades after World War II.

Answer: C
Diff: 1

79) Dependence of the periphery upon the core states for _____ is a result of imperialism.

A) capital

B) education

C) managerial expertise

D) manufactured goods

E) all of the above

Answer: E
Diff: 1

80) In the years after World War II, this country emerged as the hegemonic power:

    A) Soviet Union

    B) Britain

    C) China

    D) United States

    E) Japan

Answer: D
Diff: 1

81) Neo-colonialism

    A) has been supplanted by globalization.

    B) is generally not considered exploitative.

    C) allows core states still to have significant influence over periphery states.

    D) is not connected with transnational corporations.

    E) all of the above

Answer: C
Diff: 2

82) Globalization

    A) is less relevant now than ten years ago.

    B) has resulted in increasingly great international economic integration.

    C) began in the early 1960s.

    D) has decreased interdependence.

Answer: B
Diff: 2

83) Over the last twenty-five years globalization has resulted in

    A) homogenization of international consumer markets.

    B) a new international division of labor.

    C) the internationalization of finance.

    D) all of the above

Answer: D
Diff: 1

84) Which of the following is NOT in the current world-system's core?

A) Japan   B) South America

C) Western Europe   D) North America

Answer: B
Diff: 1

85) Which of the following regions was the last to be discovered by Europeans?

A) West Africa

B) South America

C) North America

D) Australia and New Zealand

E) Japan

Answer: D
Diff: 1

86) Which world region is least a part of the current world system's core?

A) Africa

B) Asia

C) North America

D) Europe

E) South America

Answer: A
Diff: 2

87) Which of the following was NOT a hearth area?

A) Fertile Crescent

B) Ganges floodplain

C) Anatolian plateau

D) Arizona and New Mexico

E) Scandinavia

Answer: E
Diff: 2

88) In 1750 this was NOT part of the world system:

    A) Australia

    B) Brazil

    C) Caribbean

    D) eastern North America

    E) Mediterranean North Africa

Answer: A
Diff: 2

89) The Berlin Conference

    A) occurred in the first decade of the twentieth century.

    B) focused on North America.

    C) decreased the probability of war between European states.

    D) removed most of Africa from further European settlement.

Answer: C
Diff: 2

90) Internet access is

    A) increasing at slower and slower rates.

    B) limited to fewer than 150 million people.

    C) about the same for most regions of the world.

    D) most frequent in upper income households in core countries.

Answer: D
Diff: 2

2.3 True or False

1) Most of the world's remaining external arenas are above the Arctic Circle and in Siberia.

Answer: FALSE
Diff: 3

2) The world's major hearth areas, from where new practices emerged and subsequently spread, eventually grew into the world's core.

Answer: FALSE
Diff: 3

3) Based on the history of the world system, once a country is in the periphery, it always remains in the periphery.

Answer: FALSE
Diff: 2

4) World empires in Asia that relied upon large-scale irrigation and drainage schemes for agricultural productivity are known as hydraulic societies.

Answer: TRUE
Diff: 1

5) Ann Arbor, 50 miles west of Detroit, is reasonably considered to be part of Detroit's external arena.

Answer: FALSE
Diff: 3

6) The only hinterlands remaining in the world today are found in remote areas of the world's South.

Answer: FALSE
Diff: 2

7) Geography (including map making and geographical description) was essential for commercial success in the competitive world of the European Renaissance.

Answer: TRUE
Diff: 2

8) The world system has stopped evolving and been stable since the end of colonialism after WWII.

Answer: FALSE
Diff: 1

9) The Manufacturing Belt in the United States is an example of a core within a core.

Answer: TRUE
Diff: 1

10) Because early modern geography (late eighteenth and early nineteenth century) was so involved in exploration, it ended up contributing to colonialism and imperialism.

Answer: TRUE
Diff: 2

11) After WWII, the United States emerged as the world's hegemonic power.

Answer: TRUE
Diff: 1

12) The generally recognized beginning of globalization is the end of WWII and the beginning of international organizations like NATO and the United Nations.

Answer: FALSE
Diff: 2

13) With political independence in the 1950s and 1960s, the former European colonies of Africa were finally able to achieve economic independence from the world's core.

Answer: FALSE
Diff: 2

14) As explained by Knox and Marston, the fast world encompasses almost every *where* but not every*body*.

Answer: TRUE
Diff: 2

15) Brazil has some characteristics of a core state and a periphery state.

Answer: TRUE
Diff: 1

16) Many of Western Europe's important cities were once Roman settlements.

Answer: TRUE
Diff: 2

17) The states that were best able to resist European incursions during the first three centuries of the modern world–system were located primarily in South and East Asia.

Answer: TRUE
Diff: 2

18) Until the late 1700s, European economic expansion was significantly limited by dependence on wind and water for power, and wood for building materials.

Answer: TRUE
Diff: 1

19) States become world hegemons through imperial overstretch.

Answer: FALSE
Diff: 2

20) Britain maintained world dominance in two successive cycles.

Answer: TRUE
Diff: 2

21) The United States in now considered to be the world's hegemonic power.

Answer: TRUE
Diff: 1

22) Japan has been a member of the core since the beginning of the world-system.

Answer: FALSE
Diff: 2

23) Improvements in transportation technologies make it easier to access agrarian interiors.

Answer: TRUE
Diff: 1

24) Barge transport is no longer used in Europe.

Answer: FALSE
Diff: 2

25) The nineteenth-century growth of core states would not have been possible without the use of colonies for foodstuffs, raw materials, and as markets for core-state products.

Answer: TRUE
Diff: 2

26) Most colonies produced a wide range of agricultural and manufactured products.

Answer: FALSE
Diff: 1

27) In the late nineteenth century, Britain was virtually alone in striving to gain new colonies.

Answer: FALSE
Diff: 1

28) Port cities in colonies tended to be significantly larger than interior colonial cities.

Answer: TRUE
Diff: 2

29) After World War II, the peripheral states were commonly known as the Second World.

Answer: FALSE
Diff: 1

30) A resident of a peripheral country is more likely to belong to the slow world than the fast world.

Answer: TRUE
Diff: 1

31) Core regions usually have a higher per-capita income than do periphery regions.

Answer: TRUE
Diff: 1

32) In 1895 most of South America was semi-periphery.

Answer: FALSE
Diff: 2

33) Slash-and-burn cultivation was a characteristic of Paleolithic agricultural practices.

Answer: FALSE
Diff: 1

34) The rise of the railroads led to a significant increase in the use of canals for shipping.

Answer: FALSE
Diff: 1

35) The rise of the trucking industry gave industries greater freedom in deciding where to locate factories.

Answer: TRUE
Diff: 1

36) In general, the more countries and regions plan their economies around the concept of comparative advantage, the greater overall global economic output will be.

Answer: TRUE
Diff: 2

37) Even during the height of the colonial era, none of the peripheral areas had a significant impact on global trade.

Answer: FALSE
Diff: 2

38) The amount of global trade relative to global production has increased over the last 25 years.

Answer: TRUE
Diff: 2

39) Over the last 40 or so years, the gap between the world's richest fifth and the world's poorest fifth has decreased.

Answer: FALSE
Diff: 1

2.4 Matching

SYSTEMS & SITES: Match the specific countries and regions to the entities or groups they exemplify.

1) Tripolar core
   Diff: 2

2) World's South
   Diff: 2

3) Agricultural hearths
   Diff: 2

4) Industrial hearth
   Diff: 2

5) World Empires
   Diff: 2

A) Egypt, China, Byzantium

B) Subsaharan Africa, Central America, Southeast Asia

C) Britain, France, Germany

D) Fertile Crescent, South Asian Floodplains, Tehuacan Valley

E) Europe, Japan, North America

1) E   2) B   3) D   4) C   5) A

CORE – PERIPHERY: Match the characteristic to the group of countries.

6) colonizers and imperialists
Diff: 2

7) undeveloped economies
Diff: 2

8) Fast World
Diff: 2

9) Brazil, India, Mexico
Diff: 3

10) diversified economies and
advanced technologies
Diff: 3

11) Japan and the United States
Diff: 3

12) dependent and
disadvantageous trade
relations
Diff: 3

A) Core

B) Periphery

C) Semiperiphery

6) A   7) B   8) A   9) C   10) A   11) A
12) B

PEOPLE, PLACES, THINGS: Match the device or description with the people or places.

13) Samarkand & Khiva
   Diff: 2

14) Quadrant & Astrolabe
   Diff: 2

15) Tallinn & Riga
   Diff: 2

16) Strabo & Ptolemy
   Diff: 3

17) Colon & da Gama
   Diff: 3

18) Ritter & von Humboldt
   Diff: 3

19) Mosul, Damascus & Kashmir
   Diff: 3

A) first & second–century Greek Geographers

B) nineteenth–century German Geographers

C) Hanseatic League city–states

D) fifteenth–century navigational tools

E) places after which textiles have been named

F) Silk Road Cities

G) Portuguese Explorers

13) F   14) D   15) C   16) A   17) G   18) B
19) E

EXAMPLES: Match the example to the term or phrase.

20) Increasing use of solar energy to reduce need for imported oil
Diff: 3

A) hearth area

B) import substitution

C) mini-systems

21) Middle East/Fertile Crescent as origin of wheat, olives and sheep
Diff: 3

D) hinterland

E) hegemony

22) British control and administration of political and legal affairs in India
Diff: 2

F) technology systems

G) colonialism

23) the Italian countryside as the region under Rome's sphere of influence
Diff: 2

24) nineteenth-century British domination over the world economy
Diff: 2

25) Indian Tribes of N. America before the arrival of Europeans
Diff: 2

26) clusters of energy, transportation, and production practices
Diff: 2

20) B   21) A   22) G   23) D   24) E   25) C
26) F

DATES: Match the event(s) to the approximate time at which it (they) occurred

27) Beginning of the first
agricultural revolution
Diff: 2

A) end of eighteenth century

B) fifteenth century

28) Beginning of the industrial
revolution
Diff: 2

C) 9000 BC

D) First century

29) Beginning of Cold War
Diff: 2

E) mid–nineteenth century

30) Beginning of the Age of
Discovery
Diff: 2

31) Strabo, Ptolemy & the
foundations of modern
geography
Diff: 2

27) C   28) A   29) E   30) B   31) D

2.5 Map Identification

World Map

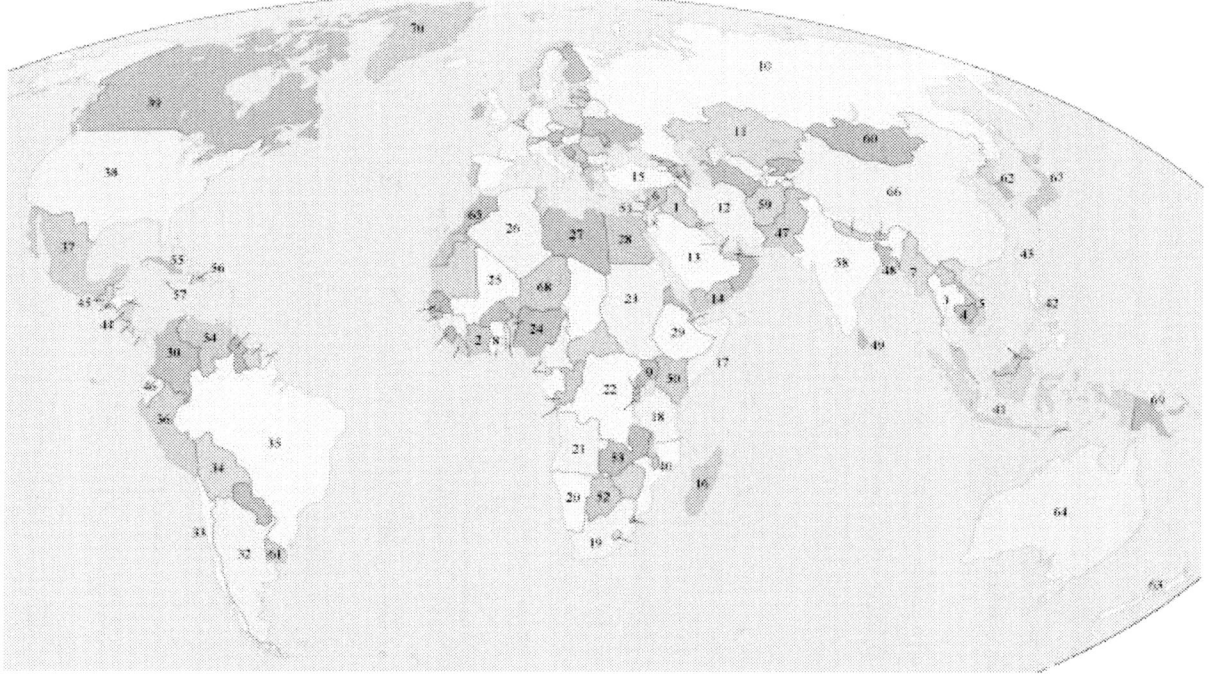

1) To drive from Portugal to France, one must drive through

    A) Morocco.

    B) Turkey.

    C) Argentina.

    D) India.

    E) Spain.

    Answer: E
    Diff: 1

2) The country of Argentina is identified by the number

    A) 2.   B) 12.   C) 22.   D) 32.   E) 42.

    Answer: D
    Diff: 1

3) Which of the following is not in Africa?

    A) Kazakhstan

    B) Kenya

    C) Ghana

    D) Ethiopia

    E) Morocco

Answer: A
Diff: 1

4) Lisbon is the capital of

    A) Portugal.

    B) Canada.

    C) Argentina.

    D) Kenya.

    E) India.

Answer: A
Diff: 1

5) Which of the following is a North African country?

    A) Ghana   B) Kenya   C) Spain   D) Morocco   E) Ethiopia

Answer: D
Diff: 2

6) Countries 26, 27 and 28 are all part of

    A) North Africa.

    B) Sub-Saharan Africa.

    C) Southeast Asia.

    D) the Middle East.

    E) North America.

Answer: A
Diff: 2

7) The European country nearest to Morocco is

    A) Spain.   B) Portugal.   C) France.   D) Canada.   E) Ghana.

Answer: A
Diff: 2

8) Rabat is the capital of country labeled with the number

   A) 8.   B) 24.   C) 45.   D) 58.   E) 65.

   Answer: E
   Diff: 2

9) The capital city of country #58 is . . .

   A) Tokyo.

   B) Dacca.

   C) New Delhi.

   D) Accra.

   E) Dakar.

   Answer: C
   Diff: 1

10) The capital city of #35 is

   A) Nairobi.

   B) Mexico City.

   C) Buenos Aires.

   D) Beijing.

   E) Madrid.

   Answer: C
   Diff: 1

11) Which pair of countries are nearest each other?

   A) Spain & Morocco

   B) Argentina & Ghana

   C) Kenya & Ghana

   D) USA & Japan

   E) Portugal & Ghana

   Answer: A
   Diff: 2

Europe

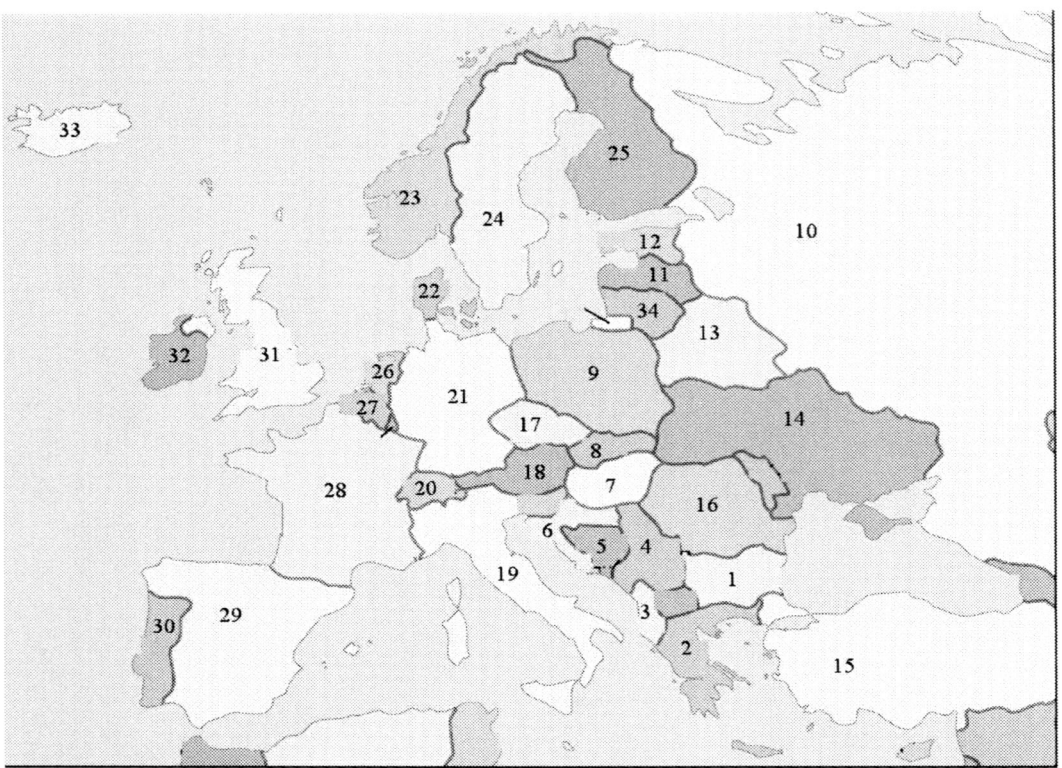

12) Lisbon is the country of the capital labeled by with which number?

A) 32   B) 31   C) 30   D) 28   E) 22

Answer: C
Diff: 1

13) Country #29 is

A) Morocco.   B) France.   C) Spain.   D) Portugal.   E) Italy.

Answer: C
Diff: 1

2.6 Chapter 2 Questions with images

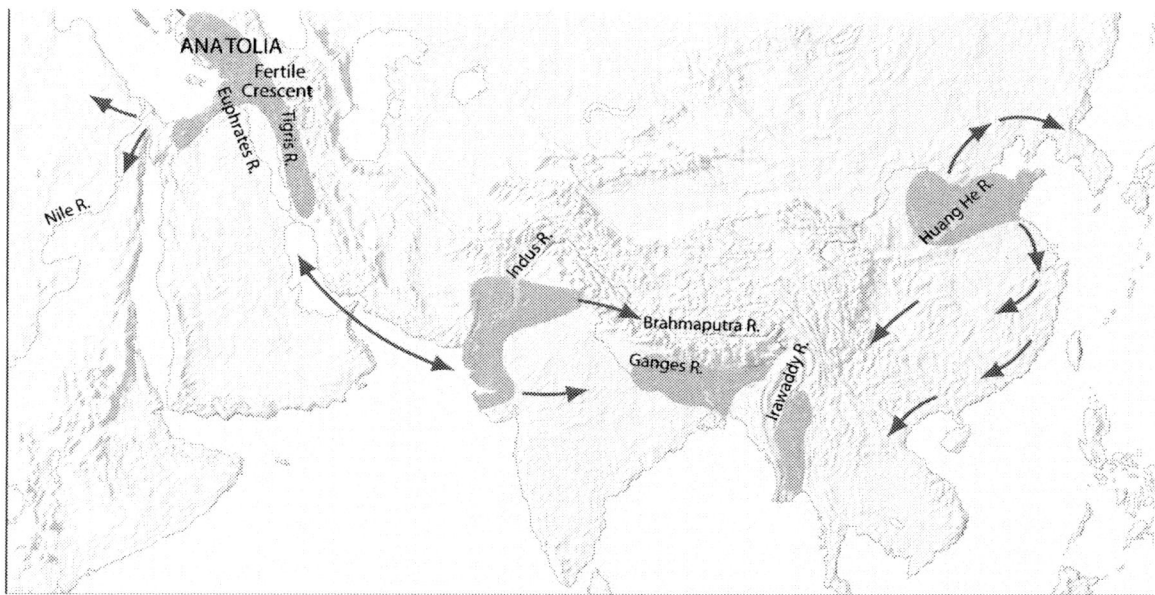

1) The regions highlighted in the above map represent

    A) sites of the first agricultural revolution.

    B) colonies of Roman Empire.

    C) New World hearth areas.

    D) the world's core regions.

    E) centers in the spread of the industrial revolution.

Answer: A
Diff: 3

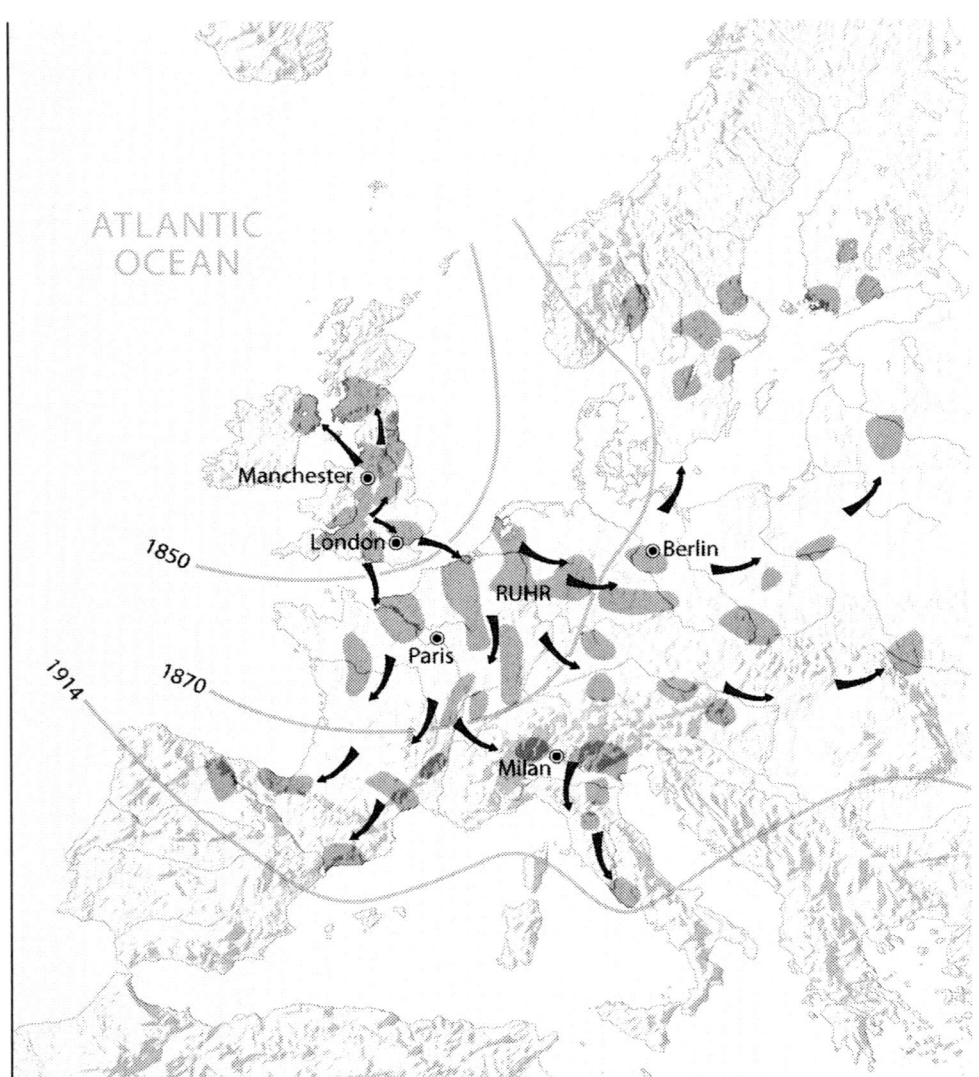

2) The above map represents

    A) the spread of the Industrial Revolution across Europe.

    B) the expansion of British colonialism.

    C) the occurrance of local conflicts that led to World War I.

    D) the migration of refugees from England.

    E) the diffusion of nuclear power plants across Europe.

Answer: A
Diff: 3

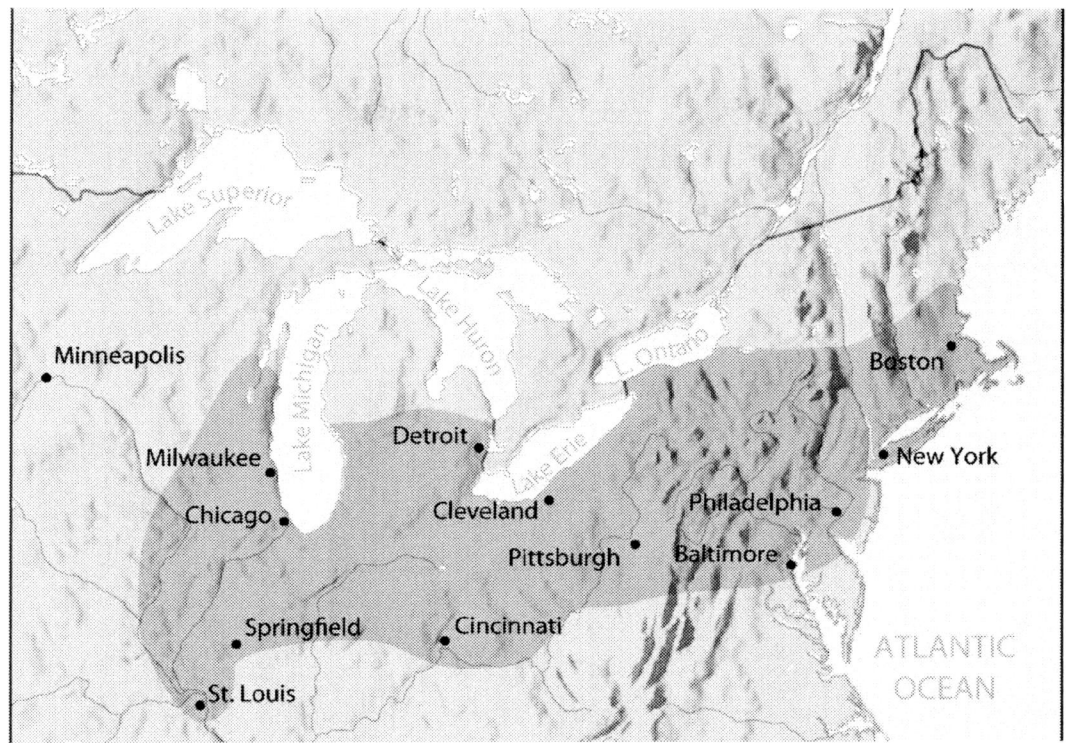

3) The shaded region in the above map represents the

    A) historical industrial region of the United States.

    B) core of the world system.

    C) original British colony in North America.

    D) coal producing region of the United States.

    E) United States' external arena.

Answer: A
Diff: 2

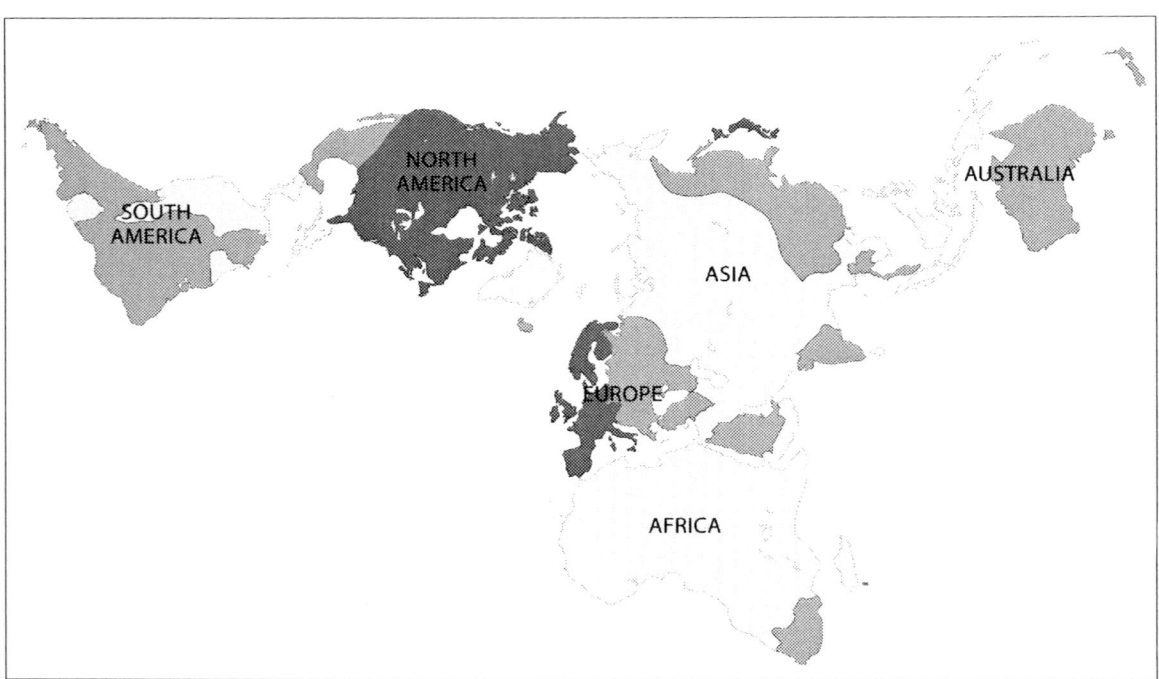

4) In the above map, the darkest shaded regions represent the world's

    A) core.

    B) periphery.

    C) external arenas.

    D) hearth areas.

    E) wealthiest colonies.

Answer: A
Diff: 3

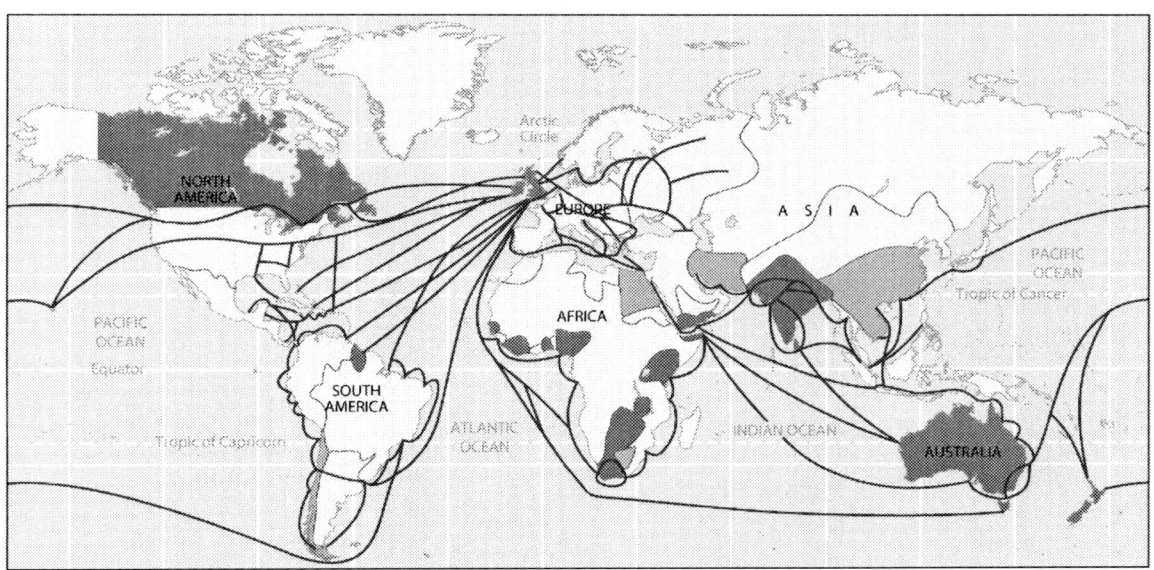

5) The above map best represents

    A) colonies and trading patterns of the British Empire.

    B) today's world core.

    C) the Silk Road and its trading routes.

    D) global internet connectivity.

    E) the Columbian Exchange.

Answer: A
Diff: 3

Chapter 3 Geographies of Population

3.1 Minimal Choice

1) Geographers are more likely than other scientists to study

    A) the biological basis of human longevity.

    B) the spatial patterns of human populations.

Answer: B
Diff: 1

2) Population increase in the twentieth century was the result of a phenomenal

    A) rise in birth rates.   B) decline in death rates.

Answer: B
Diff: 1

3) In 1985, the United States introduced the _____ census to make sure population
information is as current and accurate as possible.

    A) quinquennial   B) geodemographic

Answer: A
Diff: 1

4) Since 1790, the United States has conducted a census every

    A) 10 years.   B) 5 years.

Answer: A
Diff: 1

5) Despite the fact that the 2000 census overcounted the U.S. population by 1.3 million, it
undercounted

    A) Non–Hispanic Whites.   B) Native peoples.

Answer: B
Diff: 2

6) Nutritional density refers to the ratio of

    A) total population to land being farmed.   B) unhealthy people to total population.

Answer: A
Diff: 2

7) In 2000, the median age of the world's population was about 27 years old. By 2050, it is estimated to be

    A) 38.   B) 22.

Answer: A
Diff: 2

8) The children of Baby Boomers are known as

    A) Generation Y.   B) Generation X.

Answer: A
Diff: 3

9) The baby bust refers to the cohort(s) immediately _____ the baby boomers.

    A) before   B) after

Answer: B
Diff: 2

10) The _____ is most likely to have Baby Boomer parents.

    A) Net Generation (Generation Y)   B) Mac Generation (Generation X)

Answer: A
Diff: 3

11) Which of the following has no -- or at least very little -- impact on the doubling time?

    A) size of the population   B) education levels of the population

Answer: A
Diff: 3

12) For a given population, infant mortality rate is a more accurate indicator of which of the following?

    A) access to health care   B) medical advancements

Answer: A
Diff: 3

13) African-Americans have a(n) _____ twice that of the the national average for the United States.

    A) infant mortality rate   B) life expectancy

Answer: A
Diff: 1

14) The rise in HIV/AIDS infections is rising most steeply in

A) Eastern Europe.   B) Latin America.

Answer: A
Diff: 2

15) The demographic transition model was based on the experience of

A) core countries.   B) peripheral countries.

Answer: A
Diff: 2

16) For refugees, _____ are the most influential set of forces behind the migration experience.

A) push factors   B) pull factors

Answer: A
Diff: 2

17) The better example of voluntary migrants are

A) overseas contract workers.   B) internally displaced persons.

Answer: A
Diff: 1

18) _____ are forced migrants.

A) IDPs   B) OCWs

Answer: A
Diff: 1

19) The better explanation for the Rustbelt to Sunbelt internal wave of migration in the U.S. is

A) the pull of economic opportunity. B) the pull of cold weather.

Answer: A
Diff: 1

20) World population was 6 billion in 2005. By 2050, world population is expected to reach about 10 billion; by 2150, it is project to be about

A) 12 billion.   B) 22 billion.

Answer: A
Diff: 1

21) The livelihoods wiped out by the South Asian tsunami of 2005 created a new

A) wave of eco-migrants.   B) demographic transition.

Answer: A
Diff: 1

3.2 Multiple Choice

1) In providing millions of migrants to the world's economic core, countries like Mexico and Turkey benefit greatly from the resulting

    A) brain drain.

    B) remittance payments.

    C) beaten path.

    D) eco-migration.

    E) structural adjustment programs.

Answer: B
Diff: 3

2) A measure of the economic impact of the young and old on the more economically active and productive members of a population is known as the

    A) dependency ratio.

    B) expectancy ratio.

    C) youth-elderly cohort.

    D) infant mortality rate.

    E) crude death rate.

Answer: A
Diff: 2

3) In 1998, Ecuador had a population of 12 million and Mexico had a population of 97 million. Both had an RNI of 2.2. This means that

    A) Ecuador's population will double more quickly than Mexico's.

    B) Mexico's population will double more quickly than Ecuador's.

    C) Ecuador's and Mexico's populations will double in the same amount of time.

    D) Ecuador's and Mexico's populations will never double with such a low RNI.

Answer: C
Diff: 3

4) According to the textbook, which of the following is a major reason for falling birthrates during the 1990s in the former Soviet/Eastern bloc countries?

    A) high levels of sterility among men and women due to environmental pollution

    B) an increase in job opportunities for women, who put off having kids until later

    C) couples decide against having kids because of bleak economic prospects

    D) strict enforcement of population control policies to limit population growth

Answer: C
Diff: 2

5) For which of the following populations is total population change equal to the rate of natural increase?

    A) Los Angeles

    B) Egypt

    C) North America

    D) World

    E) None, because total population change includes migration.

Answer: D
Diff: 3

6) The twentieth century's great growth in world population is due to a phenomenal

    A) global baby boom.

    B) rise in birth rates.

    C) decline in death rates.

    D) increase in migration rates.

    E) all of the above

Answer: C
Diff: 2

7) Demography is the study of population

    A) characteristics.

    B) politics.

    C) attitudes.

    D) pressures.

    E) distribution.

Answer: A
Diff: 1

8) The most widely used tool to assess the size, distribution and characteristics of a population is

    A) the census.

    B) geodemographic analysis.

    C) geographic information systems.

    D) demographic transition.

    E) conducting a vital record.

Answer: A
Diff: 1

9) Inaccuracies in U.S. censuses

    A) do not occur with any degree of significance.

    B) are no big deal – they are just a count of the population, anyway.

    C) are the result of big government inefficiencies.

    D) are a big deal – they affect the distribution of federal revenues and congressional seats.

    E) are a big deal – they affect the distribution of professional sports franchises around the country.

Answer: D
Diff: 1

10) A population density map of the world shows that the distribution of people is most obviously affected by

    A) environmental factors such as natural resources, climate, water availability, topography.

    B) political and economic factors such as development, types of government, trade history.

    C) cultural factors such as language, cuisine and religion.

    D) preferences for places with tropical landscapes.

    E) all of the above

Answer: A
Diff: 3

11) The number of people per unit of area (such as people per square kilometer) is a measure of

    A) nutritional density.

    B) agricultural density.

    C) health density.

    D) crude density.

    E) natural density.

Answer: D
Diff: 1

12) For countries of similar area and population, the one with the greatest amount of _____ is most likely to have the highest nutritional density.

    A) forest land

    B) farmland

    C) desert lands

    D) lakes, rivers and swamps

    E) mountains

Answer: B
Diff: 3

13) Of the following, which of the following generally has the highest population density?

    A) core countries

    B) peripheral countries

    C) urban areas

    D) rural areas

    E) areas with high birth rates

Answer: C
Diff: 2

14) Age-sex pyramids are graphical representations of

    A) the structure of population at a moment in time.

    B) the distribution of a population over space.

    C) birth rates and death rates of a country.

    D) the rankings of countries around the world.

    E) a hierarchy of core-periphery relationships.

Answer: A
Diff: 2

15) If an age-sex pyramid is asymmetrical, lopsided from left to right, it means that

    A) males experienced events differently than females of the same cohorts.

    B) generation gaps are evident.

    C) the rate of natural increase is declining.

    D) the population is in the middle of the demographic transition.

    E) the demographer needs to redo the pyramid – they should always be symmetrical.

Answer: A
Diff: 3

16) To a demographer, a group of people that begin something at the same time is known as

    A) a cohort.

    B) a team.

    C) a dependency ratio.

    D) a transnational migrant.

    E) a baby boom.

Answer: A
Diff: 1

17) Which of the following best explains a population pyramid (age–sex pyramid) that looks like an umbrella, with very narrow cohorts at the bottom that widen broadly near the top?

    A) The population pyramid is upside down.

    B) The population is a retirement village.

    C) The population is a college town.

    D) Migrants are dominant in the community.

    E) The population has an open–door migration policy.

Answer: B
Diff: 3

18) As the Baby Boomers age and the elderly cohorts get larger, the dependency ratio in the United States will

    A) drop.

    B) rise.

    C) disappear.

    D) stay the same.

    E) fluctuate more and more.

Answer: B
Diff: 2

19) The Crude Birth Rate (CBR) is *not* affected by which of the following?

    A) level of economic development

    B) opportunities for women

    C) religion and other cultural practices

    D) the availability of birth control

    E) The CBR is influenced by all of the above.

Answer: E
Diff: 2

20) A population in which the total fertility rate is 2 means that

    A) birth rates and death rates are roughly equal.

    B) the population is stable (no increase or decline).

    C) the population will double in about 40 years.

    D) the population will decline by half in 40 years.

    E) both A and B

Answer: E
Diff: 3

21) Crude death rates refer to the annual ratio of

    A) deaths to every 1000 live births.

    B) deaths to every 1000 people.

    C) accidental deaths to deaths from natural causes

    D) deaths from preventable diseases to deaths from natural causes.

    E) deaths to births.

Answer: B
Diff: 1

22) Whether or not a given population grows is a function of

    A) birth rates.

    B) death rates.

    C) immigration.

    D) emigration.

    E) all of the above

Answer: E
Diff: 1

23) The combination of the CBR and the CDR is (the)

    A) rate of natural increase.

    B) infant mortality rate.

    C) dependency ratio.

    D) life expectancy.

    E) net migration.

Answer: A
Diff: 1

24) The rate of natural increase is a useful indicator for examining

    A) levels of economic development and growth.

    B) population growth.

    C) impacts of migration.

    D) access to nutrition and health.

    E) nutritional density.

Answer: B
Diff: 1

25) When calculating the rate of natural increase, one does not include

    A) birth rates.

    B) death rates.

    C) migration.

    D) the rate of natural increase uses all of the above.

    E) both A and B

Answer: C
Diff: 2

26) Infant mortality rates vary between countries. However, they do not vary among the peoples and regions inside

    A) the United States, Canada and Western Europe.

    B) Mexico and other Central American countries.

    C) Zimbabwe, Nigeria and other sub–Saharan countries.

    D) India, Bangladesh and other South Asian countries.

    E) Infant mortality rates vary between the people and regions of all countries.

Answer: E
Diff: 3

27) In sub–Saharan African countries hit hard by HIV/AIDS _____ have dropped most sharply.

    A) crude death rates

    B) crude birth rates

    C) life expectancies

    D) migration rates

    E) dependency ratios

Answer: C
Diff: 3

28) The demographic transition is a model of population change used to explain high population growth rates. According to the theory,

    A) birth rates decline, eventually followed by a decline in death rates.

    B) death rates decline, eventually followed by a decline in birth rates.

    C) birth rates and death rates decline simultaneously.

    D) birth rates rise, eventually followed by a rise in death rates.

    E) death rates rise, eventually followed by a rise in birth rates.

Answer: B
Diff: 2

29) According to the demographic transition model, the rate of natural (RNI) at the beginning (preindustrial phase) is generally _____ than the RNI at the end (industrial phase).

    A) higher

    B) lower

    C) the same as

    D) cannot generalize -- it depends on the starting and ending birth and death rates

Answer: C
Diff: 3

30) A Texan that moves to Canada _____ from Texas and _____ to Canada.

    A) immigrates/immigrates   B) immigrates/emigrates

    C) emigrates/immigrates   D) emigrates/emigrates

Answer: C
Diff: 2

31) If 1,500 people migrate into Goodhue, MN and 1000 people move out, gross migration is

    A) 2500.

    B) 1500.

    C) 1000.

    D) 500.

    E) negative 500.

Answer: A
Diff: 2

32) If 1,500 people migrate into Goodhue, MN and 1000 people move out, net migration is

    A) 2500.

    B) 1500.

    C) 1000.

    D) 500.

    E) negative 500.

Answer: D
Diff: 2

33) Of the following, a typical example of a push factor of migration would be

    A) abundant job opportunities.

    B) beautiful weather.

    C) social conflict.

    D) close family ties.

    E) good schools.

Answer: C
Diff: 3

34) Hong Kong Chinese that maintain residences and businesses in Hong Kong and Vancouver, like Turks that work in Germany while maintaining close connections and property in Turkey, are specifically known as

    A) voluntary migrants.

    B) voluntary emigrants.

    C) international emigrants.

    D) transnational migrants.

    E) guest workers.

Answer: D
Diff: 3

35) _____ temporarily migrate to take jobs in other countries and send remittance payments to their home communities.

    A) Guest workers

    B) Refugees

    C) Voluntary migrants

    D) International forced migrants

    E) Transmigrants

Answer: A
Diff: 2

36) In the United States, there have been numerous waves of internal voluntary migration. These include all of the following *except*

    A) the westward expansion of the frontier.

    B) rural–to–urban migration of agricultural workers.

    C) the great northward migration of African–Americans.

    D) the Snowbelt to Sunbelt migration.

    E) the Trail of Tears.

Answer: E
Diff: 2

37) Moderate Neo–Malthusians believe that solutions to the global population issue are best found in

    A) reducing the size of the periphery's population.

    B) technological innovations.

    C) neoliberalism and the ability of market forces to regulate population growth.

    D) the redistribution of wealth and resources.

    E) letting diseases thin out human populations.

Answer: D
Diff: 3

38) Writing on the eve of the Industrial Revolution, Thomas Malthus argued that population growth

    A) would exceed the ability of people to feed themselves.

    B) was insufficient to meet the needs of industry.

    C) presented numerous opportunities for technological innovation.

    D) was so low, and food so abundant, that people would become increasingly obese.

    E) and procreation were fundamental rights of human beings.

Answer: A
Diff: 2

39) People who share Thomas Malthus' perspectives on population growth are known as

    A) Proto–Malthusians.

    B) Neo–Malthusians.

    C) Neoliberals.

    D) Thomasians.

    E) Proto–Thomasians.

Answer: B
Diff: 1

40) Most international population policies at the end of the twentieth century have emphasized

    A) reduced birth rates.

    B) economic development.

    C) increased opportunities for women.

    D) increased health care for children.

    E) both C and D

Answer: A
Diff: 1

41) The diffusion of HIV/AIDS in sub–Saharan Africa has been most prominent

    A) among children and the elderly.

    B) in jungles and other similarly remote areas.

    C) in urban centers.

    D) along transportation routes.

    E) among homosexuals and drug users.

Answer: D
Diff: 2

42) In recognition of the complex and changing population of the United States, the 2000 census included a new category with which respondents could choose to identify:

    A) Latino/Latina.

    B) multiracial.

    C) transcendental.

    D) polyglot.

    E) world citizen.

Answer: B
Diff: 2

43) With almost 4 billion people, Asia has nearly 2/3 of the world's population. From among those below, the world region with the smallest population is

    A) Africa.   B) Europe.

    C) North America.   D) Latin America & the Caribbean.

Answer: C
Diff: 2

44) The value and power of geographic information systems come with linking demographic data to particular

    A) populations.

    B) cohorts.

    C) locations.

    D) censuses.

    E) policies.

Answer: C
Diff: 2

45) The 15 year period of low total fertility rates after the baby boom, is known as the baby

    A) bomb.

    B) boom echo.

    C) boomlet.

    D) bust.

    E) bear.

Answer: D
Diff: 2

46) In addition to the economic burden of caring for the large, aging Baby Boom population, the Net Generation carries a cultural burden --

    A) a declining geographic literacy and not understanding world cultures.

    B) not understanding the difference between high and low culture.

    C) having to watch endless reruns of Gilligan's Island and The Three Stooges.

    D) the difficulty of establishing a distinct identity.

    E) all of the above

Answer: D
Diff: 2

47) For which of the following is the U.S. national average the same as that for minority groups in the U.S.?

    A) birth rate

    B) infant mortality rate

    C) death rate

    D) all of the above

    E) none of the above

Answer: E
Diff: 1

48) The world region with by far the greatest number of internally displaced persons -- nearly half of all 25 million -- is

    A) North America.

    B) Latin America.

    C) Africa.

    D) the Middle East.

    E) Asia.

Answer: D
Diff: 2

49) Generally, internally displaced persons (IDPs) suffer more than international refugees because

    A) their own governments are unable or unwilling to help.

    B) foreign governments governments don't care.

    C) foreign governments don't know about the IDPs.

    D) their own governments do not have the military might to protect the IDPs.

    E) the world community treats refugees so well.

Answer: A
Diff: 2

50) In which of the following is Sweden, Poland, Yemen and Cambodia most similar?

    A) infant mortality rate

    B) rate of natural increase

    C) crude birth rate

    D) crude death rate

    E) total fertility rate

Answer: D
Diff: 3

51) For over 200 years, a census of the entire United States population has occurred every

    A) year.

    B) two years.

    C) five years.

    D) ten years.

    E) twenty years.

Answer: D
Diff: 1

52) Which continent has the greatest number of inhabitants?

    A) North America

    B) South America

    C) Europe

    D) Africa

    E) Asia

Answer: E
Diff: 1

53) Which continent has the fewest inhabitants?

    A) Africa

    B) Australia

    C) North America

    D) South America

    E) Asia

Answer: B
Diff: 1

54) In general, a geographer would least expect to find population clusters

    A) in areas with fertile soils.   B) in mountainous interiors.

    C) along navigable rivers.   D) beside seaports.

Answer: B
Diff: 2

55) The baby boom refers to people who were born between the years of

    A) 1928 and 1945.   B) 1946 and 1964.

    C) 1965 and 1990.   D) 1990 and the present.

Answer: B
Diff: 1

56) In which of the following countries does one expect the fastest population growth?

    A) Denmark

    B) Germany

    C) New Zealand

    D) Russia

    E) Guatemala

Answer: E
Diff: 2

57) Businesses and marketers use Geographic Information Systems to

   A) match demographic data with specific locations.

   B) coordinate the shipment of goods around the world.

   C) calculate exchange rates of currencies around the world.

   D) forecast national population growth rates.

   E) Geographic Information Systems are used for all of the above.

Answer: A
Diff: 1

58) Which of the following types of data is useful in Geographic Information Systems?

   A) income level

   B) age

   C) size of household

   D) maps

   E) all of the above

Answer: E
Diff: 2

59) From an age–sex pyramid for the USA (2000), it is clear that the largest age group is _____ years old

   A) 0–15.   B) 15–35.   C) 35–55.   D) 55–75.

Answer: C
Diff: 3

60) In an age–sex pyramid for the United States (2000), the biggest bulge in males and females is due to

   A) the sexual revolution of the 1960s/70s and the end of the Vietnam war.

   B) large families between the two World Wars.

   C) the baby boom.

   D) the baby boom echo.

   E) the baby boom bust.

Answer: C
Diff: 2

61) For which country would you expect the age-sex pyramid to look most like an actual pyramid?

A) United States

B) France

C) Japan

D) Bolivia

E) Australia

Answer: D
Diff: 3

62) In the 1950s, the outlook for the parents of baby boomers was generally positive because they

A) got educational help from the government, if they were veterans.

B) faced an expanding labor market.

C) were generally able to attain a better standard of living than their parents.

D) all of the above

Answer: D
Diff: 1

63) Baby boomers

A) have less education than the previous generation.

B) get married younger than any previous generation.

C) are more likely to get divorced than any previous generation.

D) have a lower standard of living than any previous generation.

Answer: C
Diff: 2

64) Which of the following cohorts is the most economically productive?

A) youth cohort

B) middle cohort

C) old-age cohort

D) All three cohorts are about equally economically productive.

Answer: B
Diff: 2

65) The youth cohort

    A) are not fully active in the labor force.

    B) are between the ages of 16 and 30.

    C) have little effect on the dependency ratio.

    D) refers to increasing number of young people in the service sector of the labor force.

Answer: A
Diff: 1

66) Generation X is (are)

    A) another name for the baby boom generation.

    B) the name given to the parents of baby boomers.

    C) members of the baby bust.

    D) the result of high birth rates.

    E) the children of migrants to the United States.

Answer: C
Diff: 2

67) The crude death rate

    A) is the sum total of infant mortality rate, youth mortality rate and the elderly mortality rate.

    B) typically declines as overall levels of economic development go up.

    C) is typically higher in core countries than in periphery countries.

    D) is not considered a useful measure by most population geographers.

Answer: B
Diff: 3

68) When crude birth rates are higher than crude death rates, the difference between them is known as the

    A) infant mortality rate.

    B) infant natality rate

    C) total fertility rate.

    D) natural decrease.

    E) natural increase.

Answer: E
Diff: 1

69) Infant mortality rates are lowest in which of the following areas?

    A) Western Europe   B) Africa

    C) Asia   D) South America

Answer: A
Diff: 1

70) Which of the following groups of states has been affected the least by the AIDS epidemic?

    A) North America

    B) Central Africa

    C) Asia

    D) the Middle East

    E) Western Europe

Answer: D
Diff: 2

71) In central Africa AIDS primarily strikes

    A) homosexuals.   B) drug users.   C) heterosexuals.   D) hemophiliacs.

Answer: C
Diff: 2

72) Demographic transition theory holds that

    A) advanced industrial states will have high rates of population growth.

    B) preindustrial states will have both low birth rates and death rates.

    C) high levels of economic production will lower birth rates.

    D) periphery and semi-periphery states cannot become core states.

    E) their is a maximum population size for every place.

Answer: C
Diff: 2

73) In which phase(s) of the demographic transition model are birth rate and death rate about equal?

    A) Preindustrial

    B) Transitional

    C) Industrial

    D) Preindustrial and Transitional

    E) Preindustrial and Industrial

Answer: D
Diff: 3

74) Critics of demographic transition theory argue that the theory

    A) is not very relevant for countries on the periphery.

    B) does not work for European countries.

    C) has a Marxist ideological bias.

    D) birth rates and death rates have nothing to do with each other.

Answer: A
Diff: 2

75) Emigration

    A) refers to a move *from* a place.

    B) is the same as gross migration.

    C) does not involve push factors.

    D) is equal to the difference between voluntary migration and forced migration.

Answer: A
Diff: 1

76) International voluntary migration

    A) is insignificant now compared to prehistoric times.

    B) is most likely to be from the periphery to the core.

    C) is done typically for religious reasons.

    D) is usually coordinated by the United Nations.

    E) is a combination of all of the above.

Answer: B
Diff: 2

77) The first wave of internal voluntary migration within the United States had two parts, westward expansion and

    A) the movement of Native Americans to reservations.

    B) a rural–to–urban shift.

    C) the shift of a large part of the population below the thirty–seventh parallel.

    D) the active participation of the British government.

Answer: B
Diff: 2

78) In the second wave of internal voluntary migration within the United States, African–Americans moved from the

    A) Frostbelt to the Sunbelt.

    B) rural South to cities.

    C) eastern cities to rural areas in the West.

    D) rural South to New York City and Boston.

Answer: B
Diff: 1

79) The third wave of internal voluntary migration within the United States

    A) emerged from the expansionist settlement policy of the American Revolution.

    B) brought people back to the cities through national urban renewal programs Kennedy and Johnson administrations.

    C) saw many people move to the Sun Belt.

    D) resulted in the passing of federal laws restricting internal migration.

Answer: C
Diff: 1

80) The demographic center of the United States

    A) is currently along the California and Nevada boundary.

    B) has been New York City since the late 1800s.

    C) is a sociological concept to help us understand the aging of a population.

    D) has been moving westward for the last two hundred years.

Answer: D
Diff: 1

81) The best explanation for the third internal voluntary migration wave in the United States is

    A) the desire for greater economic opportunity.

    B) the high degree of racism in the United States.

    C) the environmental problems in large cities.

    D) the romantic longing for a simple country life.

Answer: A
Diff: 2

82) The term "Trail of Tears" refers to

    A) the forced movement of Jews to concentration camps during World War II.

    B) the interment of Japanese Americans in U.S. camps during World War II.

    C) the "Long March" of the Chinese communists in the 1930s.

    D) the forced migration of the Cherokee Nation in the nineteenth century.

    E) the suffering of Indonesians forced to leave their home islands.

Answer: D
Diff: 1

83) Malthus argued that the factor limiting population size was

    A) money.

    B) food.

    C) housing.

    D) land.

    E) environmental pollution.

Answer: B
Diff: 1

84) Neomalthusians think that the greatest danger to the environment is

    A) Marxism.

    B) politicians.

    C) population growth.

    D) computer technology.

    E) industrial agriculture.

Answer: C
Diff: 1

85) Most demographers and policymakers think that the best way to control population is to

    A) hold annual conferences hosted by the UN.

    B) educate women and give them equal status with men.

    C) increase the power of religious institutions that preach abstinence and celibacy.

    D) pass laws that limit families to one one child.

    E) let HIV/AIDs, tropical diseases, plagues and epidemics run freely.

Answer: B
Diff: 1

86) Currently the global population is about

    A) 4.2 billion.

    B) 6.1 billion.

    C) 7.3 billion.

    D) 7.8 billion.

    E) 8.7 billion.

Answer: B
Diff: 1

87) In general, _____ has the highest crude birth rates.

    A) Africa

    B) South America

    C) Europe

    D) North America

    E) China and India

Answer: A
Diff: 1

88) In general, _____ has the highest crude death rates.

    A) Africa

    B) South America

    C) Europe

    D) North America

    E) China and India

Answer: A
Diff: 1

89) In general, the world region of Sub–Saharan Africa is highest for all of the following *except*

    A) life expectancy.

    B) birth rates.

    C) death rates.

    D) rate of natural increase.

    E) infant mortality rates.

Answer: A
Diff: 1

90) Which world region has the lowest rate of natural increase?

    A) Europe

    B) Oceania

    C) Latin America

    D) Asia

    E) North America

Answer: A
Diff: 1

91) Which world region has the highest GNP per capita?

    A) Europe

    B) Oceania

    C) Latin America

    D) Asia

    E) North America

Answer: E
Diff: 1

3.3 True or False

1) Things like weather and family can be pull factors for some and push factors for others.

Answer: TRUE
Diff: 2

2) The U.S. baby boom echo is the result of the prosperity of the 1990s.

Answer: FALSE
Diff: 1

3) The African diaspora includes people of African descent in the United States.

Answer: TRUE
Diff: 2

4) EPZs, RNIs, SAPs, IMRs, BLTs, and LDCs are all demographic measures.

Answer: FALSE
Diff: 2

5) The African diaspora does not include people of African descent in the United States.

Answer: FALSE
Diff: 2

6) Education and income are among a population's achieved characteristics.

Answer: TRUE
Diff: 1

7) In contrast to significantly different birth rates, more and less developed countries of the world have much more similar death rates.

Answer: TRUE
Diff: 2

8) One problem with censuses – even in the United States – is that they tend to undercount minority groups.

Answer: TRUE
Diff: 1

9) From Australia to Mexico, from Bangladesh to Egypt, the populations of all countries around the world are clustered along their coasts.

Answer: FALSE
Diff: 3

10) Age–sex pyramids can be constructed for any population, from those of counties and cities to populations of countries and continents.

Answer: TRUE
Diff: 3

11) The birth rate for all cohorts within a population is the same.

Answer: FALSE
Diff: 3

12) According to the demographic transition, people seem to be more willing to adopt measures that reduce death rates than those that reduce birth rates.

Answer: TRUE
Diff: 3

13) Typically, forced migration is a response to push factors of migration.

Answer: TRUE
Diff: 3

14) Around the world, most people who migrate do so voluntarily.

Answer: FALSE
Diff: 2

15) Historical evidence has proved Malthus correct.

Answer: FALSE
Diff: 3

16) Effective HIV/AIDS reduction and prevention programs have been established throughout sub-Saharan Africa.

Answer: TRUE
Diff: 2

17) Around the world, the larger the populations the shorter the doubling times.

Answer: FALSE
Diff: 3

18) Birth rates in almost every country on earth are dropping.

Answer: TRUE
Diff: 2

19) Diasporic populations can be comprised of either (or both) forced or voluntary migrants.

Answer: TRUE
Diff: 3

20) The population of the United States is ageing. In contrast, the average age of the population of the periphery is declining.

Answer: FALSE
Diff: 3

21) Transnational migrants include both Mexican migrants to the U.S. and Hong Kong Chinese to Canada.

Answer: TRUE
Diff: 2

22) Due mainly to the large number of displaced Palestinians, the Middle East has more refugees than any other world region.

Answer: TRUE
Diff: 2

23) The U.S.-led, international "war on terror" has helped reduce the number of the world's IDPs .

Answer: FALSE
Diff: 3

24) Generally, the plight of international refugees is better that that of internally displaced persons.

Answer: TRUE
Diff: 2

25) Differences in the enumeration dates and content of censuses in different countries makes cross-national comparisons difficult.

Answer: TRUE
Diff: 2

26) The population of Egypt is distributed relatively uniformly throughout the country.

Answer: FALSE
Diff: 1

27) As a comparison of Canada and Egypt shows, countries with deserts have lower population densities.

Answer: FALSE
Diff: 3

28) The majority of the world's population lives south of the equator.

Answer: FALSE
Diff: 1

29) An area with a high nutritional density almost always has a low agricultural density.

Answer: FALSE
Diff: 2

30) On average, periphery states have a lower ratio of doctors to inhabitants than do core states.

Answer: TRUE
Diff: 1

31) In the 1950s and early 1960s, young women married later *and* had children later.

Answer: FALSE
Diff: 2

32) It was primarily Whites who participated in the baby boom.

Answer: FALSE
Diff: 2

33) A country's infant mortality rate is a good indicator of the state of its health care system.

Answer: TRUE
Diff: 2

34) Most non-core countries continue to suffer from high mortality rates.

Answer: FALSE
Diff: 2

35) Demographic transition theory better explains changes in non-core countries than changes in core countries.

Answer: FALSE
Diff: 2

36) North African guest workers are less welcome now in France than they were in the 1960s.

Answer: TRUE
Diff: 2

37) Advances in transportation technology helped make suburbanization possible.

Answer: TRUE
Diff: 2

38) Karl Marx provided the theoretical basis for Malthus' conclusions about population.

Answer: FALSE
Diff: 2

39) Most international conferences on population have sought to decrease birth rates.

Answer: TRUE
Diff: 1

40) World population growth is projected to be slowest in core countries.

Answer: TRUE
Diff: 2

41) Most policymakers and demographers believe that the more education a woman has, the greater the number of children she will have.

Answer: FALSE
Diff: 2

42) To compute the agricultural density of a given area you must know how many people live in that area.

Answer: FALSE
Diff: 2

43) For an entire country, the crude density can never be lower than the agricultural density.

Answer: TRUE
Diff: 3

44) Generation X can best be thought of as an extension of the baby boom generation.

Answer: FALSE
Diff: 2

45) The doubling time of a population is inversely proportional to its total fertility rate.

Answer: FALSE
Diff: 2

46) In the 1990s, it was more difficult to gain political asylum in many European countries than it was in the 1980s.

Answer: TRUE
Diff: 1

47) Throughout much of the second half of the twentieth century, African–Americans immigrated in large numbers into the South.

Answer: FALSE
Diff: 1

48) Thomas Malthus' policies were based on the theory that people would eventually have less sex as the world became more civilized.

Answer: FALSE
Diff: 2

3.4 Matching

POPULATION: Match the population characteristics to the groups of countries.

1) benefit from brain drain
   Diff: 3

2) low rate of natural increase
   Diff: 3

3) high infant mortality rate
   Diff: 3

4) countries with small
   populations
   Diff: 3

5) low population density
   Diff: 3

6) large youth cohort
   Diff: 3

7) roughly 80% of the world's
   people
   Diff: 3

8) stalled in the middle of the
   demographic transition
   Diff: 3

9) principal sources of refugees
   Diff: 3

A) core countries

B) either – cannot generalize

C) peripheral countries

1) A	2) A	3) C	4) B	5) B	6) C
7) C	8) C	9) C			

MIGRATION: Match the type of migration to the example.

10) Jews, Armenians and
Palestinians spread all over
the world
Diff: 3

A) internal voluntary migration

B) international voluntary migration

C) diaspora

11) World War II internment of
Japanese
Diff: 3

D) internal forced migration

12) westward expansion of U.S.
Diff: 3

E) international forced migration

13) suburbanization
Diff: 3

14) rural–to–urban migration
Diff: 3

15) Palestinian refugees in Jordan,
Lebanon and Syria
Diff: 3

16) guest workers
Diff: 3

10) C   11) D   12) A   13) A   14) A   15) E
16) B

INTERNAL MIGRATION: Match the migration wave to the time period.

17) Westward migration
Diff: 2

18) rural–to–urban migration
Diff: 2

19) rural South to urban North,
South & West
Diff: 2

20) Rustbelt to Snowbelt
Diff: 2

21) suburbanization
Diff: 2

A) mid–nineteenth to mid–twentieth centuries

B) twentieth century

C) 1970s & 1980s

D) 1940s to 1970s

E) nineteenth & twentieth centuries

17) E   18) A   19) D   20) C   21) B

3.5 Map Identification

World Map

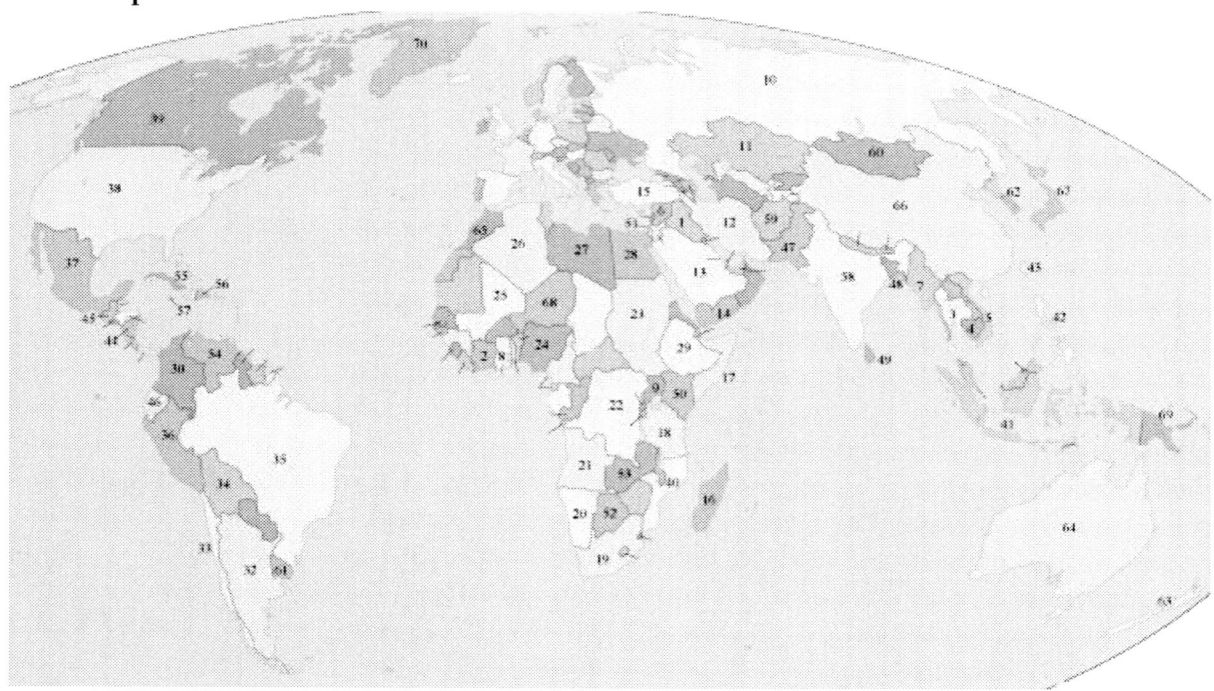

1) Which of the following is in the Fertile Crescent?

  A) Morocco

  B) India

  C) Argentina

  D) Bangladesh

  E) Egypt

  Answer: E
  Diff: 2

2) The country of Bangladesh is identified by the number

  A) 28.   B) 30.   C) 47.   D) 48.   E) 58.

  Answer: D
  Diff: 1

3) Accra is the capital of

A) Bangladesh.

B) Ghana.

C) Kazakhstan.

D) Cote D'Ivoire.

E) India.

Answer: B
Diff: 1

4) The capital(s) of country #2 is (are)

A) Abidjan & Yamoussoukro.

B) Pretoria, Johannesburg & Capetown.

C) Berlin & Amsterdam.

D) Cairo.

E) Brasilia.

Answer: A
Diff: 2

5) Brasilia is the capital of

A) 32.   B) 34.   C) 35.   D) 37.   E) 38.

Answer: E
Diff: 1

6) Which of the following is a European country?

A) Canada

B) Jamaica

C) Bangladesh

D) Netherlands

E) Kenya

Answer: D
Diff: 1

7) Which pair of countries share a border?

    A) Germany & Holland (the Netherlands)

    B) Cote D'Ivoire & Egypt

    C) Brazil & Bangladesh

    D) Holland & South Africa

    E) Brazil & South Africa

Answer: A
Diff: 2

Europe

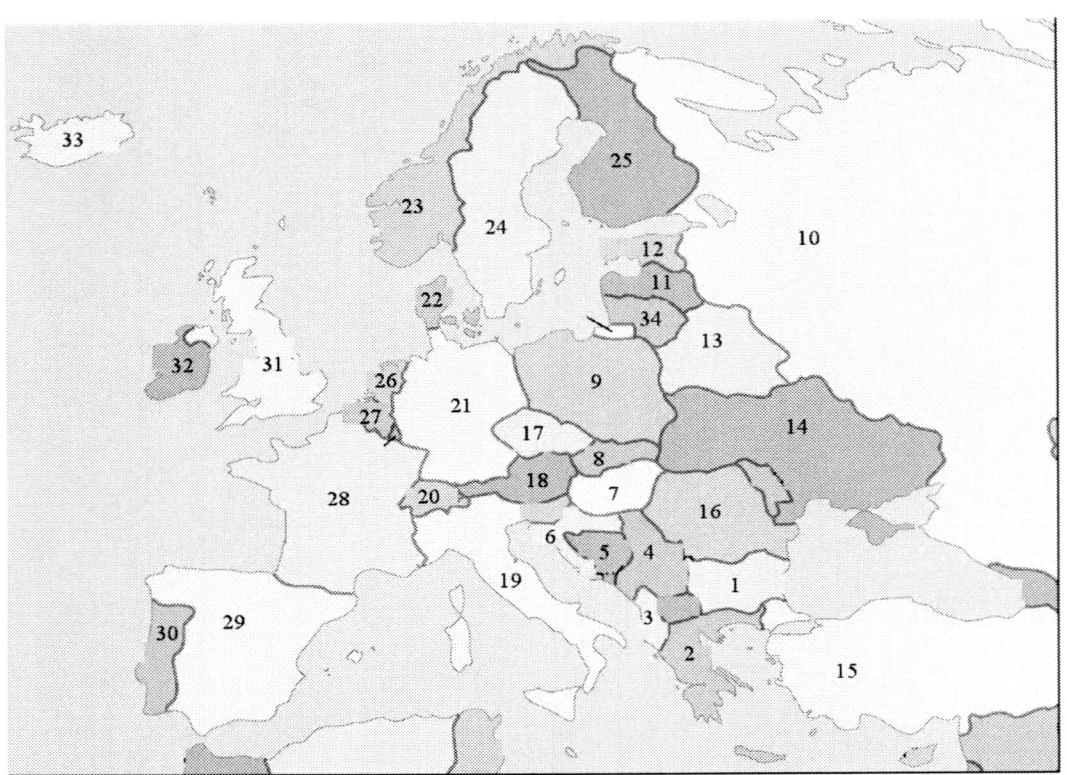

8) Berlin is the capital of the country labeled with which number?

    A) 9   B) 21   C) 30   D) 28   E) 22

Answer: B
Diff: 2

9) The Netherlands is the country labeled with the number

    A) 11.   B) 20.   C) 26.   D) 27.   E) 34.

Answer: C
Diff: 2

3.6 Chapter 3 Questions with images

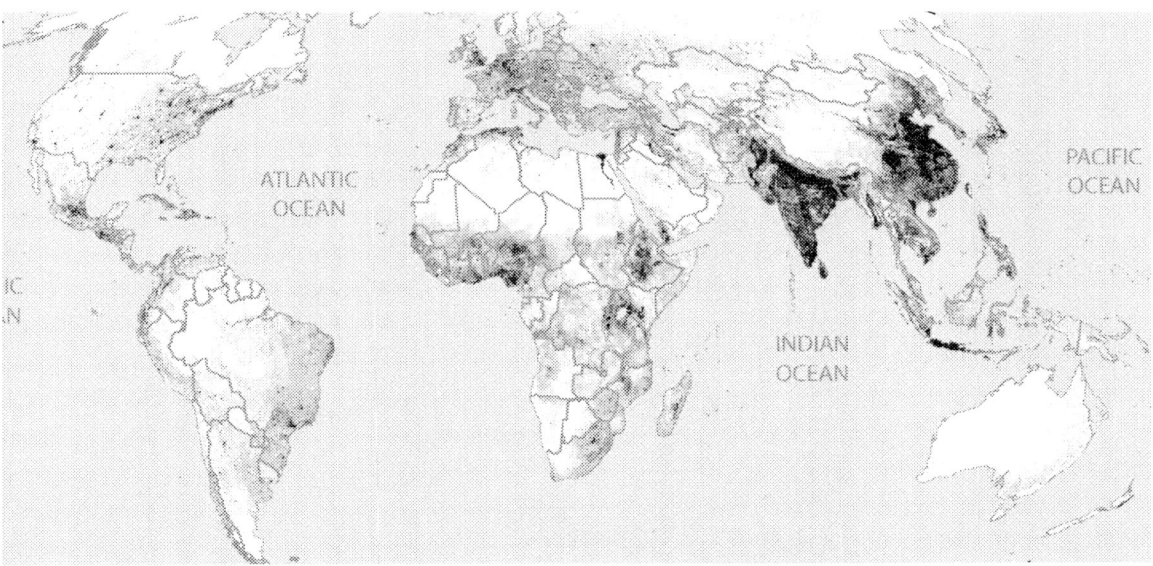

1) If the darker shadings represent greater intensity, the above map best represents

    A) population density.

    B) GDP per capita.

    C) total GDP.

    D) life expectancy.

    E) Any of the above.

Answer: A
Diff: 3

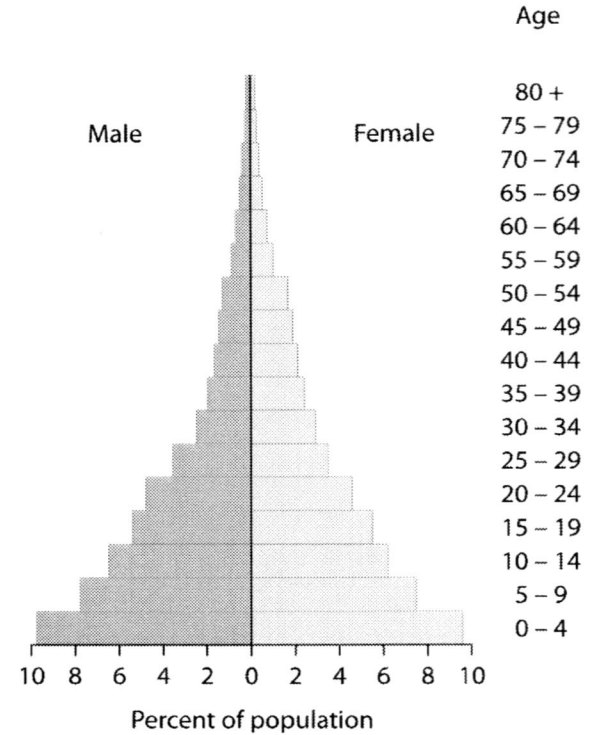

Age

80 +
75 – 79
70 – 74
65 – 69
60 – 64
55 – 59
50 – 54
45 – 49
40 – 44
35 – 39
30 – 34
25 – 29
20 – 24
15 – 19
10 – 14
5 – 9
0 – 4

Male   Female

10 8 6 4 2 0 2 4 6 8 10

Percent of population

2) The above population pyramid would most likely represent a(n) _____ country.

   A) Sub–Saharan

   B) West European

   C) East European

   D) North American

   E) Island

   Answer: A
   Diff: 3

3) The above population pyramid represents the population of

   A) Mali.   B) Finland.   C) Poland.   D) Canada.   E) Japan.

   Answer: A
   Diff: 3

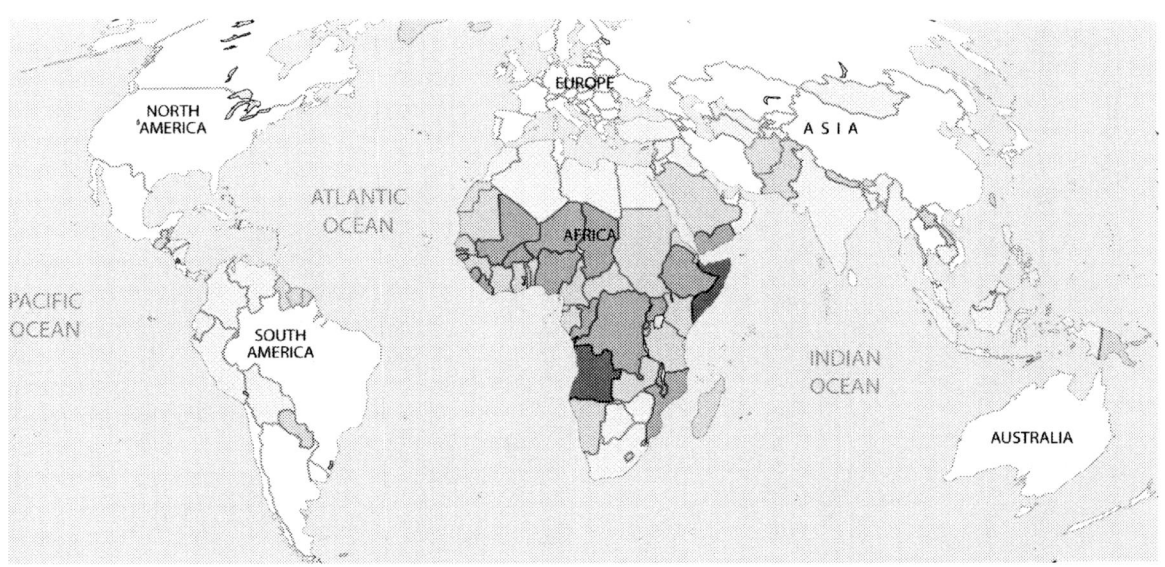

4) In the above map, the darker areas most likely represent areas of higher

    A) birth rates.

    B) death rates.

    C) refugee populations.

    D) education levels.

    E) nutritional densities.

Answer: A
Diff: 3

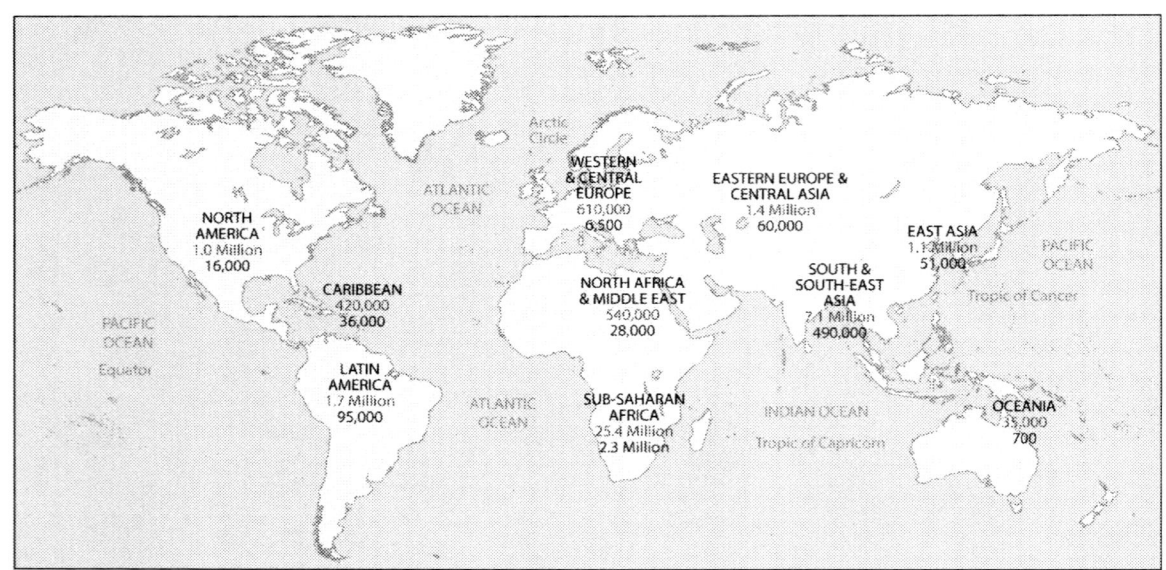

5) The statistics on the above map represent people living with and dying from

   A) HIV/AIDS.

   B) famine.

   C) war.

   D) internal displacement.

   E) diasporas.

Answer: A
Diff: 3

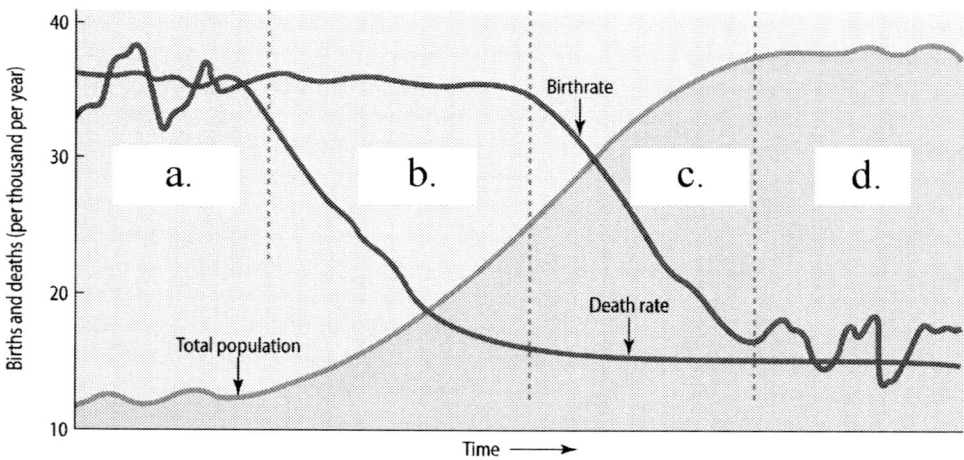

6) According to some demographers, the high rates of natural increase in the world's periphery are because the countries are stalled in which phase?

   A) a.   B) b.   C) c.   D) d.

Answer: B
Diff: 3

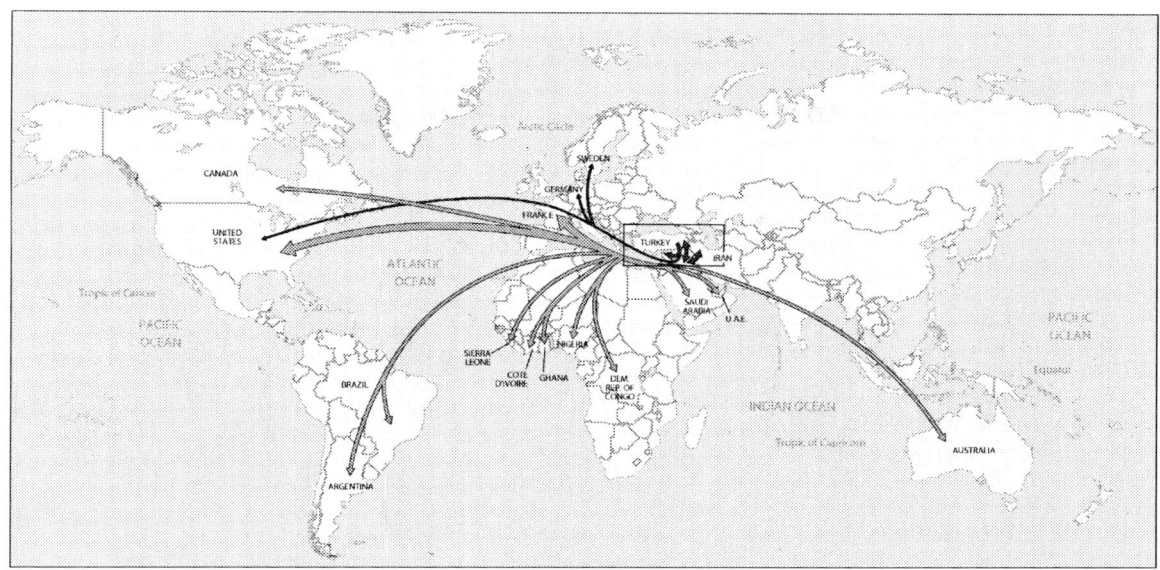

7) The above map graphically represents the Kurdish and Lebanese

    A) diaspora.

    B) demographic transition

    C) eco–migration.

    D) IDP.

    E) baby boom.

Answer: A
Diff: 3

Age–Sex Diagrams: Match the diagram to the population it represents.

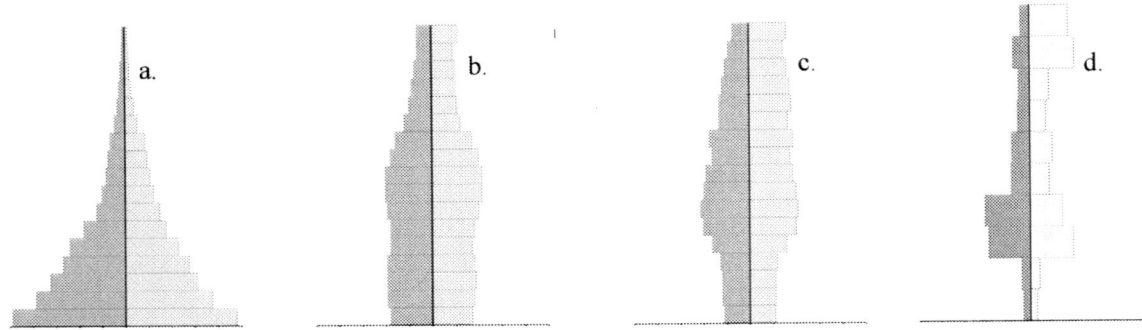

8) Population with a low RNI
   Diff: 3

9) Elderly population
   Diff: 3

10) Population with negative RNI
    Diff: 3

11) Population with a high RNI
    Diff: 3

A) a.

B) d.

C) b.

E) c.

8) C   9) B   10) E   11) A

Chapter 4 Nature and Society

4.1 Minimal Choice

1) Wangari Maathai, received the 2004 Nobel Peace Prize for addressing the linkages between environmental conservation and economic development through her work in

    A) tree planting.   B) refugee assistance.

Answer: A
Diff: 1

2) Kenya's Green Belt Movement is a grass-roots program that asssists marginal people and environments through

    A) preserving and improving local biodiversity.

    B) technological innovations & genetically modified plants.

Answer: A
Diff: 1

3) According to some scienticsts, one sign of global climate change and human induced changes to the environment is the alarming _____ in worldwide frog populations.

    A) decline   B) increase

Answer: A
Diff: 1

4) Global climate change is causing a(n)

    A) increase in the frequency of violent storms.

    B) decrease in sea levels.

Answer: A
Diff: 1

5) After Hurricane Ivan (2004), the United Nations International Secretariat for Disaster Reduction recognized _____ as a model in hurricane preparation.

    A) Cuba   B) Miami-Dade County, Florida

Answer: A
Diff: 1

6) Your textbook authors point out that to represent the disastrous impact of Hurricane Katrina (2005) as a "natural" disaster it misleading because it ignores

    A) political & social factors.   B) cultural and religious factors.

Answer: A
Diff: 1

7) Cultral ecologogists attempt to understand how cultural processes affect adaptation to

    A) the environment.   B) the world system.

Answer: A
Diff: 1

8) The hybrid rural culture of the the Central Andean region contains a combination of _____ practices.

    A) Spaniard and Inca   B) Peruvian and Mexican

Answer: A
Diff: 1

9) Understanding human–environment interactions within the context of the surrounding political and economic relationships is an approach taken by

    A) political ecologists.   B) eco–economists.

Answer: A
Diff: 1

10) At the bottom of the food chain are the

    A) photosynthesizers.   B) invertebrates.

Answer: A
Diff: 1

11) The belief that nature is sacred and should not be used at all is (was) held by

    A) preservationists like Earth First!   B) conservationists like Teddy Roosevelt.

Answer: A
Diff: 1

12) Archaeologists are still trying to figure out why certain megafauna (ie., _____) became extinct around 11,000 years ago and others did not.

    A) mammoths & cave bears.   B) fruit trees and ferns

Answer: A
Diff: 1

13) Deforestation typically precedes

    A) siltation.   B) virgin soil epidemics.

Answer: A
Diff: 1

14) The greatest loss of human life in history followed the Columbian Exchange and its associated

    A) virgin soil epidemics.   B) slavery and forced labor.

Answer: A
Diff: 2

15) France generates _____ of its electricity from nuclear sources.

    A) 90%   B) almost 0%

Answer: A
Diff: 1

16) The Bolivian portion of the Amazon is under threat from hardwood logging and the production of

    A) coca.   B) cocoa.

Answer: A
Diff: 2

17) Ecofeminists attribute environmental problems to the _____ biases in Western culture.

    A) patriarchal   B) matriarchal

Answer: A
Diff: 1

18) According to our text, to date, no accidents have been associated with nuclear energy production in the

    A) periphery.   B) core.

Answer: B
Diff: 1

19) The Kyoto Protocol targets _____ in the attempt to balance economic development with environmental protection.

    A) core countries   B) peripheral countries

Answer: A
Diff: 1

20) After the United States, the world's biggest per capita emitter of carbon dioxide -- one of the most problematic greenhouse gases -- is

    A) Canada.   B) China.

Answer: A
Diff: 1

4.2 Multiple Choice

1) The immediate cause of the Aral Sea ecological catastrophe can be tied to

    A) unsustainable agricultural practices.

    B) industrial pollution.

    C) a nuclear accident.

    D) acid rain.

    E) global warming.

Answer: A
Diff: 1

2) According to our text, which of the following is *not* true?

    A) Affluent core countries are more effective at protecting their environments than poor peripheral countries.

    B) Core countries are more interested in protecting the environment because of their Judeo–Christian perspective on nature.

    C) Core countries help protect their environments by exporting industrial wastes to peripheral countries.

    D) Core countries help protect their environments through technological innovations.

    E) Both A and B are *not* true.

Answer: B
Diff: 1

3) Even though _____ has been banned from use in the United States since 1972, it continues to persist in the environment throughout the U.S., for example in fish.

    A) DDT   B) PAT   C) CFC   D) BLT   E) CO2

Answer: A
Diff: 1

4) The production of hydropower is most strongly associated with

    A) river resources.

    B) ground water resources.

    C) no oil or natural gas.

    D) the periphery.

    E) the core.

Answer: A
Diff: 3

5) All of the following are renewable energy resources *except*

    A) hydropower.

    B) wind power.

    C) tidal power.

    D) geothermal energy.

    E) All of the above are renewable energy sources.

Answer: E
Diff: 1

6) National and State Parks across the United States, from the Rockies to the Smokies, operate under a view of natural resource use built on the idea of

    A) preservation.

    B) conservation.

    C) deforestation.

    D) modernization.

    E) both A and B

Answer: B
Diff: 1

7) The idea that "nature is a social creation" means that

    A) humans have built the physical world and its landscapes -- nothing is natural.

    B) the physical world means different things to different people at different times.

    C) God created the earth in six days.

    D) the evolutionary process concluded with the emergence of humans.

    E) the physical world and its resources were made for human use.

Answer: B
Diff: 2

8) Rachel Carson is probably most well known for

    A) being the first woman Chief of the United States Forest Service.

    B) her life and experiences at Walden Pond.

    C) writing *Silent Spring*.

    D) identifying the benefits of agricultural pesticides.

    E) inventing the Clovis Point.

Answer: C
Diff: 1

9) One conceptual theory (i.e., IPAT) for understanding the factors contributing to environmental impacts relates them to

    A) technological level.

    B) level of affluence.

    C) population size.

    D) all of the above

    E) both A and B

Answer: D
Diff: 1

10) The nature of the relationship between humans and their environment is based mostly on

    A) technological understanding and ability.

    B) prevailing religious beliefs.

    C) population size.

    D) the hegemonic political system.

    E) core–periphery relationships.

Answer: A
Diff: 2

11) Human adaptations to the natural environment

    A) have been occurring for hundreds and thousands of years.

    B) no longer occur with globalization of the late twentieth century.

    C) began with the Industrial Revolution.

    D) almost never result in pollution or environmental degradation.

    E) occur in only hearth areas – many regions of the world remain pristine and untouched by human activity.

Answer: A
Diff: 1

12) The social production of nature refers to

    A) cultural and political ecology.

    B) the transformation of landscapes and species by human activity.

    C) cloning, surrogate mothering and in vitro fertilization.

    D) ecological imperialism.

    E) preservation and conservation of unique environments and biosphere reserves.

Answer: B
Diff: 2

13) Political ecologists emphasize

    A) the impact of political and economic forces on local cultures and resource use.

    B) traditional groups' involvement in the political process.

    C) environmental and resource policy.

    D) environmental ethics and the ethics of resource use.

    E) the impact of globalization on resource trade.

Answer: A
Diff: 1

14) Human contributions to global climate warming are primarily from

    A) carbon dioxide emissions in the core.

    B) deforestation in the periphery.

    C) oil spills in the core and the periphery.

    D) the proliferation of pavement in both the core and the periphery.

    E) the hole in the ozone layer created by the space shuttle.

Answer: A
Diff: 1

15) The contemporary view of nature dominant in the United States is most strongly linked to the

    A) Judeo–Christian tradition, in which nature is to be dominated or tamed by Man.

    B) North American Indian tradition, which emphasized the interrelatedness of the natural world.

    C) romantic philosophies of Henry David Thoreau, in which all creatures have divine qualities – humans are not exceptional.

    D) transcendental poet Ralph Waldo Emerson, who encouraged a mystical and spiritual alternative to the primitive and savage life.

Answer: A
Diff: 1

16) The lower an organism on the food chain, the

    A) more energy efficient it is.

    B) more energetic it is.

    C) less of them there are.

    D) more meat it eats.

    E) more tasty it is, especially with a little bit of garlic and olive oil.

Answer: A
Diff: 1

17) The foundations of the U.S. environmental movement of the twentieth century are drawn from the ideas of

    A) Sally Marston.

    B) George Perkins Marsh.

    C) Rachel Carson.

    D) Teddy Roosevelt.

    E) Karl Marx.

Answer: B
Diff: 1

18) Earth First! and other groups that use extralegal tactics to protect the environment are, generally,

    A) conservationists.

    B) preservationists.

    C) political ecologists.

    D) cultural ecologists.

    E) ecological imperialists.

Answer: B
Diff: 1

19) Whereas environmental preservation advocates that certain habitats, species, and resources should be off-limits and left entirely alone, conservation approaches encourage

    A) respectful and sustainable used of natural resources.

    B) exploitation of natural resources.

    C) a return to "natural" life-styles like those lived by Native Americans.

    D) re-creation and reclamation of natural landscapes.

    E) rights for animals, trees and landscapes equal to those given humans.

Answer: A
Diff: 1

20) _____ the view of nature as a nurturing and bountiful mother was replaced by a view in which it was subordinate to man and something to be exploited.

    A) Already in the sixteenth century,

    B) After the Industrial Revolution,

    C) With globalization of the late twentieth century,

    D) As part of Reaganomics,

    E) With the emergence of the World Bank,

Answer: A
Diff: 2

21) Groups such as the Environmental Defense Fund, Sierra Club, World Watch Institute and the Nature Conservancy are known as "mainstream" environmental groups because they

    A) work within the established political and economic system.

    B) serve multinational business interests.

    C) reflect the opinions and attitudes of the majority of the U. S. public.

    D) receive their funding from the government.

    E) concentrate their efforts on lakes, rivers and streams.

Answer: A
Diff: 2

22) The book *Silent Spring* explores the environmental impacts of

    A) pesticides.

    B) global warming.

    C) a world without lawn mowers.

    D) the Green Revolution.

    E) nuclear power, wastes and weapons.

Answer: A
Diff: 1

23) Radical environmental groups like Earth First! and Greenpeace

    A) combine religious fundamentalism and the environment.

    B) operate outside the bounds of mainstream institutional frameworks.

    C) represent the views of people on the fringe and in the periphery.

    D) share the interests of developers, transnational corporations and the WTO.

    E) try to get the states of California, Oregon and Washington to secede from the Union.

Answer: B
Diff: 3

24) The environmental justice movement emphasizes the disproportional burdens that the _____ face from the negative consequences of economic development.

    A) core

    B) periphery

    C) rich

    D) middle-class

    E) poor

Answer: E
Diff: 2

25) A tool with which early Stone Age (Paleolithic) people extensively altered their environment was

    A) fire.

    B) the wheel.

    C) irrigation.

    D) the plow.

    E) terraces.

Answer: A
Diff: 1

26) The Clovis point helped North America's early peoples

    A) hunt large animals for meat.

    B) plow up the grasslands.

    C) defend against the first Europeans.

    D) navigate featureless terrains.

    E) cut down forests for timber.

Answer: A
Diff: 1

27) Among other differences, Neolithic peoples were separated from Paleolithic peoples by the

    A) First Agricultural Revolution.

    B) Continental Divide.

    C) Fertile Crescent.

    D) Atlantic Ocean (separating the New and Old Worlds).

    E) introduction of globalization.

Answer: A
Diff: 2

28) The term megafauna is another way of referring to large

    A) animals.

    B) plants.

    C) trees.

    D) people.

    E) animals in the deer family.

    Answer: A
    Diff: 1

29) The most reasonable explanation for the selective extinction of large animals like mastodons, mammoths, cave bears and giant deer at the end of the Pleistocene around 10,000 years ago is (are)

    A) global climate change.

    B) natural disasters.

    C) Stone Age over-hunting.

    D) pesticides.

    E) ecological imperialism.

    Answer: C
    Diff: 2

30) The simplification of ecosystems and the loss of biodiversity began with

    A) Neolithic peoples.

    B) the Columbian Exchange.

    C) the Crusades.

    D) the beginnings of the Judeo-Christian tradition.

    E) the Industrial Revolution.

    Answer: A
    Diff: 2

31) Cities of ancient Mesopotamia in the Fertile Crescent grew and relied upon a vast irrigation network. It is thought that the region eventually collapsed about 4,000 years ago because of

    A) environmental mismanagement.

    B) climate change.

    C) species extinction.

    D) religious conflict.

    E) the discovery of oil.

    Answer: A
    Diff: 2

32) The same problem that plagued early agricultural civilization in Mesopotamia currently plague contemporary irrigation agriculture from such places as California and SW Arizona to India and Central Asia. This problem is

A) salinazation -- salt build-up in soils.

B) population growth onto agricultural lands.

C) drought.

D) climate change.

E) the lack of labor and expertise.

Answer: A
Diff: 2

33) Well before the start of European colonialism, Europe had already

A) cut down most of its forests.

B) established a strong record of environmental preservation.

C) doubled its area by reclaiming land from the sea.

D) polluted its air, water and soils through industrialization.

E) identified the relationship between human actions and global warming.

Answer: A
Diff: 1

34) European colonization of the New World resulted in the greatest loss of human life in history. The primary factor responsible was

A) disease.　　B) war.　　C) slavery.　　D) fire.　　E) famine.

Answer: A
Diff: 1

35) Which of the following is *not* true? The Columbian Exchange resulted in the introduction of

A) virgin soil epidemics to the New World.

B) wheat, sugarcane, pigs, oxen and cattle to the New World.

C) pests like dandelions and thistles, rats and starlings to the New World.

D) potatoes, corn, tomatoes, cotton to the Old World.

E) None of the above *are* not true. The Columbian Exchange resulted in all of them.

Answer: E
Diff: 1

36) The introduction of exotic plants and animals into new ecosystems, such as the introduction of African bees to Brazil in the 1950s to improve the local bee-keeping industry, is an example of

  A) ecological imperialism.

  B) demographic collapse.

  C) virgin soil epidemic.

  D) transcendentalism.

  E) the Columbian exchange.

  Answer: A
  Diff: 1

37) Numerous small islands of Oceania in the South Pacific continue to suffer environmental consequences of the Cold War arms race because they were

  A) used as massive naval and military bases.

  B) used as nuclear weapons testing sites.

  C) depleted of mineral resources for high tech materials.

  D) used as testing sites for biological weapons.

  E) littered with depleted uranium and other military trash.

  Answer: B
  Diff: 1

38) Russia holds about one-third of the world's known reserves of _____, predicted to be this century's fastest growing energy source.

  A) natural gas

  B) hydropower

  C) nuclear power

  D) low-sulfur coal

  E) geothermal energy

  Answer: A
  Diff: 1

39) The great environmental benefit of hydropower as an energy source is that it

    A) produces few atmospheric pollutants.

    B) benefits water quality.

    C) has no impact on local plant and animal life.

    D) maintains the pristine quality of the body of water on which it is built.

    E) All of the above are among the benefits of hydropower.

Answer: A
Diff: 1

40) The world's largest generator of the greenhouse gases that lead to global warming is

    A) the United States.

    B) China.

    C) Mexico.

    D) France.

    E) Japan.

Answer: A
Diff: 1

41) The greatest estimated area of deforestation since pre-agricultural times has occurred in

    A) Europe.

    B) Latin America.

    C) Africa.

    D) North America.

    E) the Former USSR.

Answer: A
Diff: 1

42) Marshes, bogs, peatlands, and swamps are all in the _____ category of land cover.

    A) wetland

    B) steppe

    C) archipelago

    D) forest

    E) grassland

Answer: A
Diff: 1

43) International efforts to protect biodiversity have included efforts to halt "bioprospecting," the corporate practice of

A) intentionally reducing the varieties of fruits and vegetables found in the grocery store.

B) replacing traditional and native species of plants with crops for export.

C) overharvesting non-traditional crops like hemp and seaweed from public areas.

D) exploiting indigenous knowledge of medicinal plants for commercial purposes.

Answer: D
Diff: 2

44) Desertification occurring in the grasslands of the Sahel, bordering the Sahara is the result of

A) careless overgrazing by thoughtles͏ herders.

B) expanding beef production for U.S. and European markets.

C) a complex set of environmental, cultural and political economic factors.

D) industrialization and urbanization.

E) droughts and other acts of nature or God.

Answer: C
Diff: 2

45) The new logging frontier for U.S. and South Korean timber multinationals are the _____ forests, the largest in the world.

A) Siberian

B) Indonesian

C) Amazonian

D) Canadian

E) Alaskan

Answer: A
Diff: 1

46) Which of the following is *not* true about Wangari Maathai, the 2004 Noble Peace Prize Laureate?

A) She founded Africa's first biotech research facility.

B) Her work is built around the wide-spread benefits of tree planting & reforestation.

C) She is the first African woman to receive the prize.

D) She is Kenya's Assistant Minister for Environment and Natural Resources

Answer: A
Diff: 1

47) In general, the biggest water user in the U.S. Southwest is the _____ sector.

    A) agricultural

    B) residential

    C) commercial

    D) government

    E) tourism

Answer: A
Diff: 1

48) According to Knox and Marston, the high number of deaths in New Orleans from hurricane Katrina (2005) was primarily the result of

    A) social and political factors.

    B) global warming.

    C) "Mother Nature."

    D) terrorists.

    E) pollution.

Answer: A
Diff: 1

49) The largest cause of oil pollution in the world's oceans is

    A) oil extraction.

    B) oil tanker accidents.

    C) home heating oil emissions.

    D) surface run-off of oil from core countries.

    E) natural causes.

Answer: A
Diff: 1

50) Australia contributes to the world's energy supply by supplying 27% of the world's

    A) uranium.

    B) oil.

    C) hydroelectric power.

    D) coal.

    E) thermal energy.

Answer: A
Diff: 1

51) The 1992 Earth Summit was concerned primarily with this type of issue:

    A) population growth

    B) the status of women

    C) local environmental issues

    D) global environmental issues

Answer: D
Diff: 2

52) Society is composed of

    A) human institutions.

    B) human inventions.

    C) human relationships.

    D) all of the above

Answer: D
Diff: 1

53) Some argue that population growth is a way to solve the global environmental crisis because a large population

    A) will lead to the quick spread of lethal diseases, which will drastically reduce population.

    B) makes it more likely that the technological innovations necessary to solve the global crisis will be developed.

    C) will have more power in pressuring politicians to address the problems.

    D) makes it more likely that there will be pressure to colonize other planets.

Answer: B
Diff: 3

54) Which religious perspective on nature is most likely to advocate that humans dominate nature?

    A) Taoist perspective

    B) Buddhist perspective

    C) Judeo–Christian perspective

    D) Animistic perspective

Answer: C
Diff: 2

55) The Buddhist perspective on nature

    A) is more like the Islamic perspective than the Taoist perspective.

    B) holds that humans must safeguard all life.

    C) teaches that all forms of life are separate and independent from one another.

    D) was actually developed by Nepali Armenians.

    E) allows consumption of meat only if the animal is not killed before being eaten.

Answer: B
Diff: 2

56) Which religious perspective believes that all animate and inanimate natural phenomena have a spirit or consciousness?

    A) Judeo–Christian perspective

    B) Buddhist perspective

    C) Taoist perspective

    D) Islamic perspective

    E) Animist perspective

Answer: E
Diff: 2

57) Henry David Thoreau

    A) lived during the early part of the twentieth century.

    B) stressed man's domination of nature.

    C) denounced transcendentalism.

    D) is often credited as the founder of the American environmental movement.

    E) was Amish.

Answer: D
Diff: 2

58) Which of the following environmental philosophies is the most mainstream?

    A) conservation

    B) environmental ethics

    C) deep ecology

    D) ecofeminism

    E) preservation

Answer: A
Diff: 1

59) In the energy flow diagram presented in the text, herbivores are

    A) above top carnivores and below photosynthesizers.

    B) at the top of the diagram.

    C) above photosynthesizers and below carnivores.

    D) in–between carnivores and top carnivores.

    E) surrounded by omnivores.

Answer: C
Diff: 1

60) Ecofeminism

    A) rejects Goddess worship.

    B) has found significant acceptance primarily in core countries.

    C) argues that men equate nature with women.

    D) calls for the creation of a strong patriarchy.

Answer: C
Diff: 2

61) The idea that humans could and should dominate nature became prevalent in Western culture

    A) in direct opposition to Christian teachings.

    B) despite the opposing efforts of Thomas Hobbes and Francis Bacon.

    C) during the sixteenth century.

    D) because of the writings of Henry David Thoreau and the early nineteenth-century transcendentalists.

Answer: C
Diff: 2

62) The Paleolithic Period

    A) saw the first use of chipped stone tools.

    B) began about 10,000 years ago.

    C) is also called the late Stone Age.

    D) was when humans started creating significant numbers of permanent settlements.

Answer: A
Diff: 2

63) Humans dispersed so widely during the Paleolithic period primarily because

    A) they wished to avoid infectious diseases.

    B) they needed new areas with sufficient food for survival.

    C) wars made it necessary.

    D) of the innate desire to explore new lands.

Answer: B
Diff: 2

64) Which of the following is the least plausible explanation for the extinction of many of the large animal species in North America about 11,000 years ago?

    A) climate change   B) large–scale natural disasters

    C) a devastating comet impact   D) human hunting activities

Answer: C
Diff: 1

65) The Neolithic Period

    A) ended with the end of the last Ice Age.

    B) saw significant development of agriculture.

    C) was characterized by hunting as the primary food–producing activity of humans.

    D) saw little religious activity by humans.

Answer: B
Diff: 1

66) During the Neolithic Period, human societies produced the first significant numbers of craftspeople and religious and political elites; this was primarily due to

    A) the ability of agricultural workers to produce surplus food.

    B) religious creeds prevalent in those societies.

    C) laws proclaimed by rulers.

    D) the large increase in human intellect during the Neolithic Period.

Answer: A
Diff: 2

67) The failure of many of the first Neolithic societies was due in significant part to

    A) environmental mismanagement.   B) increased salinity in soils.

    C) siltation.   D) all of the above

Answer: D
Diff: 1

68) During the era of internal European expansion, the most obvious change in the land was

    A) siltation.   B) soil salination.   C) sheep grazing.   D) deforestation.

Answer: D
Diff: 2

69) Prior to the Colombian Exchange, the only large domestic animals in the Americas use for work/protein were

    A) dogs.

    B) dogs and llamas.

    C) dogs, llamas and horses.

    D) dogs, llamas, horses, and oxen

    E) dogs, llamas, horses, oxen and pigs

Answer: B
Diff: 2

70) The greatest factor behind the New World's large population decrease after the arrival of the Europeans was

    A) disease.   B) war.   C) genocide.   D) migration.

Answer: A
Diff: 1

71) Fossil fuel use increased dramatically during the

    A) demographic collapse.

    B) Neolithic Period.

    C) early Middle Ages.

    D) Industrial Revolution.

    E) Age of Exploration.

Answer: D
Diff: 1

72) Which of the following energy resources is renewable?

    A) hydropower

    B) coal

    C) oil

    D) uranium

    E) All of the above are renewable.

Answer: A
Diff: 1

73) Of the energy consumed by humans around the world, the greatest proportion comes from

   A) coal.

   B) oil.

   C) hydropower.

   D) nuclear power.

   E) natural gas.

Answer: B
Diff: 2

74) This region has the highest commercial energy consumption per capita:

   A) Asia   B) Africa

   C) South America   D) North America

Answer: D
Diff: 1

75) Which of the following energy resources produces the fewest toxic chemicals when burned?

   A) natural gas   B) coal   C) heating oil   D) petroleum

Answer: A
Diff: 2

76) Nuclear energy as a source of energy

   A) is more common in the periphery than in the core.

   B) was more popular in core countries in the 1960s than now.

   C) produces no significant waste by-products.

   D) was banned by the French government in the mid–1990s.

   E) is a leading cause of air pollution.

Answer: B
Diff: 2

77) Most of the population in the periphery relies on _____ as their main energy source.

   A) coal

   B) hydropower

   C) wood

   D) dung

   E) animals

Answer: C
Diff: 1

78) Of the following, which is a positive aspect of hydropower?

    A) increased acidity of dammed water from submerged trees

    B) improved habitat for fish and wildlife

    C) negligible contribution to atmospheric pollution

    D) increased number of reservoirs and artificial lakes for tourism

Answer: C
Diff: 1

79) The problem of acidic air emissions and acid rain are worst in

    A) Africa.

    B) North America and Western Europe.

    C) Asia.

    D) Australia.

    E) Antarctica.

Answer: B
Diff: 1

80) The world's worst cases of deforestation are currently occurring in

    A) the boreal forests of Canada.

    B) the temperate forests of western North America.

    C) the rain forests in peripheral countries.

    D) the desert forests of the Middle East.

Answer: C
Diff: 1

81) Destruction of rain forests results in

    A) disruption in the oxygen and carbon dioxide cycles of forests.

    B) an increase in biological diversity.

    C) stabilization of the global temperature.

    D) increased agricultural production and less hunger.

    E) all of the above

Answer: A
Diff: 2

82) The expansion of cropland

    A) has led to an increase in grasslands.

    B) has occurred simultaneously with a drop in overall global food production.

    C) has increased significantly over the last few decades in peripheral countries.

    D) has increased significantly over the last few decades in core countries.

Answer: C
Diff: 2

83) The term "global change" includes this type of problem:

    A) environmental   B) political

    C) economic   D) all of the above

Answer: D
Diff: 1

84) The Islamic perspective on nature has the most in common with the perspective on nature of this religion:

    A) Judaism   B) Buddhism   C) Taoism   D) Animism

Answer: A
Diff: 2

85) In the energy pyramid accompanying a generalized food chain, _____ produce the least amount of energy.

    A) top carnivores   B) carnivores

    C) photosynthesizers   D) herbivores

Answer: A
Diff: 3

86) The main reason for the slowing of continental expansion in Europe in the 1300s was

    A) prolonged and bloody warfare.

    B) the bubonic plague.

    C) the unwillingness to use paper money as a form of currency.

    D) the opposition of the Church.

    E) memories of bad experiences during the Crusades.

Answer: B
Diff: 2

87) Of the following, which was domesticated in the Old World and to the New World?

A) corn
B) potatoes
C) tomatoes
D) wheat

Answer: D
Diff: 1

4.3 True or False

1) Most environmentalists agree that environmental consciousness is a luxury more than a necessity.

Answer: FALSE
Diff: 2

2) The higher an animal is in the food chain, the fewer there are of that animal.

Answer: TRUE
Diff: 1

3) Preservation, deep ecology, and eco-feminism are radical environmental perspectives found only in the core.

Answer: FALSE
Diff: 2

4) There are not enough resources for all people around the globe to have living standards like those of the core.

Answer: TRUE
Diff: 1

5) Until the Columbian Exchange, humans did not noticeably alter the natural environment.

Answer: FALSE
Diff: 1

6) The Clovis point is known to archaeologists for its role in helping to win arguments and influence people.

Answer: FALSE
Diff: 1

7) The common factor among all eco-feminists is to replace male leaders with females in the work place, at home and in the environmental movement.

Answer: FALSE
Diff: 1

8) Late Stone Age Neolithic peoples are credited with developing agriculture.

Answer: TRUE
Diff: 2

9) The second phase of European expansion was external and also known as colonialism.

Answer: TRUE
Diff: 2

10) The dip in Europe's population from 1300 to 1500 was due mostly to food shortages.

Answer: FALSE
Diff: 1

11) Since it began, the Columbian Exchange continues.

Answer: TRUE
Diff: 2

12) Before the arrival of the Spaniards and Portuguese, horses were not known in the Americas.

Answer: TRUE
Diff: 1

13) None of the beneficial impacts of the Columbian Exchange went to the peoples of the New World.

Answer: FALSE
Diff: 2

14) The majority of the energy consumed in the world today comes from nonrenewable sources.

Answer: TRUE
Diff: 1

15) Land use change occurs through conversion from one use to another or by modifications of existing cover.

Answer: TRUE
Diff: 2

16) With global warming, the rising sea level could realistically flood over half of Bangladesh.

Answer: TRUE
Diff: 1

17) Peppers, tomatoes and potatoes were introduced to the New World from Europe.

Answer: FALSE
Diff: 1

18) The goal of the Kyoto Protocol is to limit logging and reduce worldwide deforestation.

Answer: FALSE
Diff: 1

19) Technological development in the core has helped it avoid the soil salinization associated with early civilizations and the periphery.

Answer: FALSE
Diff: 1

20) Though Australia produces about a quarter of the world's uranium, they produce no electricity from it.

Answer: TRUE
Diff: 2

21) According to your text, the pair of processes with the greatest impact on humans and their environment are industrialization and urbanization.

Answer: TRUE
Diff: 2

22) Solar power and fuelwood for heating and cooking are being encouraged in the periphery as sustainable and renewable forms of energy.

Answer: FALSE
Diff: 1

23) The environmental determinism model holds that nature is molded and controlled by human societies.

Answer: FALSE
Diff: 2

24) Nature is in part a social creation.

Answer: TRUE
Diff: 2

25) Prevailing views and concepts of nature have remained fairly constant over the last 2,000 years.

Answer: FALSE
Diff: 1

26) In general, peripheral countries do a better job protecting the environment than core countries do.

Answer: FALSE
Diff: 2

27) The Taoist perspective on nature values nature for its own sake, not for any practical uses it might have for humans.

Answer: TRUE
Diff: 2

28) Members of Earth First! and Greenpeace are more likely to hold the preservationist view than the conservationist view.

Answer: TRUE
Diff: 1

29) The organic view of nature that prevailed in medieval Europe viewed both earth and nature as male.

Answer: FALSE
Diff: 1

30) Paleolithic peoples had little impact on their environments.

Answer: FALSE
Diff: 1

31) Human domestication of plants brought a corresponding increase in the appreciation of nature as a provider of rain, sunlight, and fertile soil.

Answer: TRUE
Diff: 1

32) The European human population has grown more in the last 2,000 years than in the previous 400,000 years.

Answer: TRUE
Diff: 2

33) During the period of European external expansion, the introduction of plants and animals flowed from the Old World to the New World, but not in the reverse direction.

Answer: FALSE
Diff: 1

34) The United States is both the largest producer and consumer of the world's energy resources.

Answer: TRUE
Diff: 2

35) Over the last four decades, global energy consumption has decreased.

Answer: FALSE
Diff: 1

36) Most of the oil that enters the ocean is due to oil spills from tankers.

Answer: FALSE
Diff: 2

37) The majority of countries in the core are not expanding their nuclear power capabilities.

Answer: TRUE
Diff: 2

38) The increased incidence of acid rain is primarily due to the burning of fossil fuels.

Answer: TRUE
Diff: 1

39) Thinning of some trees from a forest is conversion of the land, not modification.

Answer: FALSE
Diff: 1

40) There are fewer acres of rain forest now than fifty years ago.

Answer: TRUE
Diff: 1

41) San Francisco Bay has been little modified by humans, and thus has a thriving ecosystem very similar to the one that existed 200 years ago.

Answer: FALSE
Diff: 1

42) The Judeo–Christian perspective places humans on the same level as all other mammals in creation.

Answer: FALSE
Diff: 1

43) Buddhism stresses the separate nature of all individuals, human and non–human.

Answer: FALSE
Diff: 2

44) Deep ecology includes the concept of biospherical egalitarianism.

Answer: TRUE
Diff: 1

45) From its earliest days, Christian leaders have actively promoted domination of nature.

Answer: FALSE
Diff: 2

46) The mammoth and the cave bear disappeared from North America around the same time the dinosaurs did.

Answer: FALSE
Diff: 1

47) Neolithic peoples had a more sedentary life than did Paleolithic peoples.

Answer: TRUE
Diff: 1

48) Few peripheral regions continue to use wood as a significant source of energy.

Answer: FALSE
Diff: 2

49) Desertification is most common in tropical and subtropical areas.

Answer: FALSE
Diff: 1

4.4 Matching

ENERGY & RESOURCES: Match the activity or phenomena with the group of countries in which is most likely to be found.

1) use of woodfuels
   Diff: 3

   A) core

   B) periphery

2) nuclear power generation
   Diff: 3

3) high CO_2 emissions
   Diff: 3

4) current high rates of deforestation
   Diff: 3

5) high energy consumption per capita
   Diff: 3

6) acid rain
   Diff: 3

7) declining cropland
   Diff: 3

1) B   2) A   3) A   4) B   5) A   6) A
7) A

ENVIRONMENTAL PHILOSOPHIES: Match the description to the group of countries.

8) environmental ethics
   Diff: 2

9) ecofeminism
   Diff: 2

10) deep ecology
    Diff: 2

11) environmental justice
    Diff: 2

A) concerned with inequitable
   distribution of pollution and
   environmental degradation

B) nature has been subordinated and
   exploited in the same way that
   women are

C) humans are part of the nonhuman
   world & the biosphere is the
   center of creation

D) rights should be given to
   nonhuman nature

8) D   9) B   10) C   11) A

4.5 Map Identification

World Map

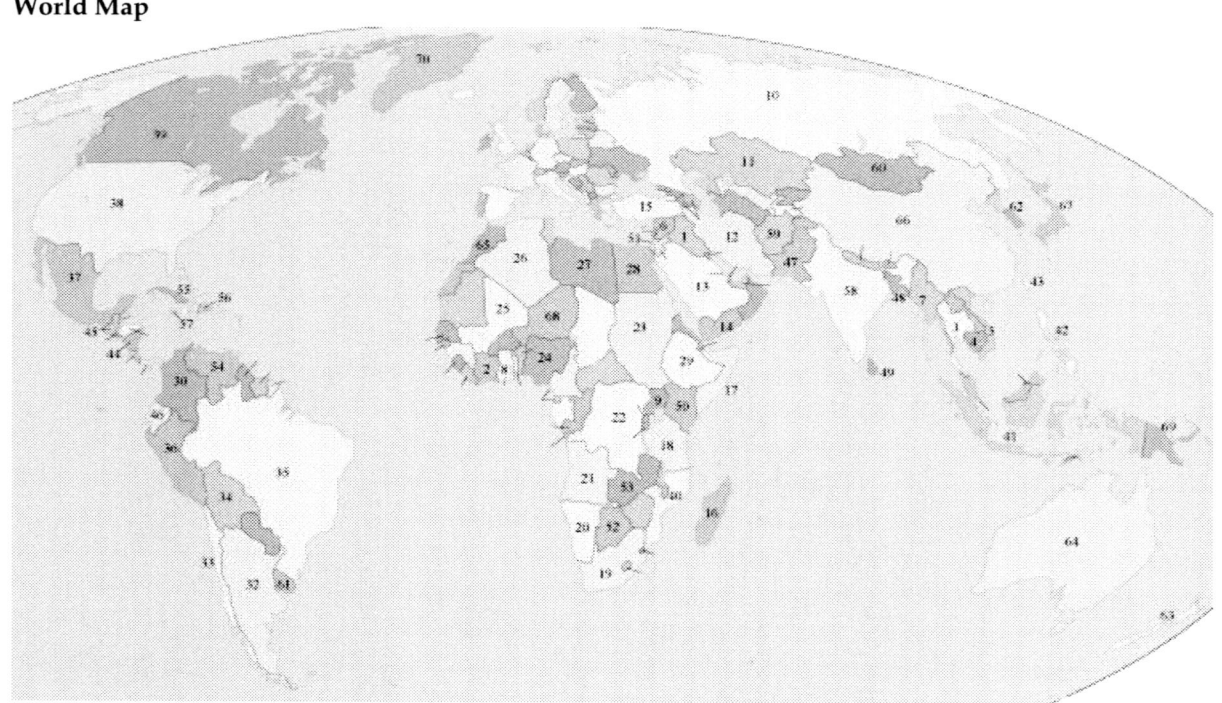

1) Haiti and the Dominican Republic share this island.

   A) 16   B) 43   C) 49   D) 56   E) 67

   Answer: D
   Diff: 1

2) The country of Australia is identified by the number

   A) 16.   B) 35.   C) 70.   D) 41.   E) 64.

   Answer: E
   Diff: 1

3) La Paz is the capital of

   A) 36.   B) 32.   C) 24.   D) 23.   E) 7.

   Answer: B
   Diff: 1

4) The capital of country #17 is

   A) Mogadishu.

   B) Lima.

   C) Kampala.

   D) Hispaniola.

   E) Islamabad.

   Answer: A
   Diff: 1

5) Port–au–Prince is the Capital of

   A) Canada.

   B) France.

   C) Ghana.

   D) Cote D'Ivoire.

   E) Haiti.

   Answer: E
   Diff: 1

6) Which of the following is in the Andean Region?

   A) Peru

   B) Dominican Republic

   C) Australia

   D) Mexico

   E) Bangladesh

   Answer: A
   Diff: 2

7) Which of the following is in the world's core?

    A) Australia   B) Bolivia   C) Haiti   D) Somalia   E) Uganda

Answer: A
Diff: 2

8) Which pair of countries share a continent?

    A) Haiti & the Dominican Republic

    B) Bolivia & Somalia

    C) Peru & Uganda

    D) Australia & Bolivia

    E) Australia & Somalia

Answer: A
Diff: 2

9) Which pair of countries do NOT share a continent?

    A) Haiti & the Dominican Republic

    B) Bolivia & Peru

    C) Somalia & Uganda

    D) Somalia & Bolivia

    E) Each of the above pairs share the same continent.

Answer: D
Diff: 2

10) Canberra is the capital of the country labeled with which number?

    A) 24   B) 34   C) 44   D) 54   E) 64

Answer: E
Diff: 1

11) The capital of Uganda is

    A) Addis Ababa.

    B) Accra.

    C) Kampala.

    D) Nairobi.

    E) Pretoria.

Answer: C
Diff: 1

4.6 Chapter 4 Questions with images

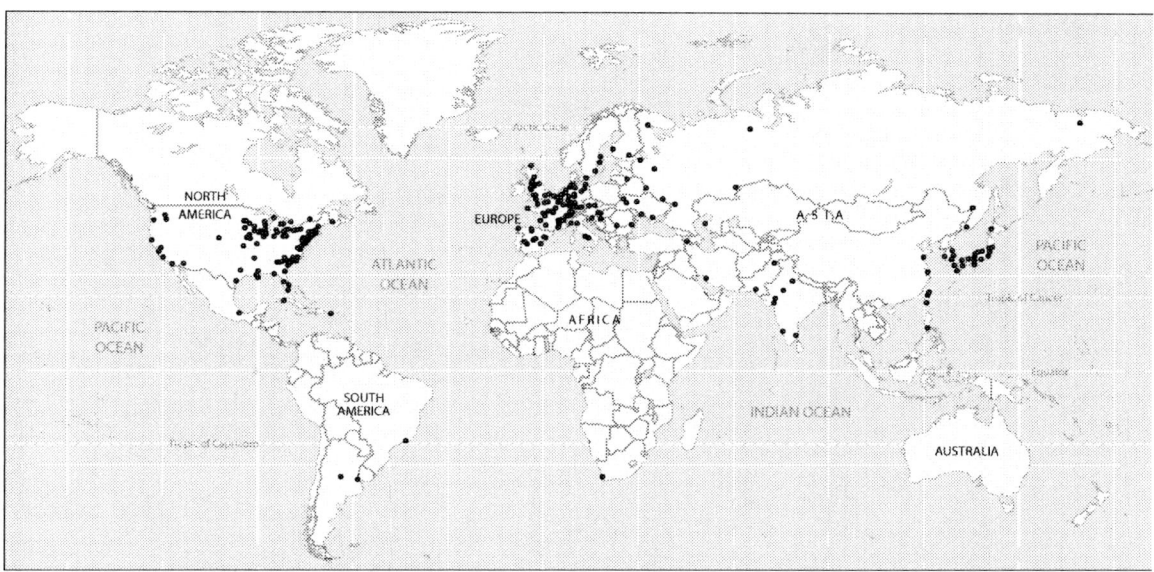

1) The above map shows the world distribution of

    A) nuclear reactors.

    B) hydropower facilities.

    C) wood–fired power plants.

    D) natural gas fields.

    E) oil refineries.

Answer: A
Diff: 3

Chapter 5 Cultural Geographies

5.1 Minimal Choice

1) Which of the following is the "humanized" version of the other?

   A) cultural landscape   B) natural landscape

   Answer: A
   Diff: 1

2) The french, geographical concept of *genre de vie* most closely resembles what we call a cultural

   A) complex.   B) trait.

   Answer: A
   Diff: 2

3) *Descansos* along roadsides in Mexico and Spain are examples of cultural

   A) traits.   B) systems.

   Answer: A
   Diff: 1

4) Ceremonies or celebrations that mark transitions in human life are known as

   A) rites of passage.   B) *genres de vie.*

   Answer: A
   Diff: 1

5) From the following belief systems, which is newer and evolved from the other?

   A) Buddhism   B) Hinduism

   Answer: A
   Diff: 1

6) The majority of Muslims are

   A) Sunni.   B) Shi'ite.

   Answer: A
   Diff: 1

7) The fastest growing religion in the United States is

   A) Islam.   B) Orthodox Christianity.

   Answer: A
   Diff: 1

8) All Indo-European languages (including Russian, Hindi, English, Spanish, German) are all part of the same language

A) family.   B) branch.

Answer: A
Diff: 1

9) India's internal state identities are fairly closely aligned with different

A) languages.   B) religions.

Answer: A
Diff: 2

10) Regional variations in language are common, and referred to as

A) dialects.   B) language branches.

Answer: A
Diff: 1

11) Islam's most holy city is

A) Mecca.   B) Jerusalem.

Answer: A
Diff: 1

12) The set of practical, behavioral guidelines observed by Muslims based on the words and action of the Prophet Mohammed is known as the

A) Sunna.   B) Qur'an.

Answer: A
Diff: 2

13) According to our text, the political preference of increasing numbers of Quebec residents is for

A) sovereignty.   B) separatism.

Answer: A
Diff: 2

14) Gender is an identity, and reflects _____ differences between men and women.

A) social   B) biological

Answer: A
Diff: 1

15) The Grameen Bank emerged in Bangladesh as a way of empowering women through

A) providing small business loans.   B) subsidizing the cost of education.

Answer: A
Diff: 2

5.2 Multiple Choice

1) Missionizing religions

A) actively seek converts.

B) are identified with particular ethnic or tribal groups.

C) do not seek converts.

D) are place based.

E) eschew missionaries.

Answer: A
Diff: 2

2) A(n) _____ is needed and used where many languages are spoken and a single language of communication, commerce, and government is needed. English, Spanish, French and Russian are all examples.

A) *lingua franca*

B) pidgin

C) dialect

D) Indo–European language

E) isogloss

Answer: A
Diff: 1

3) To human geographers, which of the following statements is *not* true. Culture

A) is a shared sets of meanings.

B) is lived through the materials and symbolic practices of everyday live.

C) is based on our genetic inheritance.

D) can be transformed by forces internal and external to particular groups.

E) includes values, beliefs, practices, language, identities.

Answer: C
Diff: 1

4) At the end of the twentieth century, according to your textbook, the fastest growing religion in the U.S. was

   A) Islam.

   B) Christianity.

   C) Buddhism.

   D) Animism.

   E) Hinduism.

Answer: A
Diff: 1

5) The late twentieth century impacts of Western cultural media products (e.g., television) on the people of Fiji has been likened to

   A) disease brought by nineteenth–century colonialists.

   B) economic development brought by the World Bank after WW II.

   C) literacy brought by U.S. and European aid programs in the 1960s and 1970s.

   D) democracy brought by academics from the United States.

   E) liberation brought at the end of WW I.

Answer: A
Diff: 2

6) _____ is/are the heart and soul of the globalized Hip–Hop Nation.

   A) Music

   B) African–Americans

   C) Gangs

   D) Justice for minorities

   E) The Bronx, New York

Answer: A
Diff: 1

7) _____ was an American pioneer in exploring and understanding the many ways that humans transform the surface of the earth to create cultural landscapes.

   A) Carl Sauer

   B) Notorious B.I.G.

   C) the Dalai Lama

   D) Paul Knox

   E) Paul Vidal de la Blache

Answer: A
Diff: 1

8) Human-built features over a land surface - such as small dairy farms over the Wisconsin countryside or vineyards over California's Napa Valley - are examples of

   A) cultural landscapes.

   B) cultural agents.

   C) cultural media.

   D) natural landscapes.

   E) natural agents.

   Answer: A
   Diff: 1

9) Carl Sauer, H.C. Darby and Paul Vidal de la Blache placed _____ at the heart and center of their studies of human-environment interactions.

   A) cultural landscapes

   B) natural landscapes

   C) climatological factors

   D) language and religion

   E) economics and politics

   Answer: A
   Diff: 1

10) Early French geographers interested in cultural landscapes examined how France's various *genres de vie* emerged from the constraints and possibilities posed by local

   A) physical environments.

   B) political and economic systems.

   C) cultures.

   D) diasporas.

   E) cultural environments.

   Answer: A
   Diff: 2

11) Pork avoidance among Muslims, eating fish on Fridays among Roman Catholics, bar mitzvahs among Jews and eating black-eyed peas on New Year's Day in the U.S. South are all

   A) cultural traits.

   B) rites of passage.

   C) coming-of-age ceremonies.

   D) dietary restrictions.

   E) *genres de vie.*

Answer: A
Diff: 1

12) Coming of age ceremonies – marking the transition from childhood into adulthood – are examples of

   A) rites of passage.

   B) cultural transitions.

   C) *genre de vie.*

   D) folk culture.

   E) sexual identity.

Answer: A
Diff: 1

13) A cultural region is an area where certain cultural practices, beliefs, and values

   A) are shared by the majority.

   B) share the same origins.

   C) originate.

   D) are linked by an official language or *lingua franca.*

   E) are linked by the same religion.

Answer: A
Diff: 2

14) A cultural system of traits, territorial affiliation and shared history

   A) does not allow for internal variation within the system.

   B) helps shape a group's collective identity.

   C) means that all group members speak the same language.

   D) means that all group members practices the same religion.

   E) both C and D

Answer: B
Diff: 2

15) Diasporas have contributed *especially* to the spread of _____ around the world.

    A) religion   B) disease   C) dialects   D) conflict   E) trade

Answer: A
Diff: 1

16) The world's four major world religions

    A) originated from Old World agricultural and urban hearth areas.

    B) emerged from the world's core regions.

    C) diffused from the New World following the Columbian Exchange.

    D) began in the region of modern–day Israel/Palestine/Arabian Peninsula.

    E) were spread around the world with European imperialism.

Answer: A
Diff: 1

17) Which of the following does not share religious and regional roots with the others?

    A) Islam

    B) Buddhism

    C) Sikhism

    D) Hinduism

    E) All of the above emerged from the same religious and regional roots.

Answer: A
Diff: 3

18) Despite having a long history and followers around the world, Judaism does not have many followers. In large part, this is because Judaism

    A) does not seek converts.

    B) is a polytheistic religion.

    C) is an off–shoot of the much more popular Sikhism.

    D) like Feng Shui, is just a passing fad.

    E) recognizes Saturday as the holy day, which conflicts with Saturday as a day of work, play and college football.

Answer: A
Diff: 2

19) In our postcolonial era, the flow of religious influence is increasingly from

    A) periphery to core.　　　　　　　B) core to periphery.

    C) core to core.　　　　　　　　　D) periphery to periphery.

Answer: A
Diff: 1

20) Before the Colombian Exchange and contact with the Old World, the people of the Americas practiced

    A) Shamanism and Animism.

    B) Buddhism and Sikhism.

    C) Orthodox Christianity.

    D) Liberation theology.

    E) Shiism and Sunnism.

Answer: A
Diff: 1

21) Candomble, Umbanda, Voudou and Santeria are religions of Latin America that merge indigenous beliefs of Native Americans with

    A) Roman Catholicism brought by colonizers.

    B) Roman Catholicism and traditional African beliefs brought by slaves.

    C) Mormonism brought by missionaries.

    D) Mormonism and Roman Catholicism.

    E) all of the above

Answer: B
Diff: 2

22) The Dalai Lama travels the world supporting the people of Tibet and promoting

    A) Buddhism.

    B) Catholicism.

    C) Hinduism.

    D) Islam.

    E) non-violent protestantism.

Answer: A
Diff: 1

23) Before attaining enlightenment and becoming the Buddha, Prince Guatama was a(n)

   A) Hindu.

   B) Muslim.

   C) Christian.

   D) Sikh.

   E) animist.

Answer: A
Diff: 2

24) Swahili, Arabic, English, French and Hausa are all spoken by many people across Africa. What they have in common is that they are all

   A) languages of trade and business in Africa.

   B) Indo-European languages.

   C) languages indigenous to Africa.

   D) languages brought to Africa by European colonizers.

   E) spoken by the bushmen of southern Africa.

Answer: A
Diff: 3

25) To be in the same family, languages must share the same

   A) vocabulary.

   B) alphabet (or script).

   C) origins.

   D) grammar.

   E) dialect.

Answer: C
Diff: 2

26) The English spoken in Minnesota and the English spoken in Australia can best be characterized as two different

   A) dialects.

   B) language families.

   C) language groups.

   D) languages.

   E) language branches.

Answer: A
Diff: 3

27) The use of language distinctive of a particular group is known as a(n)

   A) dialect.

   B) idiom.

   C) diaspora.

   D) drawl.

   E) colloquialism.

Answer: A
Diff: 2

28) Some countries, like France (at least until recently) suppress local and regional languages in an attempt to

   A) unify the country.

   B) keep English and globalization out.

   C) keep out migrants.

   D) abide by European Union requirements.

   E) make their country more attractive to tourists.

Answer: A
Diff: 2

29) Currently, around the world, there are roughly _____ living languages.

   A) 5   B) 50   C) 500   D) 5000   E) 50,000

Answer: D
Diff: 1

30) In 1995, in response to political, economic and social threats to their cultural identity, the people of Quebec narrowly voted to

   A) remain part of Canada.

   B) secede from Canada.

   C) become part of the United States.

   D) keep French as their official language.

   E) become part of NAFTA.

Answer: A
Diff: 2

31) Kinship is a form of social organization in which bonds between people are based on

    A) blood relations.

    B) marriage.

    C) adoption.

    D) solidarity.

    E) all of the above

Answer: E
Diff: 2

32) The effort to protect regional and national cultures from Americanization and the homogenizing effects of globalization is known as

    A) cultural nationalism.

    B) anti–Americanism.

    C) cultural imperialism.

    D) traditional nationalism.

    E) religious fundamentalism.

Answer: A
Diff: 2

33) The *hajj*, fasting during Ramadan, and giving alms (charitable donations) are

    A) among the primary obligations of Muslims.

    B) rites of passage for Muslims.

    C) cultural traits of Islamic countries.

    D) cultural traits of Arabs.

    E) among the five prayers of Islam.

Answer: A
Diff: 2

34) The split of Islam into two sects, Sunni and Shi'i,

    A) emerged over who should succeed Mohammed.

    B) emerged with the rise in twentieth–century globalization.

    C) emerged over who should control access to Mecca.

    D) has been resolved by Islamism.

    E) reflects the differences between the Arab and the non–Arab Muslims.

Answer: A
Diff: 2

35) The most widespread and effective anticolonial, anti-imperialist, and generally anticore movement to challenge the modernizing and secularizing forces of globalization has been

   A) Islamism.

   B) postmodernism.

   C) jihad.

   D) cultural nationalism.

   E) postcolonialism.

Answer: A
Diff: 2

36) Islamism attempts to protect the purity and centrality of Islamic precepts through

   A) a return to a universal Islamic state.

   B) jihad.

   C) hajj.

   D) the Five Pillars.

   E) secular democracy.

Answer: A
Diff: 2

37) Muslim is to Islam as

   A) Christian is to Christianity.

   B) Hindu is to Hindi.

   C) Turkish is to Arabic.

   D) English is to Latin.

   E) both A and B

Answer: A
Diff: 3

38) Which of the following spread around the world with the purpose of making converts and saving souls (as well as for the purposes of political control)?

   A) Islam

   B) Christianity

   C) Judaism

   D) both A and B

   E) all of the above

Answer: D
Diff: 2

39) Based on battles over country music broadcasting in Canada in the mid-1990s, the United States demonstrated an approach to culture in which music was treated as a

    A) commodity to be bought, sold and traded.

    B) national treasure to be protected.

    C) form of identity to be supported and developed.

    D) tool of imperialism.

    E) nationalist icon of propaganda.

Answer: A
Diff: 3

40) Canadians are very aware of U.S. cultural products because

    A) 90 percent of Canadians live within 200 miles of the U.S./Canadian border.

    B) 90 percent of Americans live within 200 miles of the U.S./Canadian border.

    C) most Canadians have U.S. passports.

    D) of all the American professional ice hockey teams.

    E) all Canadian retirees winter in Florida and Arizona.

Answer: A
Diff: 2

41) Whereas race is a problematic way of differentiating human beings based on physical characteristics such as skin color, _____ creates differences out of cultural traits and complexes.

    A) ethnicity

    B) gender

    C) class

    D) racism

    E) cultural nationalism

Answer: A
Diff: 2

42) A human geographer studying gender issues would most likely study

    A) men's compared to women's salaries.

    B) prostitution in and around red-light districts.

    C) the international sex-trade.

    D) fashions and attitudes of homosexuals.

    E) pink spending.

Answer: A
Diff: 2

43) The British historical geographer H.C. Darby was best know for

A) reconstructing past landscapes from the Domesday Book.

B) starting the first geography department in England (at Oxford).

C) writing the Domesday Book documenting England's dialects.

D) interpreting the Old English dialect spoken by William the Conqueror.

E) Making the first religious map of Asia.

Answer: A
Diff: 1

44) According to your text, Hip-hop music is the coming together of all of the following *except*

A) grace.   B) place.   C) space.   D) race.

Answer: A
Diff: 2

45) Which of the following has not been used to create social identities and/or power differences among groups?

A) sexuality

B) racialization

C) gender

D) ethnicity

E) All of the above have been the basis for identity and power differences.

Answer: E
Diff: 2

46) The "shared set of meanings" of culture generally refers to

A) religious practices.

B) family values.

C) historical understandings.

D) ideas about gender roles.

E) all of the above

Answer: E
Diff: 1

47) Cultural geography

    A) is concerned only with material culture.

    B) is no longer relevant because the world has become homogeneous.

    C) explores the interactions of culture with space, place, and landscape.

    D) was denounced for its racist and upper–class bias by Carl Sauer.

Answer: C
Diff: 1

48) According to Carl Sauer, a cultural landscape

    A) exists prior to human habitation of the given landscape.

    B) need not require a natural landscape.

    C) results from the action of a cultural group within and on a landscape.

    D) is an old–fashioned concept with limited use by contemporary geographers.

Answer: C
Diff: 2

49) According to Sauer's model, _____ is (are) important in the creation of cultural landscapes.

    A) time

    B) cultural practices

    C) natural landscapes

    D) geology and climate

    E) All of the above are important in the process of creating cultural landscapes.

Answer: E
Diff: 2

50) French geographer Vidal de la Blanche

    A) thought that how people obtained their livelihoods was important for the geographer.

    B) concentrated on studying large geographical units.

    C) found that industrialization had only a small impact on rural France.

    D) got his formal geographic training under Paul Knox and Sallie Marston.

    E) all of the above.

Answer: A
Diff: 2

51) Confirmation of 12-year-old boys and girls in the Roman Catholic Church is best described as a

    A) cultural trait.   B) rite of passage.

    C) cultural complex.   D) *bar mitzvah* or *bat mitzvah*.

Answer: B
Diff: 1

52) Diasporas

    A) occur when people of a homogeneous group are dispersed from their traditional home region.

    B) occurred frequently during biblical times, but have been rare since.

    C) has been the most common reason for conversion to Christianity.

    D) refers solely to the emigration of people from the region of Palestine.

Answer: A
Diff: 1

53) On world maps of religion, Central and South America are represented as

    A) Roman Catholic.

    B) Protestant.

    C) Eastern Orthodox.

    D) Buddhists.

    E) animists.

Answer: A
Diff: 1

54) Outside Israel, Judaism is concentrated in

    A) South America and the Caribbean.

    B) Europe and North America.

    C) Africa.

    D) West Asia.

    E) East Asia.

Answer: B
Diff: 1

55) Buddhism originated in

A) Jordan.

B) Saudi Arabia.

C) Thailand.

D) Japan.

E) India.

Answer: E
Diff: 1

56) Prior to European contact and colonization, the peoples of the Americas practiced

A) Shintoism.

B) Animism and Shamanism.

C) Buddhism and Taoism.

D) Sikhism.

E) Mormonism.

Answer: B
Diff: 1

57) Which of the following terms is most likely to encompass the largest number of languages?

A) language family   B) language branch

C) language group   D) language dialect

Answer: A
Diff: 1

58) Spanish and French

A) emerged from Arabic.

B) are mutually intelligible: if you speak one you can understand the other.

C) are related to Hindi, Farsi, Greek and other Indo–European languages.

D) used to be spoken across all of Europe.

Answer: C
Diff: 1

59) About 50 percent of the global population speaks languages belonging to the _____ language family.

    A) Caucasian

    B) Afro–Asiatic

    C) Sino–Tibetan

    D) Indo–European

    E) Amerind

Answer: D
Diff: 1

60) During which of the following time periods has the French government been most accepting of regional languages within France?

    A) from the early 1980s to the present

    B) during the presidency of DeGaulle in the 1960s

    C) during the reign of Napoleon in the early nineteenth century

    D) during the reign of Louis XVI just prior to the 1789 French Revolution

Answer: A
Diff: 2

61) Which of the following countries or regions is least likely to engage in cultural nationalism?

    A) France   B) United States   C) Quebec   D) Saudi Arabia

Answer: B
Diff: 1

62) Cultural nationalism

    A) has been on the wane over the last two decades as the world has turned more towards democracy.

    B) is exemplified by France's efforts to protect its language from "Americanization."

    C) is practiced primarily in the Islamic world.

    D) occurs when governments actively try to export their culture to other countries with the specific aim of changing the cultures of those countries.

Answer: B
Diff: 2

63) The Qu'ran

    A) was written after most of the Old Testament was written, but before the New Testament.

    B) does not recognize Jesus as a prophet.

    C) is used by the Shi'i, but not by Sunnis.

    D) was written my Muhammad.

    E) is considered by Muslims to be the word of God, delivered through Muhammad.

Answer: E
Diff: 2

64) The number of television sets per capita is highest in

    A) Africa.   B) Southeast Asia.

    C) North America.   D) South America.

Answer: C
Diff: 1

65) Islamism is, basically,

    A) a strict Islamic fundamentalism.

    B) an anti-Western or anti-core political movement.

    C) a movement advocating the integration of Western values into Islamic society.

    D) a perspective that opposes all forms of cultural nationalism.

    E) the religions introduced by the prophet Muhammad.

Answer: B
Diff: 2

66) The cultural hearth of Islam is in

    A) Saudi Arabia, in the Middle East.

    B) Egypt, North Africa.

    C) Indonesia and Malaysia, Southeast Asia.

    D) the Balkans, in Europe.

    E) China, in East Asia.

Answer: A
Diff: 1

67) Which of the following countries is NOT more than 50 percent Muslim?

    A) Egypt   B) Iran   C) India   D) Iraq   E) Turkey

Answer: C
Diff: 2

68) "Pink spending"

    A) was common in Hitler's Germany.

    B) has led to the formation of openly gay areas in many large cities.

    C) has generally backfired on the gay movement.

    D) has been more effective in peripheral countries than in core countries.

Answer: B
Diff: 2

69) "Queer activism" of such groups as ACTUP and Queer Nation has included

    A) exposing high-profile homosexuals who wanted their homosexuality kept secret.

    B) "cultural terrorism."

    C) kissing and holding hands in public.

    D) all of the above

Answer: D
Diff: 1

70) For the geographer, ethnicity deals with a particular group

    A) with perceived or actual commonality in language or religion.

    B) that may or may not engage in public displays related to its ethnicity.

    C) that has a socially created system of rules governing who is and is not a member of the group.

    D) all of the above

    E) none of the above

Answer: D
Diff: 2

71) In late-nineteenth-century America, the Irish

    A) had achieved equal status with earlier immigrant groups of Protestant stock.

    B) invented Saint Patrick, who never existed in real life.

    C) were looked down upon by many Americans.

    D) often got the highest paying jobs.

Answer: C
Diff: 2

72) From a biological standpoint, race does not exist. Practically, however, the term has come to refer to

A) is most apparent in the segregation of certain ethnic groups, such as the Chinese in a "Chinatown."

B) differences between people based on skin color and other physical characteristics.

C) differences in cultures and practice.

D) differences between people as determined by intelligence tests.

Answer: B
Diff: 2

73) Ethnic neighborhoods

A) are often created by the dominant society to affirm that society's sense of identity.

B) are the best method for breaking down systems of racial classification.

C) are rarely found in core countries.

D) evolve around great restaurants.

Answer: A
Diff: 2

74) Power differences between men and women in a society are determined primarily by

A) biological differences.   B) society and culture.

C) physical geography.   D) performance in standardized testing.

Answer: B
Diff: 2

75) Among the Hausa of northern Nigeria, which of the following groups is likely to suffer the least in a drought?

A) women   B) children   C) men   D) dogs

Answer: C
Diff: 1

76) Cultural ecology

A) is the approach taken by Sauer in his studies of the cultural landscape.

B) stresses that systemic interrelationships link cultures and the environment.

C) looks only at material elements of culture.

D) is an approach used by few modern geographers.

Answer: B
Diff: 2

77) Political ecology

    A) stresses the importance of political and economic forces.

    B) takes a narrower approach than cultural ecology.

    C) originated in the Soviet Union, and pretty much died when the Soviet Union died.

    D) none of the above

Answer: A
Diff: 3

78) This is NOT a major forefather of hip-hop:

    A) Bob Marley   B) Huey Newton   C) James Brown   D) Nat King Cole

Answer: D
Diff: 2

79) In the United States, hip-hop is least associated with

    A) Los Angeles.

    B) New York City.

    C) Oakland.

    D) Detroit.

    E) Washington, D.C.

Answer: E
Diff: 2

80) The leadership of hip-hop is predominantly

    A) black and male.

    B) black and female.

    C) white and male.

    D) white and female.

    E) Latino and male.

Answer: A
Diff: 1

81) Hinduism originated in modern-day

    A) China.   B) Iran.   C) India.   D) Burma.   E) Israel.

Answer: C
Diff: 1

82) Of the following religions, which is oldest?

   A) Hinduism

   B) Sikhism

   C) Buddhism

   D) Islam

   E) Bahai

Answer: A
Diff: 2

83) Protestantism is least prevalent in

   A) the United States.

   B) northern Europe.

   C) Australia.

   D) South America.

   E) South Africa.

Answer: D
Diff: 2

84) This religion did not have its origins in the Middle East:

   A) Islam   B) Judaism   C) Christianity   D) Sikhism

Answer: D
Diff: 1

85) Of the following religions, which was founded most recently?

   A) Islam

   B) Buddhism

   C) Christianity

   D) Hinduism

   E) Daoism

Answer: A
Diff: 2

86) Where in the United States is Sunday viewing of televangelist programs most prevalent?

   A) Southeast   B) West   C) Northwest   D) Midwest

Answer: A
Diff: 2

87) In what country is Shi'ism the official state religion?

A) Jordan

B) Egypt

C) Bangladesh

D) Iran

E) Malaysia

Answer: D
Diff: 2

88) Muslims do not make up a majority of this country:

A) South Africa

B) Algeria

C) Egypt

D) Sudan

E) Pakistan

Answer: A
Diff: 2

5.3 True or False

1) Institutions are informal & formal associations that help societies organize and operate.

Answer: TRUE
Diff: 1

2) Different cultural groups can have the same cultural trait(s).

Answer: TRUE
Diff: 1

3) Some countries have more than one official language.

Answer: TRUE
Diff: 1

4) All the people of the Middle East speak Arabic.

Answer: FALSE
Diff: 2

5) Culture is found only among ethnically homogeneous groups.

Answer: FALSE
Diff: 2

6) Culture is constantly being newly created as it shapes and is shaped by politics, economics and society.

Answer: TRUE
Diff: 1

7) Cultural landscapes precede natural landscapes.

Answer: FALSE
Diff: 1

8) The same cultural trait can be found in different cultural regions.

Answer: TRUE
Diff: 1

9) Rites of passage are limited to the world's peripheral places and traditional peoples.

Answer: FALSE
Diff: 2

10) A diaspora is the diffusion of a religion from its cultural hearth.

Answer: FALSE
Diff: 1

11) Liberation theology, which emerged to empower the poor in Latin America, combines the messages of Jesus and Karl Marx.

Answer: TRUE
Diff: 2

12) Around the world, indigenous languages are disappearing faster than new languages are emerging.

Answer: TRUE
Diff: 2

13) The establishment of official languages contributes to the extinction of languages.

Answer: TRUE
Diff: 2

14) All Muslims are Islamists.

Answer: TRUE
Diff: 1

15) All Muslims accept the Five Pillars.

   Answer: TRUE
   Diff: 1

16) Islam, Judaism and Christianity are the three great monolithic religions.

   Answer: FALSE
   Diff: 1

17) Islam is monotheistic but not monolithic.

   Answer: TRUE
   Diff: 2

18) The term (and concept) *fundamentalism* is only accurately applied to Islam.

   Answer: FALSE
   Diff: 1

19) Only peripheral countries are struggling to resist U.S. cultural hegemony.

   Answer: FALSE
   Diff: 2

20) Based on the evidence to date, there is not yet a global culture.

   Answer: TRUE
   Diff: 2

21) In the case of world music, globalization has helped cultural diversity to flourish.

   Answer: TRUE
   Diff: 1

22) Cultural traits can vary within a cultural system.

   Answer: TRUE
   Diff: 2

23) Computers and cellular phones are changing languages like English but not the nature of our personal relationships.

   Answer: FALSE
   Diff: 2

24) Patriarchal gender systems distinguish the world's periphery from the core.

   Answer: FALSE
   Diff: 2

25) South Africa's is the first constitution to prohibit discrimination on the grounds of sexual orientation.

Answer: TRUE
Diff: 2

26) Around the world, women recognize their subordination as cultural and negotiable; men see it as biological and given.

Answer: TRUE
Diff: 2

27) For Carl Sauer, culture is the agent that transforms a natural landscape into a cultural landscape.

Answer: TRUE
Diff: 2

28) A cultural complex consists of those cultural traits characteristic of a particular group.

Answer: TRUE
Diff: 1

29) A cultural region is by definition large with no discontinuous sections.

Answer: FALSE
Diff: 1

30) Language hearths are the source regions of languages.

Answer: TRUE
Diff: 2

31) It is believed by most scholars that the Indo–European language family had its origins in southern India.

Answer: FALSE
Diff: 1

32) Islam has more adherents than any other religion.

Answer: FALSE
Diff: 1

33) Followers of Islamism place the rights of the individual above the common good.

Answer: FALSE
Diff: 3

34) Canada enthusiastically embraces American culture.

Answer: FALSE
Diff: 1

35) From the cultural geographer's viewpoint, sexuality is the same everywhere on earth.

Answer: FALSE
Diff: 2

36) Ethnic parades in America used to be very political, although they are not so now.

Answer: FALSE
Diff: 2

37) Among the Hausa in northern Nigeria, the women have fewer resources to help them cope with drought than do the men.

Answer: TRUE
Diff: 1

38) Cultural ecology examines how cultural practices affect adaptation to the environment.

Answer: TRUE
Diff: 2

39) In comparison to Sauer's approach to the cultural landscape, cultural ecology places more emphasis on the cultural processes of groups rather than on the impact of the groups on the environment.

Answer: TRUE
Diff: 3

40) After colonization by the Spanish, the indigenous people of the Andes found the dog more useful than any other domestic animal.

Answer: FALSE
Diff: 1

41) Political ecologists place less emphasis on economic forces than cultural ecologists do.

Answer: FALSE
Diff: 2

42) While many of the world's people are familiar with common products, symbols, and events, there is as of yet no "global culture."

Answer: TRUE
Diff: 2

43) So far, hip-hop seems to be primarily an American phenomenon.

Answer: FALSE
Diff: 1

44) Although many Chinese cannot read the writing of other Chinese, they all speak and understand the same oral language.

Answer: FALSE
Diff: 2

45) Canada's government actively supports the development and retention of Canadian culture.

Answer: TRUE
Diff: 1

46) The native Andean people lost more than half their population after the coming of the Spanish.

Answer: TRUE
Diff: 1

5.4 Matching

CULTURE: Match the example to the term or phrase. There is one best set of answers.

1) cultural trait
   Diff: 2

2) cultural complex
   Diff: 2

3) cultural region
   Diff: 2

4) cultural hearth
   Diff: 2

5) cultural system
   Diff: 2

A) pork avoidance among Muslims

B) Judaism as a set of dietary, religious and social practices

C) Latin America as unique countries with broad similarities (language, religion, colonial history)

D) Quebec as predominantly French and Catholic

E) South Asia as the origin of Hinduism

1) A   2) B   3) D   4) E   5) C

RELIGIONS: *Match the religion to the approximate time of its emergence.*

6) Hinduism
Diff: 2

7) Buddhism
Diff: 2

8) Christianity
Diff: 2

9) Sikhism
Diff: 2

10) Judaism
Diff: 2

11) Islam
Diff: 2

A) 0 B.C./A.D.

B) 500 B.C.

C) 2,000 B.C.

D) fifteenth century A.D.

E) seventh century

6) C   7) B   8) A   9) D   10) C   11) E

5.5 Map Identification

World Map

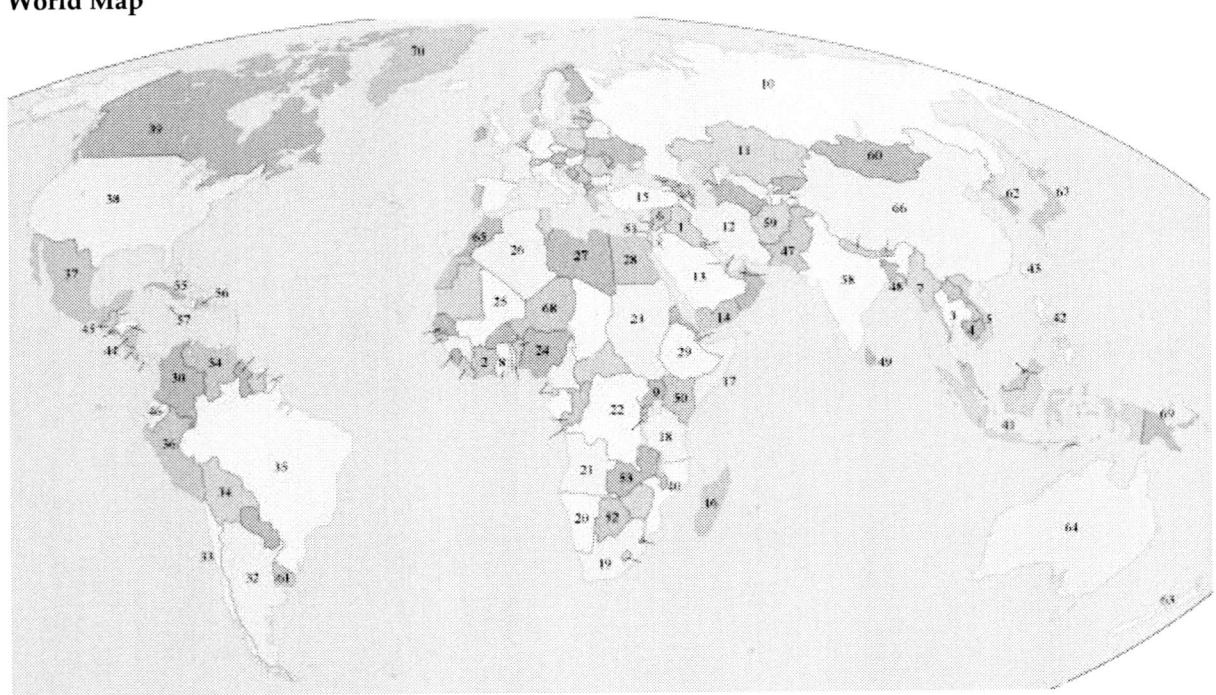

1) Saudi Arabia shares a border with which of the following countries?

    A) Iran   B) Iraq   C) Mongolia   D) Pakistan   E) Sri Lanka

Answer: B
Diff: 2

2) All of the following countries are Asian except

    A) Iran.

    B) Mongolia.

    C) Nigeria.

    D) Pakistan.

    E) Sri Lanka.

Answer: C
Diff: 2

3) The country of Mongolia is identified by the number

    A) 20.   B) 30.   C) 40.   D) 50.   E) 60.

Answer: E
Diff: 1

4) Islamabad is the capital of

    A) Iran.

    B) Pakistan.

    C) Iraq.

    D) Saudi Arabia.

    E) Nigeria.

Answer: B
Diff: 1

5) The capital of country #60 is

    A) Ulan Bator.

    B) Addis Ababa.

    C) Sri Lanka.

    D) Buenos Aires.

    E) Hong Kong.

Answer: A
Diff: 1

6) Colombo is the capital of

    A) 6.   B) 30.   C) 42..   D) 49.   E) 57.

Answer: D
Diff: 1

7) The countries of which two capitals share a border?

    A) Baghdad & Tehran

    B) Islamabad & Riyadh

    C) Ulan Bator & Colombo

    D) Abuja & Colombo

    E) Baghdad & Islamabad

Answer: A
Diff: 2

8) Which of the following is landlocked?

    A) Mongolia   B) Nigeria   C) Iran   D) Sri Lanka   E) Pakistan

Answer: A
Diff: 2

9) Which pair of countries share a continent?

    A) Haiti & the Dominican Republic

    B) Bolivia & Somalia

    C) Peru & Uganda

    D) Australia & Bolivia

    E) Australia & Somalia

Answer: A
Diff: 2

10) Which pair of countries do NOT share a continent?

    A) Mongolia & Iraq

    B) Pakistan & Iran

    C) Iran & Sri Lanka

    D) Sri Lanka & Saudi Arabia

    E) Each of the above pairs share the same continent.

Answer: E
Diff: 2

11) Abuja is the capital of the country labeled with which number?

    A) 24   B) 34   C) 44   D) 54   E) 64

Answer: E
Diff: 1

12) The capital of Iran is

    A) Baghdad.

    B) Riyadh.

    C) Tehran.

    D) Islamabad.

    E) Cairo.

Answer: C
Diff: 1

5.6 Chapter 5 Questions with images

Origin areas of major religions: Match the letter of the region to the religion that originated there.

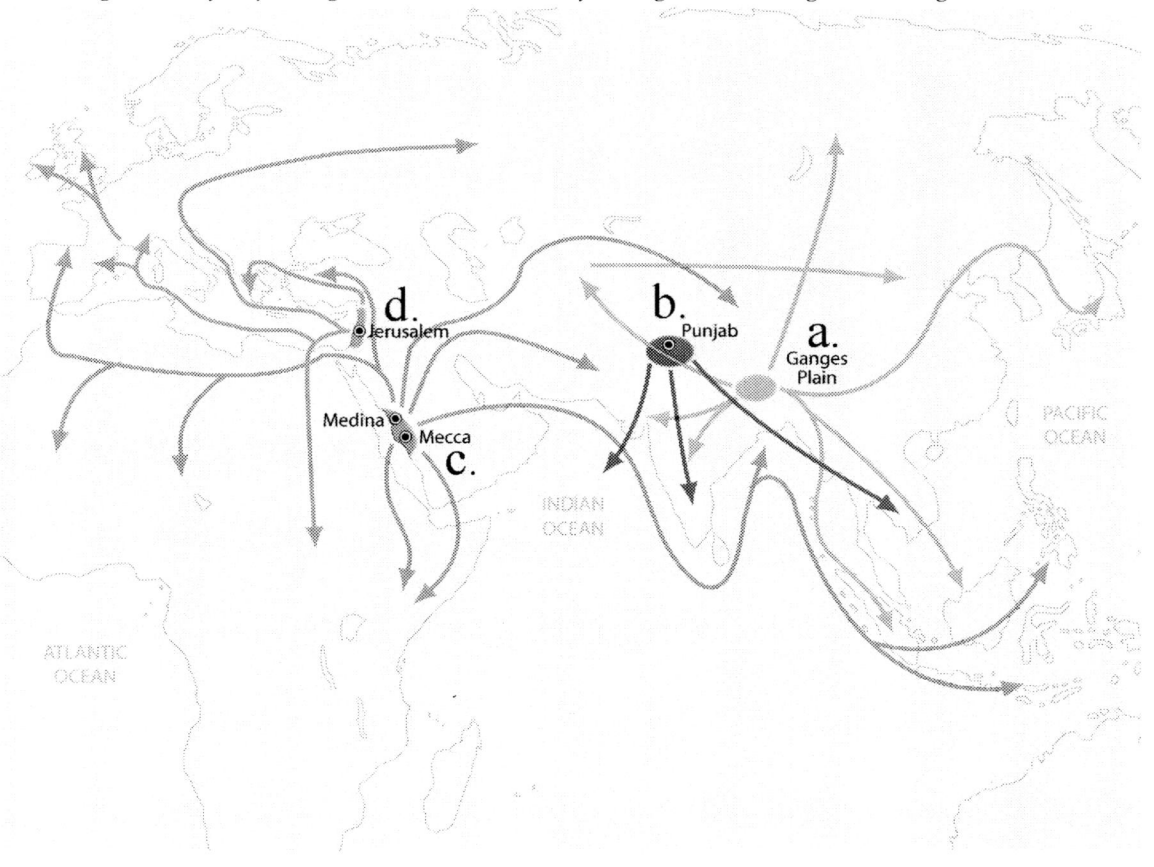

1) Buddhism
   Diff: 2

2) Hinduism
   Diff: 2

3) Islam
   Diff: 2

4) Christianity
   Diff: 2

A) a.

B) b.

C) c.

D) d.

1) A   2) B   3) C   4) D

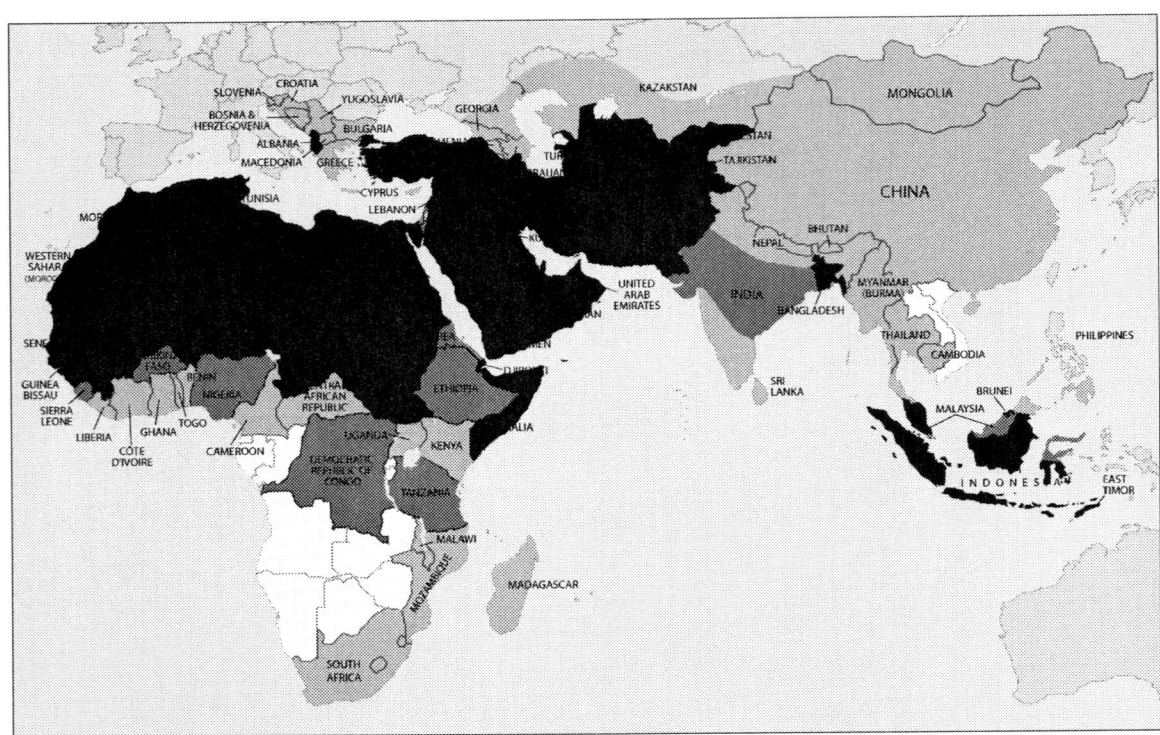

5) In the above map, the darkest shadings indicate countries where the population of _____ is over 50%.

    A) Muslims

    B) Buddhists

    C) Seikhs

    D) Jews

    E) Hindus

Answer: A
Diff: 3

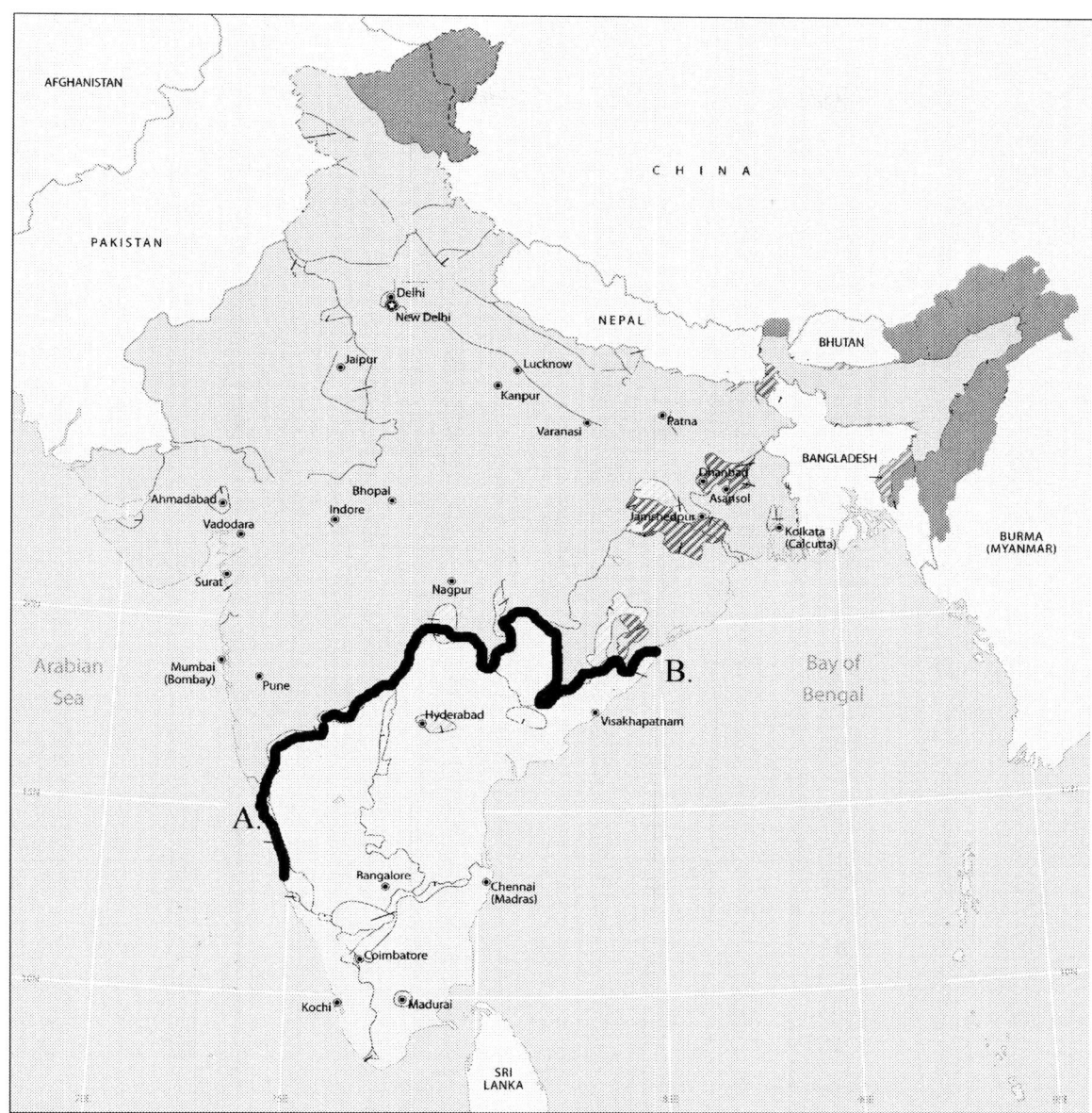

6) The line that stretches from A to B in the above map separates which of the following two general groups?

    A) Indo–Aryan language speakers from Dravidian language speakers

    B) Desert dwellers from mountain peoples

    C) Muslims from Hindus

    D) Christians from Muslims

    E) English speakers from non–English speakers

Answer: A
Diff: 3

Chapter 6 Interpreting Places and Landscapes

6.1 Minimal Choice

1) The study of the social and cultural meanings people give to personal space -- like how far we stand from others when speaking to them -- is known as

   A) proxemics.   B) ethology.

   Answer: A
   Diff: 1

2) The irony, according to Knox and Marston, is that places become "placeless" as

   A) developers try to make them more distinctive.

   B) they take on characteristics of the slow world.

   Answer: A
   Diff: 2

3) Vulgaria is distinguished by landscapes of

   A) bigness and ostentation.   B) moral decay.

   Answer: A
   Diff: 2

4) The tendency for people to have places to which they have a special attachment or sense of identity is known as

   A) topophilia.   B) proxemia.

   Answer: A
   Diff: 1

5) The humanistic approach in geography focuses on

   A) the perception of individuals.   B) factors that shape the views of society.

   Answer: A
   Diff: 2

6) Signs and symbols embedded in the landscape that send messages about identity, beliefs, practices and values, and which we can learn to read and interpret, is an example of

   A) semiotics.   B) geographic literacy.

   Answer: A
   Diff: 1

7) New urbanism and the slow city movements attempt to

     A) rediscover the culture of place.   B) recover derelict landscapes.

Answer: A
Diff: 2

8) The slow city movement has emerged and is growing in the world's

     A) core countries.   B) peripheral countries.

Answer: A
Diff: 2

9) The purchase of images and the experience of spectacular and distinctive places, physical settings and landscapes are combined in the concept of place

     A) consumption.   B) marketing.

Answer: A
Diff: 2

10) _____ is based on the commercial exploitation of the histories of people and places.

     A) The heritage industry   B) Place consumption

Answer: A
Diff: 1

11) Overwhelming _____ is one of the biggest dangers facing successful slow cities.

     A) tourism   B) urban sprawl

Answer: A
Diff: 2

12) Varanasi -- on the Ganges River -- is an exceptionally sacred pilgrimage site to

     A) Hindus.   B) Muslims.

Answer: A
Diff: 1

13) Malls are complex

     A) derelict landscapes.   B) semiotic sites.

Answer: B
Diff: 1

14) An ethologist would be more likely to study

     A) dialects.   B) proxemics.

Answer: B
Diff: 1

15) Geographers using the humanistic approach share a great deal with other social sciences, but especially

A) pyschology.   B) sociology.

Answer: A
Diff: 2

6.2 Multiple Choice

1) The study of peoples' sense of _____ is part of what ethologists study.

A) ethics

B) ethnicity

C) territoriality

D) space

E) landscape

Answer: C
Diff: 1

2) To an ethologist, graffiti in an high-density urban area is least likely to be explained as a(n)

A) response to overcrowding.   B) act of vandalism.

C) expression of identity.   D) claim to territory.

Answer: B
Diff: 2

3) The concept of territoriality helps to classify people and resources in terms of location in

A) space.

B) society.

C) the economy.

D) history.

E) the political system.

Answer: A
Diff: 2

4) Territoriality helps helps us understand how rules, laws and the exercise of power have become associated with

A) spaces and places.   B) individuals and groups.

C) cultures and ethnicities.   D) political and economic systems.

Answer: A
Diff: 2

5) Social affairs involving property rights, political jurisdictions, market areas, ethnic claims to specific areas and efforts to protect traditional land uses all involve issues of

    A) proxemics.

    B) territoriality.

    C) sacred spaces.

    D) cosmopolitanism.

    E) race.

Answer: B
Diff: 2

6) The images that come to mind when we think of a place, any place, like Tucson, Arizona or Damascus, Syria are known as our

    A) cognitive images.

    B) stereotypical images.

    C) territorial markers.

    D) semiotic markers.

    E) topophobic images.

Answer: A
Diff: 1

7) Distortions in our cognitive images are the result of

    A) partial or incomplete information.

    B) biased information.

    C) our likes and dislikes.

    D) the strength of our memories.

    E) all of the above

Answer: E
Diff: 1

8) Paths, edges, districts, nodes and landmarks are used to organize

    A) our cognitive images.

    B) our landscapes.

    C) our individual topophilias.

    D) sacred space.

    E) semiotic landscapes.

Answer: A
Diff: 1

9) In somebody's cognitive image of the United States, it is *least* likely that the Mississippi River is a

    A) node.   B) path.   C) edge.   D) landmark.

Answer: A
Diff: 3

10) Generally, the more experience and first-hand information we have of a place, the more our cognitive images

    A) reflect reality.

    B) are simplified.

    C) converge on topophilia.

    D) are like derelict landscapes.

    E) become territorial.

Answer: A
Diff: 2

11) The parking lot down the street would best be characterized as a

    A) landscape of despair.

    B) derelict landscape.

    C) sacred site.

    D) symbolic landscape.

    E) vernacular landscape.

Answer: E
Diff: 2

12) A study of the social and cultural meanings that people give to personal space – for example, how near or distant you like to sit near others in class – is known as

    A) semiotics.

    B) proxemics.

    C) territoriality.

    D) sacred space.

    E) sense of place.

Answer: B
Diff: 1

13) The longing and ongoing attachments that a migrant may have to her home land is an example of

    A) topophilia.

    B) usufruct.

    C) semiotics.

    D) sacred space.

    E) ethology.

Answer: A
Diff: 1

14) Though Route 66 no longer exists as originally constructed, it still exists as a symbolic landscape that represents

    A) optimism and new opportunities.

    B) despair and decline.

    C) sex, drugs and rock and roll.

    D) the decline of U.S. automobile manufacturing.

    E) the baby boom generation.

Answer: A
Diff: 1

15) The best example of a landscape of power as discussed in our text is

    A) the Pentagon.

    B) a weight–training facility like Gold's gymnasium.

    C) a wind farm.

    D) an electricity–generating station.

    E) a landscape destroyed by a natural disaster like a tornado or earthquake.

Answer: A
Diff: 3

16) When we talk about landscapes as texts, we are referring to

    A) books on landscapes.

    B) the categorization of landscapes based on their features.

    C) landscapes as things of meaning, that can be written and read, like books.

    D) the physical geography underlying cultural landscapes.

    E) an encyclopedia of geographic terms.

Answer: C
Diff: 2

17) Recognizing that landscapes both produce and communicate meaning allows us to

   A) interpret local & national values, priorities, histories, cultural practices.

   B) build a cultural landscape out of a natural landscape.

   C) form cognitive images of places to which we have never been.

   D) build cultural complexes.

   E) dance the hokey pokey.

Answer: A
Diff: 3

18) The humanistic approach in geography emphasizes _____ values, meanings, intentions and behaviors.

   A) an individual's

   B) human-kind's

   C) a specific culture's

   D) cultural

   E) social

Answer: A
Diff: 1

19) Reading, writing and recognizing signs and symbols (such as those that are written into landscapes) is known as

   A) semiotics.

   B) proxemics.

   C) eurhythmics.

   D) semantics.

   E) prosthetics.

Answer: A
Diff: 1

20) Sacred spaces are sacred because

   A) of a miracle that occurred there.

   B) God makes it so.

   C) people make them so.

   D) houses of worship (e.g., temples, mosques, churches, monasteries) are located there.

   E) all of the above

Answer: C
Diff: 2

21) The *hajj* is among the world's very largest

    A) annual pilgrimages.

    B) sacred spaces.

    C) sacred sites.

    D) mosques.

    E) religious conflicts.

Answer: A
Diff: 1

22) To participate in the *hajj* is to be a Muslim and participate in commemorative & symbolic acts in

    A) Mecca.

    B) Jerusalem

    C) Rome.

    D) the Taj Mahal.

    E) Constantinople.

Answer: A
Diff: 1

23) A semiotic reading of Brasilia suggests that the capital city of Brazil was built in the shape of a(n)

    A) airplane, to represent Brasilia as the engine and symbol of Brazil's rapid modernization.

    B) series of crosses, suggesting its sacred or blessed place in Brazil.

    C) colorful rainforest bird, to represent the diversity of people and environments that make up Brazil.

    D) coffee bean, acknowledging Brazil's connection and contribution to the world economy & culture.

    E) both A and B

Answer: E
Diff: 2

24) Mecca, Jerusalem, the Ganges and Lourdes are among the world's most important

   A) religious hearths of monotheism.

   B) pilgrimage sites.

   C) districts, nodes and landmarks.

   D) landscapes of despair.

   E) landscapes-as-text.

   Answer: B
   Diff: 1

25) Landscapes and place-making in which economic and scientific reason and progress are emphasized, are characteristics of

   A) Modernity.

   B) Postmodernity.

   C) Enlightenment.

   D) Fast Cities.

   E) cosmopolitanism.

   Answer: A
   Diff: 2

26) As a view of the world that embraces and combines a range of perspectives, Postmodernity focuses on

   A) environmentally and socially sustainable Modernity.

   B) a return to traditional approaches and religion.

   C) consumption and living for the moment.

   D) all of the above

   E) both A and B

   Answer: C
   Diff: 2

27) Just as we can consume food and other material goods, contemporary culture encourages us to consume *places*, meaning, to

   A) purchase images, symbols and experiences of places.

   B) deplete resource through destroying landscapes.

   C) destroy unique places to build franchises.

   D) travel to other places to learn about their geographies and histories.

   E) all of the above

   Answer: A
   Diff: 2

28) The "Slow Food" movement emerged in response to

    A) the speed of globalization.

    B) mass production and cultural homogenization.

    C) the diffusion of U.S.–based fast food franchises around the world.

    D) emergence of genetically engineered foods.

    E) all of the above

Answer: E
Diff: 2

29) To geographers, the heritage industry is based on the commodification and commercial exploitation of

    A) history.

    B) ideas.

    C) ethnicities

    D) styles.

    E) technologies.

Answer: A
Diff: 1

30) An important consequence of the heritage industry in urban areas is

    A) the loss of authentic histories and landscapes.

    B) the spread of interest in geography and history.

    C) a shift in place marketing from from an emphasis on consumption to one on preservation.

    D) the dissemination of people and their cultures, like the migration of the Swiss to Georgia or the British to Tokyo.

Answer: A
Diff: 2

31) Route 66 is important today for its place in the global

    A) imagination.

    B) highway system.

    C) trucking network.

    D) telecommunications network.

    E) defense system.

Answer: A
Diff: 1

32) An SUV in a megachurch parking lot, surrounded by box stores is a classic landscape most likely seen in

    A) Botoxia.

    B) Inauthentica.

    C) Privatopia.

    D) Semiotica.

    E) Vulgaria.

Answer: E
Diff: 2

33) The study of embedding signs and symbols in the landscape that send messages about identity, beliefs, practices and values -- and which we can learn to read and interpret, -- is an example of

    A) semiotics.

    B) geographic literacy.

    C) topo-linguistics.

    D) environmental perception.

    E) semantics.

Answer: A
Diff: 1

34) The cultural hearth of the slow cities movement is

    A) Italy.

    B) Canada.

    C) Texas.

    D) Southern California.

    E) Brazil.

Answer: A
Diff: 3

35) Among the core principals of the slow cities movement is the concept of

    A) "dwelling."

    B) "visulalizing geography."

    C) "Disneyfication."

    D) "place commodification."

    E) "pseudoplace."

Answer: A
Diff: 2

36) Bra, Greve, Orvieto and Positano are

A) the founding municipalities of the slow cities movement.

B) Roman Catholic sacred sites and pilgrimage destinations.

C) Europe's most affluent shopping malls and sites of consumption.

D) derelict inner–city neighborhoods of Los Angeles of which people have a vague cognitive image.

E) famous sites along Route 66.

Answer: A
Diff: 1

37) Jerusalem is not a sacred city to which of the following groups?

A) Hindus

B) Jews

C) Christians

D) Muslims

E) Jerusalem is believed sacred by *all* of the above groups.

Answer: A
Diff: 2

38) One negative outgrowth of the heritage industry is the tendency toward "Disneyfication," whereby

A) authentic histories and cultures are trivialized, sanitized and glossed over.

B) images and symbols from movies, advertising and popular culture become part of what we believe to be part of the authentic history and landscape of a place.

C) local identity is manufactured to aid marketing and attract tourists.

D) histories of peoples and their places are commercially exploited for widespread consumption.

E) all of the above.

Answer: E
Diff: 2

39) In their study of how humans perceive the environment, geographers have the most in common with

 A) historians.

 B) psychologists.

 C) sociologists.

 D) geologists.

 E) ecologists.

Answer: B
Diff: 2

40) Which of the following significantly affects environmental knowledge?

 A) gender   B) stage of life cycle

 C) religious beliefs   D) all of the above

Answer: D
Diff: 1

41) Globalization in the form of the new production of irrigated cash crops brought this change to the rural Sudanese village studied by geographer Cindi Katz:

 A) Children were required to attend school.

 B) Subsistence crops were no longer grown.

 C) The traditional roles and activities of boys and girls changed.

 D) all of the above

Answer: C
Diff: 3

42) The trailer park and the suburb are examples of

 A) derelict landscapes.   B) ordinary landscapes.

 C) symbolic landscapes.   D) gender–based landscapes.

Answer: B
Diff: 1

43) Because its buildings are modeled after those of the relatively democratic Greek city–states of ancient times, the landscape created by the federal government in Washington, D.C., is best thought of as a(n)

A) derelict landscape.

B) Aegean landscape.

C) symbolic landscape.

D) Socratic landscape.

E) ordinary landscape.

Answer: C
Diff: 2

44) The humanistic approach in geography places this at the center of analysis:

A) community

B) God

C) the State

D) the individual

E) the family

Answer: D
Diff: 2

45) Much of the recent work in cultural geography has stressed that

A) the sum of individual attitudes and views equals the views held by the group that includes those individuals.

B) there is a one–way relationship in which humans act on the environment, but not the reverse.

C) it is important to take an interdisciplinary approach.

D) it is impossible to interpret landscapes as they are all starting to look the same.

E) all of the above

Answer: C
Diff: 2

46) The landscape–as–text concept

    A) holds that some people actively shape the landscape.

    B) was developed by Carl Sauer and Sallie Marston.

    C) is dependent upon geographical publishers.

    D) argues that landscapes can produce meaning, but can't communicate meaning.

    E) requires understanding the grammar of geography -- place identification.

Answer: A
Diff: 2

47) Territoriality

    A) regulates access to people.

    B) regulates access to resources.

    C) regulates social interaction.

    D) provides a focus of group membership and identity.

    E) all of the above

Answer: E
Diff: 2

48) In terms of cognitive images, a street is more likely to be

    A) a district.   B) a path or an edge.

    C) a node beside a landmark.   D) a landmark.

Answer: B
Diff: 2

49) In the process of forming cognitive images, _____ is (are) primarily involved in both perception and cognition.

    A) senses

    B) culture

    C) brain and personality

    D) society and institutions

    E) transformed cognitive image

Answer: C
Diff: 2

50) Place marketing is least likely to target

    A) wealthy tourists.

    B) organizers of business and professional conferences.

    C) top management of large corporations.

    D) the highly skilled and well-educated.

    E) middle-class suburbanites.

Answer: E
Diff: 2

51) Portsmouth, England

    A) is more important now as a naval port than ever before.

    B) is the center of England's lake district and burgeoning water park tourist industry.

    C) has developed a substantial naval heritage industry.

    D) is the major beach destination for the English.

    E) is the the future of site of Europe's second Disneyland.

Answer: C
Diff: 1

52) Portsmouth, England has based its growing tourism industry primarily on

    A) the attractiveness of its beaches.

    B) its reputation as the base of England's gay and lesbian populations.

    C) the attractiveness and historical distinctiveness of nearby cathedrals, castles, and estates.

    D) its association with naval history and warfare.

    E) American tourists.

Answer: D
Diff: 1

53) Which of the following is usually the most important consideration for the heritage industry when it decides how to restore and develop a given landscape?

    A) commercial considerations   B) principles of preservation

    C) historical accuracy   D) UNESCO guidelines

Answer: A
Diff: 2

54) The practice of writing and reading signs is called

    A) esthetics.

    B) semiotics.

    C) image interpretation.

    D) heuristics.

    E) symbology.

Answer: B
Diff: 1

55) This message is consistently sent by malls to all, regardless of gender, age, class, or race:

    A) appreciate architecture   B) consume, consume

    C) observe social standards of behavior   D) buy low, sell high

Answer: B
Diff: 2

56) Brasilia

    A) was established by the Portuguese in the early 1800s.

    B) was intended to transform Brazilian society.

    C) is the world center of coffee culture.

    D) exists primarily in the minds of architects.

Answer: B
Diff: 2

57) Lucio Costa based his design of Brasilia on this symbol:

    A) the cross

    B) the peace sign

    C) the hammer and sickle

    D) the yin–yang circle

    E) the star of David

Answer: A
Diff: 1

58) This _____ architectural style was chosen for Brasilia to help convey what designers and supporters saw for Brazil's future.

    A) classical

    B) neo-classical

    C) authoritarian

    D) utilitarian

    E) Modernist

Answer: E
Diff: 2

59) Many of the sites that are sacred for India's Hindus are located

    A) near rivers.

    B) in the southern part of the country.

    C) on the border with Bangladesh.

    D) near the centers of major cities.

    E) in the highlands of Tibet.

Answer: A
Diff: 2

60) The *hajj* is the once-in-a-lifetime pilgrimage for practitioners of

    A) Hinduism.

    B) Judaism.

    C) Islam.

    D) Jainism.

    E) Buddhism.

Answer: C
Diff: 1

61) Islam requires Muslims to make a once-in- a-lifetime pilgrimage to

    A) Amman, Jordan.

    B) Mecca, Saudi Arabia.

    C) Marakesh, Morocco.

    D) Kuala Lumpur, Malaysia.

    E) Damascus, Syria.

Answer: B
Diff: 1

62) For which of the following groups does the Holy Lands of Palestine/Israel have the most significance?

    A) Hindus

    B) followers of Greek Orthodoxy

    C) Roman Catholics

    D) Christian Zionists

    E) Sufis

Answer: D
Diff: 2

63) Most observers of cultural change think that we now live in the age of

    A) Modernity.

    B) Postmodernity.

    C) classicism.

    D) Avant-Gardism.

    E) Aquarius.

Answer: B
Diff: 1

64) This is NOT a characteristic of Modernism:

    A) roots in the European Renaissance

    B) scientific rationality

    C) progress

    D) conformity

    E) reason

Answer: D
Diff: 2

65) Materialism

    A) is rejected by Modernity and Postmodernity.

    B) is rejected by Postmodernity, but encouraged by Modernity.

    C) is rejected by Modernity, but encouraged by Postmodernity.

    D) is encouraged by Modernity and Postmodernity.

Answer: D
Diff: 2

66) Contemporary culture relies least on this type of consumption:

   A) visual   B) material   C) mystical   D) experiential

   Answer: C
   Diff: 2

67) During the 1970s and 1980s, advertising strategies began shifting towards presenting products as

   A) more efficient.   B) representative of a desirable lifestyle.

   C) economical and practical.   D) newer and better.

   Answer: B
   Diff: 2

68) The majority of Internet communication is conducted in this language:

   A) English   B) Chinese   C) Spanish   D) Japanese   E) French

   Answer: A
   Diff: 1

69) Modernity includes all of the following, except

   A) reason.

   B) abstract design.

   C) scientific rationality.

   D) progress.

   E) creativity.

   Answer: B
   Diff: 2

70) The Internet

   A) has users distributed fairly evenly around the globe.

   B) increases the ability of states to control their citizens.

   C) uses Esperanto as the main language of communication.

   D) is difficult to regulate.

   Answer: D
   Diff: 2

6.3 True or False

1) Promoting place identity is an important way of eliminating conflicts between places and stereotypes of other people.

Answer: FALSE
Diff: 2

2) The meanings that people give to places are based only on our personalities and what we experience through our senses.

Answer: FALSE
Diff: 2

3) The environment in which we are raised influences the cognitive images we have of other places.

Answer: TRUE
Diff: 2

4) Among the great things about cognitive images is that they highlight the complexities and details of real–world environments.

Answer: FALSE
Diff: 3

5) You can have a cognitive image of a place to which you have never been.

Answer: TRUE
Diff: 2

6) Our values and belief systems contribute to our distorted cognitive images.

Answer: TRUE
Diff: 2

7) In one's cognitive image of Paris, the Eiffel Tower can be both a node and a landmark.

Answer: TRUE
Diff: 2

8) Our cognitive images affect our behavior, and influence such things as how much we like a particular place, where we travel, and the foreign policies we encourage.

Answer: TRUE
Diff: 2

9) Topophilia occurs only at the local or neighborhood scale.

Answer: FALSE
Diff: 3

10) Bulidings like the former World Trade Center can simultaneously be part of a landscape of power and a symbolic landscape.

   Answer: TRUE
   Diff: 2

11) The humanistic approach in geography recognizes that people tend to think and act similarly.

   Answer: FALSE
   Diff: 3

12) Just as people read and interpret books differently, they can read and interpret landscapes differently.

   Answer: TRUE
   Diff: 2

13) Semiotics refers to the signs and meanings that are *intentionally* embedded into landscapes.

   Answer: FALSE
   Diff: 3

14) Within one place, different spaces can send different messages to different people.

   Answer: TRUE
   Diff: 2

15) Sacred spaces are not limited to houses of worship.

   Answer: TRUE
   Diff: 2

16) Postmodernity is most evident in the world's core.

   Answer: TRUE
   Diff: 2

17) Slow Cities refer to those underdeveloped cities of the world's periphery.

   Answer: FALSE
   Diff: 2

18) As with material goods, places can be consumed.

   Answer: TRUE
   Diff: 2

19) In general, people's perceptions of the environment capture the actual characteristics of the environment.

Answer: FALSE
Diff: 2

20) Current cultural geography sees the relationship between the environment and humans as interactive.

Answer: TRUE
Diff: 2

21) Distortions in cognitive images can result from both individual biases or incomplete information.

Answer: TRUE
Diff: 2

22) Behavior influences the formation of cognitive images, and cognitive images influence behavior.

Answer: TRUE
Diff: 2

23) People with broader and more expansive images of place are less likely to travel far than those with narrower and more localized images of place.

Answer: FALSE
Diff: 2

24) Due to genetic traits, most people have a similar attitude towards risk taking.

Answer: FALSE
Diff: 1

25) Globalization has increased the importance of place marketing.

Answer: TRUE
Diff: 1

26) Place marketing typically targets blue-collar workers.

Answer: FALSE
Diff: 1

27) The heritage industry is regulated by the United Nations to ensure architectural, historical and geographical accuracy.

Answer: FALSE
Diff: 2

28) Semiotics brings together a sign "reader" and a sign "writer."

Answer: TRUE
Diff: 1

29) Shopping malls are geared to lower–middle–class consumers.

Answer: FALSE
Diff: 2

30) The architectural style of the government buildings in Brasilia was chosen to represent the country's agrarian and pastoral heritage.

Answer: FALSE
Diff: 2

31) With time, development on the outskirts of Brasilia has kept to the vision of the city's original designers.

Answer: FALSE
Diff: 2

32) Sacred spaces require the presence of a human–built temple or shrine.

Answer: FALSE
Diff: 1

33) The Ganges is the most holy of India's rivers.

Answer: TRUE
Diff: 2

34) The most visited Christian sacred site in Europe is Temppeliaukiokirkko –– "the Rock Church" –– in Helsinki, Finland.

Answer: FALSE
Diff: 1

35) Postmodernity focuses on developing the inner–self rather than on consumption and materialism.

Answer: FALSE
Diff: 2

36) Core countries have a disproportionate share of Internet use when compared to countries of the periphery.

Answer: TRUE
Diff: 1

37) A geographer would not typically classify a trailer park as being part of an ordinary landscape.

Answer: FALSE
Diff: 1

38) "Outsiders" and "insiders" will often have a different sense of place for the same place.

Answer: TRUE
Diff: 1

39) Modernity rejects the use of rationality.

Answer: FALSE
Diff: 2

40) Cosmopolitanism stresses the importance of the cultural values of large core cities such as New York and Paris.

Answer: FALSE
Diff: 1

41) Cyberspace is predominantly controlled by people in core countries.

Answer: TRUE
Diff: 1

6.4 Matching

PLACES & SPACES: Match the example to the term it best represents.

1) your annoyance when somebody sits in the seat you have been using all semester, even thought there are no "assigned" seats.
Diff: 2

A) topophilia

B) semiotics

C) ethology

D) proxemics

2) the discomfort you feel when somebody invades your personal space by standing very close to you when speaking
Diff: 3

3) graffiti as a territorial marker and physical expression of one's identity
Diff: 2

4) choosing to dress in a way that tells others that you're a fan of the Detroit Red Wings
Diff: 3

5) the sense of longing or belonging that many people feel about places special to them, such as their home towns
Diff: 2

6) the embedding of symbols in the landscape of southern Louisiana letting visitors know that they have come to "Cajun Country"
Diff: 3

1) D   2) D   3) C   4) B   5) A   6) B

Chapter 6: Interpreting Places and Landscapes

LANDSCAPES: Match the term or phrase to the landscape.

7) the Mall of America
   Diff: 2

8) urban slums
   Diff: 2

9) mainstreet of a small,
   midwestern town
   Diff: 2

10) shrines or memorials left at
    the sites of accidents
    Diff: 2

11) clusters of corporate tower
    blocks
    Diff: 2

A) vernacular landscape

B) landscape of power

C) derelict landscape

D) palace of consumption

E) Symbolic Landscape

7) D   8) C   9) A   10) E   11) B

222

6.5 Map Identification

World Map

1) Which of the following is the closest in distance to the United States?

    A) Indonesia

    B) England

    C) Mali

    D) Venezuela

    E) Cuba

Answer: E
Diff: 2

2) Country #25 is

    A) Sudan.   B) Mali.   C) Angola.   D) Kenya.   E) Ghana.

Answer: B
Diff: 1

3) The country of Venezuela is identified by the number

    A) 27.   B) 30.   C) 54.   D) 58.   E) 64.

Answer: C
Diff: 1

4) Bamako is the capital of

    A) Somalia.

    B) Mali.

    C) Malawi.

    D) Venezuela.

    E) Nigeria.

Answer: B
Diff: 1

5) The capital of country #23 is

    A) Khartoum.

    B) Djakarta.

    C) Caracas.

    D) Bamako.

    E) Bucharest.

Answer: A
Diff: 1

6) Havana is the capital of

    A) 16.   B) 30.   C) 42..   D) 55.   E) 67.

Answer: D
Diff: 1

7) Which of the following is not an island country?

    A) Venezuela

    B) Cuba

    C) England

    D) Indonesia

    E) All of the above are island countries.

Answer: A
Diff: 2

8) Which pair of countries share a continent?

    A) Mali & Sudan

    B) England & Cuba

    C) Romania & Indonesia

    D) Venezuela & England

    E) Cuba & Mali

Answer: A
Diff: 2

9) Which pair of countries do NOT share a continent?

    A) Venezuela & Cuba

    B) England & Romania

    C) Indonesia & Venezuela

    D) Mali & Sudan

    E) Each of the above pairs share the same continent.

Answer: C
Diff: 2

Europe

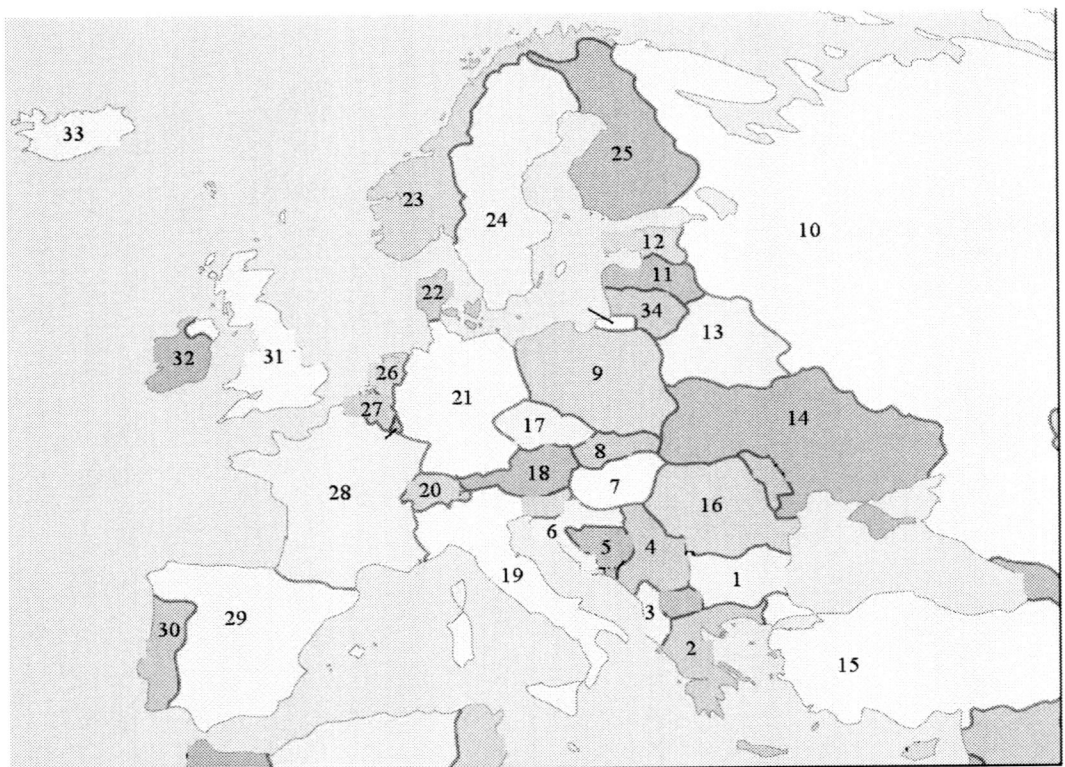

10) Bucharest is the capital of the country labeled with which number?

A) 2   B) 6   C) 13   D) 16   E) 34

Answer: D
Diff: 2

11) The capital of #31 is

A) Berlin.   B) Paris.   C) London.   D) Madrid.   E) Moscow.

Answer: C
Diff: 2

Chapter 7 Geography of Economic Development

7.1 Minimal Choice

1) A country's level of economic development is most commonly measured by

    A) GDP and GNI.   B) HDI and GEI.

    Answer: A
    Diff: 1

2) According the the UNDP's gender empowerment index, the world region with the highest scores is

    A) Scandinavia (the Nordic countries).

    B) Southeast Asia (not including Indonesia).

    Answer: A
    Diff: 1

3) The leading source of energy across Sub–Saharan Africa is

    A) fuelwood.   B) coal.

    Answer: A
    Diff: 1

4) With 15% of the world's population, the world's high income countries use _____ of its commercial energy.

    A) 50%   B) 5%

    Answer: A
    Diff: 1

5) Europeans spend more on ice cream than the world spends on

    A) basic education in the periphery.   B) military expenditures in the core.

    Answer: A
    Diff: 1

6) Countries with economies especially dependent on non–fuel minerals are more generally found in the

    A) periphery.   B) core.

    Answer: A
    Diff: 2

7) The primary sector of the economy includes

    A) mining.   B) manufacturing.

Answer: A
Diff: 1

8) NICs are countries that have moved to the semi-periphery from the

    A) periphery.   B) core.

Answer: A
Diff: 1

9) NICs are known for

    A) manufacturing.   B) mining.

Answer: A
Diff: 1

10) In the world's core, _____ is most important for economic well-being.

    A) knowledge   B) human resources

Answer: A
Diff: 1

11) Quaternary economic activities are most prevalent in the

    A) core.   B) periphery.

Answer: A
Diff: 2

12) The economic integration of the world system is reflected in great growth of global

    A) trade.   B) production.

Answer: A
Diff: 1

13) Those countries like Burkina Faso, Bolivia, Malawi and Samoa that barely contribute to the world economy's flow of imports and exports exhibit a high degree of

    A) autarky.   B) independence.

Answer: A
Diff: 1

14) China makes most of the world's

    A) toys.   B) cars.

Answer: A
Diff: 1

15) Much of China's manufacturing growth is due to

    A) import substitution.   B) initial advantage.

Answer: A
Diff: 2

16) Sharing a pool of labor with special skills and experience is an example of a

    A) localization economy.   B) flexible production system.

Answer: A
Diff: 1

17) Fundamentally, _____ is a strategy for poverty alleviation and sustainable development.

    A) Fair Trade   B) Free Trade

Answer: A
Diff: 3

18) The biggest market for Fair Trade products in the world is

    A) Britain.   B) North America.

Answer: A
Diff: 1

19) The withdrawal of investments from low-yielding activities and regions to other, higher yielding activities and regions is known as

    A) creative destruction.   B) cumulative causation.

Answer: A
Diff: 1

20) Just-in-time production relies upon

    A) vertical integration.   B) export-processing zones.

Answer: A
Diff: 2

21) Typically, traditional international outsourcing in the tertiary sector involves

    A) routine producers.   B) symbolic analysts.

Answer: A
Diff: 2

22) Among the leading exporters of outsourced service activities is

    A) India.   B) the United States.

Answer: A
Diff: 2

23) One measure of the biologically productive area needed to provide the resources and absorb the waste of a region or country is its

    A) ecological footprint.   B) carrying capacity.

Answer: A
Diff: 1

24) As explained by Gunnar Myrdal, the _____ in one region causes backwash effects in another.

    A) process of cumulative causation   B) spiral of deindustrialization

Answer: A
Diff: 1

25) The U.S. Internal Revenue Service estimates that hundreds of billions of dollars in taxes are evaded annually through schemes involving

    A) off–shore financial centers.   B) export processing zones.

Answer: A
Diff: 1

7.2 Multiple Choice

1) The cost advantages that manufacturers get from high–volume production are known as

    A) economies of scale.

    B) economic development.

    C) spatial diffusion.

    D) spatial economies.

    E) agglomeration economies.

Answer: A
Diff: 1

2) Structural adjustment programs as a condition for international loans are intended to make sure that

    A) neediest people are helped first.

    B) agricultural land is redistributed equitably so all may have a chance to earn a living.

    C) loans are repaid through reduced government spending and increased export earnings.

    D) loans are repaid through increased investments in research and development.

    E) all of the above

Answer: C
Diff: 3

3) Basic principals of commercial and industrial location are based on

    A) access to inputs.

    B) proximity to markets.

    C) the availability of labor.

    D) processing costs.

    E) all of the above

Answer: E
Diff: 2

4) Economic development is even over space in

    A) the world system.

    B) core countries.

    C) peripheral countries.

    D) all of the above

    E) none of the above

Answer: E
Diff: 2

5) To most equitably compare the relative levels of economic development of different countries, and to adjust for their different currencies, it is best to use

    A) Gross Domestic Product.

    B) Gross Domestic Product per capita.

    C) Gross National Income per capita.

    D) Purchasing Power Parity.

    E) Any of the above.

Answer: D
Diff: 2

6) The Gross Domestic Product (GDP) of a region or country includes the total value (in a given year) of all but which of the following?

    A) foodstuffs produced in the country

    B) services produced in the country

    C) machinery produced in the country

    D) profits from abroad (overseas)

    E) GDP includes all of the above.

Answer: D
Diff: 2

7) Global justice and equality (between core and periphery countries) is evident when looking at maps of

    A) personal income and GDP/capita.

    B) life expectancy and infant mortality rates.

    C) adult literacy and public expenditures on higher education.

    D) poverty and malnutrition rates.

    E) none of the above

Answer: E
Diff: 2

8) According to calculations made by the United Nations Development Program (UNDP), women around the world

    A) are better off throughout the core than anywhere in peripheral and semi-peripheral countries.

    B) are best off in the United States and Canada.

    C) are best off in Scandinavia.

    D) on the average earn about 90% of what men earn.

    E) both A and B

Answer: C
Diff: 2

9) In the context of economic development, regional inequality across the globe

    A) has declined with increased globalization over the last 25 years.

    B) has increased with increasing globalization over the last 25 years.

    C) has not worsened in countries like the United States and Scandinavia over the last 25 years.

    D) is not evident in peripheral countries.

    E) is not evident in core countries.

Answer: B
Diff: 2

10) A country's ecological footprint is calculated from all but which of the following?

   A) size of the population

   B) the education of the population

   C) the affluence of the population – calculated in terms of how much they consume

   D) the technologies being used – measured in term of the intensity of resource use

   E) all of the above

Answer: B
Diff: 2

11) Economic development that meets the needs and aspirations of the present without compromising the ability of future generations to meet their needs is the classic definition for

   A) carrying capacity.

   B) ecological footprint.

   C) sustainable development.

   D) Reaganomics.

   E) the Human Development Index.

Answer: C
Diff: 1

12) The ability of a country to explore and exploit its resources is based on all but which of the following?

   A) the value of its resources

   B) technological innovations in the country and around the world

   C) the political situation in that country

   D) economic conditions in that country

   E) All of the above factors determine a country's ability to exploit its resources.

Answer: E
Diff: 2

13) Typical of so many countries in the periphery, structural adjustment programs have

    A) turned Jamaica into a leading producer of potatoes and other essential foodstuffs in the Caribbean.

    B) helped Jamaica avoid the same kind of debt problems facing many developing countries.

    C) increased social programs in Jamaica, most notably educational and employment opportunities.

    D) increased Jamaica's dependency on imported food.

    E) introduced dairy farming to Jamaica as an important step in moving beyond neocolonialism.

Answer: D
Diff: 3

14) Jamaica's economy is heavily dependent on mining (bauxite) and tourism. These are

    A) primary sector economic activities.

    B) secondary sector economic activities.

    C) tertiary sector economic activities.

    D) primary and secondary sector economic activities, respectively.

    E) primary and tertiary sector economic activities, respectively.

Answer: E
Diff: 3

15) The largest sector in core economies is the tertiary sector; activities in this sector include

    A) agricultural production built around corn, wheat and beef.

    B) manufacturing industries built around steel, transportation and military equipment.

    C) grocery stores and other retail and wholesale sales, legal services & entertainment.

    D) all of the above

    E) both A and B

Answer: C
Diff: 3

16) Which of the following would one expect to find in a peripheral country with a large primary sector?

    A) coffee and cocoa been trees

    B) coffee roasting and chocolate making factories

    C) coffee shops, espresso bars and chocolate specialty stores

    D) research and development on how to make imitation coffee and chocolate flavors

    E) all of the above

Answer: A
Diff: 3

17) With the exception of some oil–rich economies, countries with large primary sectors of the economy have GDPs/capita _____ countries with large tertiary sectors.

    A) higher than

    B) lower than

    C) quite similar to

    D) sometimes higher/sometimes lower – cannot generalize

Answer: B
Diff: 3

18) In the world system, highest levels of per capita GDP are found in economies where the tertiary and quaternary sectors dominate the workforce – these economies are known as

    A) industrial.

    B) nonindustrial.

    C) postindustrial.

    D) sustainable.

    E) newly industrialized.

Answer: C
Diff: 2

19) In the world's major core economies, the production and distribution of _____ has become the most important contributor to gross domestic product.

    A) manufactured goods

    B) knowledge

    C) energy

    D) food

    E) computers

Answer: B
Diff: 2

20) Asia's "Four Tigers" are best characterized as

    A) NICs.

    B) core countries.

    C) peripheral countries.

    D) LDCs.

    E) MVPs.

Answer: A
Diff: 2

21) NICs & Tigers are best exemplified by

    A) Bolivia, Burkina Faso, Ghana, Malawi, Samoa and Tanzania.

    B) Slovakia, Romania, Bulgaria, Latvia, Ukraine and Yugoslavia.

    C) Canada, Finland, Russia, South Africa, Australia and New Zealand.

    D) China, Brazil, South Korea, Mexico, Taiwan, India and Argentina.

    E) Amsterdam, New York, Tokyo, London, Moscow and Beijing.

Answer: D
Diff: 3

22) International trade in the world system is built around the world's major trading blocs, including all but

    A) Western Europe and its former colonies.

    B) North America and its Latin American trading partners.

    C) the countries of the former Soviet Union.

    D) Japan, East Asian NICs and Tigers.

    E) All of the above are the basis of international trade in the world system.

Answer: A
Diff: 3

23) The world system's autarkic countries include

    A) Bolivia, Burkina Faso, Ghana, Malawi, Samoa and Tanzania.

    B) Slovakia, Romania, Bulgaria, Latvia, Slovenia and Yugoslavia.

    C) Canada, Finland, Russia, South Africa, Australia and New Zealand.

    D) China, Brazil, South Korea, Mexico, Taiwan, India and Argentina.

    E) Amsterdam, New York, Tokyo, London, Moscow and Beijing.

Answer: A
Diff: 3

24) Countries that do not contribute significantly to the world economy in terms of imports and exports

    A) have a high degree of autarky.

    B) are Third World countries.

    C) are countries of the world's South.

    D) are peripheral countries.

    E) exercise hegemony.

Answer: A
Diff: 1

25) The World Trade Organization has its origins in (the)

    A) GATT.   B) IMF.   C) UN.   D) UNDP.   E) NATO.

Answer: A
Diff: 3

26) "Dependency" for peripheral countries means that they are dependent on core countries for all of the following except

    A) demand.

    B) labor.

    C) investment.

    D) technology.

    E) imports.

Answer: B
Diff: 3

27) The peripheral country dilemma of having constantly to borrow in order to fund economic development is known as the

    A) debt service.

    B) debt trap.

    C) death trap.

    D) dependency cycle.

    E) cycle of debt.

Answer: B
Diff: 1

28) The debt crisis refers to

A) the high debt service many peripheral countries must pay on international loans.

B) the increasing debt service that banks are unable to collect from students and credit card holders.

C) the loans that entrepreneurs in core countries are unable to get from investment banks.

D) the difficulty core countries have in balancing their budgets.

E) the increasing number of bankruptcies occurring in core countries.

Answer: A
Diff: 2

29) W. W. Rostow's model of economic development encourages the perception that every country is striving for and moving toward

A) high mass consumption.

B) post–industrialism.

C) socialism.

D) economic self–sufficiency.

E) democracy.

Answer: A
Diff: 2

30) According to Andre Gunder Frank's "dependency theory" the development and prosperity of the world's core was based on the _____ of the periphery.

A) development

B) underdevelopment

C) backwardness

D) traditionalism

E) economic prosperity

Answer: B
Diff: 2

31) The cost savings and/or advantages that individual firms get when they are located in the same area as other firms of the same industry is known as a(n) _____ economy.

   A) remittance

   B) external

   C) ancillary

   D) localization

   E) deindustrialization

   Answer: D
   Diff: 1

32) Schools, roads, railroads, hospitals, retail outlets, recreational and cultural opportunities, social services and the entire framework of support services and amenities in a city or region is known as its

   A) infrastructure.

   B) initial advantage.

   C) spread effects.

   D) ancillary activities.

   E) ecological footprint.

   Answer: A
   Diff: 2

33) The process of cumulative causation in an area drains all but _____ from surrounding areas?

   A) entrepreneurial talent   B) labor

   C) investment capital   D) infrastructure

   Answer: D
   Diff: 3

34) The spiral of economic growth and advantage that emerges as external economies, agglomeration and localization economies develop in a place is called

   A) cumulative causation.

   B) creative destruction.

   C) neo–Fordism.

   D) flexible production.

   E) Reaganomics.

   Answer: A
   Diff: 1

35) According to Nobel prize-winning economist Gunnar Myrdal, cumulative causation and the spiral of local economic growth in one area tends to cause negative impacts in others called

A) backwash effects.

B) agglomeration diseconomies.

C) deindustrialization.

D) spread effects.

E) external economies.

Answer: A
Diff: 1

36) Backwash effects in a region include all but which of the following

A) out-migration of labor and talent.

B) a shrinking tax base.

C) increase in forward and backward linkages.

D) outflows of investment capital.

Answer: C
Diff: 2

37) The spiral of cumulative causation in peripheral regions and countries is assisted by

A) import substitution in the core.

B) backwash effects from the core.

C) spread effects from the core.

D) agglomeration diseconomies in the core.

E) both C and D

Answer: E
Diff: 2

38) The spiral of cumulative causation in core regions and countries is assisted by

A) import substitution in the periphery.

B) backwash effects in the periphery.

C) spread effects from the periphery.

D) agglomeration diseconomies in the periphery.

E) both C and D

Answer: B
Diff: 2

39) Growing sugar beets for sugar, as an alternative to importing sugar made from sugar cane, is an example of

A) import substitution.

B) a quaternary sector activity.

C) flexible production.

D) vertical disintegration.

E) deindustrialization.

Answer: A
Diff: 3

40) Import substitution is an important strategy for economic growth because

A) domestic (local) production is supported.

B) all imports are able to compete on a level playing field.

C) consumers pay less for imported goods.

D) import processing zones function as engines of economic development.

E) all of the above

Answer: A
Diff: 3

41) Creative destruction refers to the

A) withdrawal of investment from low profit areas and activities for reinvestment in high profit ones.

B) conversion and remodeling of old, decaying buildings into modern art facilities.

C) artistically destroying and knocking down old buildings and areas for new development.

D) removal of materials from old facilities for use in new construction, to maintain links between old and new.

E) none of the above

Answer: A
Diff: 1

42) Creative destruction refers to the withdrawal of _____ from declining areas and activities for use in new areas and activities.

    A) capital

    B) building materials

    C) culture

    D) political ideas

    E) all of the above

Answer: A
Diff: 2

43) In the context of creative destruction in the U.S., investment removed from _____ provided the capital and locational flexibility for investment in peripheral countries.

    A) the Sunbelt

    B) the Manufacturing Belt

    C) *maquiladoras*

    D) export–processing zones

    E) all of the above

Answer: B
Diff: 3

44) Core–periphery patterns are modified by

    A) deindustrialization.

    B) creative destruction.

    C) government intervention.

    D) all of the above

    E) both A and B

Answer: D
Diff: 2

45) Governments establish propulsive industries to promote

    A) regional economic development.

    B) economic growth in existing manufacturing centers.

    C) primary sector growth.

    D) local health, education and welfare.

Answer: A
Diff: 2

46) Of the following, which are generally considered "propulsive industries"?

    A) department and grocery stores

    B) local mom and pop businesses

    C) shipbuilding and automobile manufacturing plants

    D) community libraries and hospitals

    E) all of the above

Answer: C
Diff: 2

47) Places of economic activity organized around one or more high-growth industries are known as

    A) growth poles.

    B) north poles.

    C) economic poles.

    D) industrial poles.

    E) government poles.

Answer: A
Diff: 1

48) Growth poles emerge

    A) as government policies to encourage cumulative causation.

    B) through the forces of supply and demand.

    C) based on comparative advantage.

    D) based on the international division of labor.

    E) as a consequence of core-periphery relations.

Answer: A
Diff: 2

49) Transnational companies are those that are involved in

    A) international trade.

    B) production in multiple countries.

    C) manufacturing in multiple countries.

    D) foreign sales and marketing in numerous countries.

    E) all of the above

Answer: E
Diff: 1

50) Advantages to manufacturers of the global assembly line include all of the following *except*

    A) economies of scale with standardized global products.

    B) comparative advantages.

    C) multiple sources of supply.

    D) access to global markets.

    E) All of the above are advantages to manufacturers.

Answer: E
Diff: 2

51) The global assembly line refers to consumer goods that are made

    A) with raw materials, components, labor, and manufacture from around the world.

    B) in one country and designed to be marketed and sold around the world.

    C) with capital invested by people, businesses and banks from around the world.

    D) with the goal of employing as many people in the periphery as possible.

    E) in factories that are sited on both sides of an international border.

Answer: A
Diff: 1

52) According to your text, the _____ industry is one of the most globalized of all manufacturing industries.

    A) clothing

    B) chocolate

    C) small appliances

    D) computer

    E) ship–building

Answer: A
Diff: 1

53) Manufacturing based on assembly line techniques and high wages, and reliant upon mass consumption, is known as

    A) Fordism.

    B) Toyotaism.

    C) Reaganomics.

    D) Chryslerism.

    E) just–in–time manufacturing.

Answer: A
Diff: 1

54) Flexible production, distribution and marketing systems are specifically associated with

    A) Fordism.

    B) Neo-Fordism.

    C) Reaganomics.

    D) *maquiladoras.*

    E) the trickle-down theory.

Answer: B
Diff: 1

55) One of the huge benefits of just-in-time production is that the need for _____ is eliminated.

    A) large inventories

    B) labor

    C) advertising

    D) working overtime

    E) understanding cultural differences

Answer: A
Diff: 2

56) Just-in-time production relies upon all of the following *except*

    A) dependency.

    B) vertical integration.

    C) computer-aided manufacturing.

    D) computer-based information systems.

    E) strategic alliances.

Answer: A
Diff: 2

57) *Maquiladoras* (manufacturing firms that import components for assembly and re-export) are found

    A) in Mexico, clustered near the U.S. border.

    B) in Canada, clustered in and around Quebec.

    C) throughout Spanish-speaking communities of North America.

    D) throughout the world's periphery.

    E) in the Philippines, in export-processing zones.

Answer: A
Diff: 1

58) _____ have contributed to deindustrialization in the Manufacturing Belt and its corrosion into the Rust Belt.

    A) *Maquiladoras* in Mexico

    B) Export processing zones (EPZs) in labor–cheap parts of the world

    C) New and high–tech industries in the Sunbelt

    D) Pressures within Midwestern industries to reduce labor costs

    E) all of the above

Answer: E
Diff: 3

59) The vast majority of workers in *maquiladoras* and Export Processing Zones are

    A) children.

    B) women.

    C) men.

    D) the elderly.

    E) people of African descent.

Answer: B
Diff: 1

60) Countries establish Export Processing Zones (EPZs) to attract

    A) export–oriented industries.

    B) propulsive industries.

    C) foreign aid.

    D) secret, tax–sheltered monies.

    E) *maquiladoras.*

Answer: A
Diff: 2

61) Offshore financial centers are designed to attract

    A) export–oriented industries.

    B) propulsive industries.

    C) foreign aid.

    D) secret, tax–sheltered monies.

    E) *maquiladoras.*

Answer: D
Diff: 1

62) The world's largest non–agricultural employer is (are)

   A) tourism.

   B) General Motors.

   C) export processing zones.

   D) *maquiladoras.*

   E) the global office.

Answer: A
Diff: 1

63) The region of South China emerged as China's core manufacturing region due to all of the following *except*

   A) its harbors and ports.

   B) the established trade and manufacturing networks of Macau and Hong Kong.

   C) capital investment from Hong Kong, Taiwan and the Chinese Diaspora.

   D) its rich energy and natural resources base.

   E) all of the above.

Answer: D
Diff: 2

64) Most foreign investment in China comes from

   A) East Asia.

   B) Europe.

   C) North America.

   D) the Middle East.

   E) South America.

Answer: A
Diff: 1

65) The most certified Fair Trade product in the United States is

   A) coffee.

   B) bananas.

   C) tea.

   D) chocolate.

   E) chicken.

Answer: A
Diff: 1

66) In 2003, which of the following was biggest?

    A) Wal-Mart's annual sales.

    B) Chili John's Cafe (in Beaver Dam, Wisconsin) annual sales.

    C) Portugal's total GDP.

    D) Ireland's total GDP.

    E) Turkey's total GDP.

Answer: A
Diff: 1

67) The term "Third World"

    A) has been in use since the Age of Exploration.

    B) is a Cold War term referring to the periphery.

    C) is used for countries that practice neither capitalism or socialism.

    D) refers to the world's politically neutral countries.

    E) refers to those countries that are neither in the North nor the South.

Answer: B
Diff: 2

68) Tariffs

    A) refer to trade quotas.

    B) are specifically designed to increase the price of exported goods.

    C) are taxes on imported goods.

    D) require a highly developed transportation and communications infrastructure to be effective.

    E) none of above

Answer: C
Diff: 1

69) Which of the following gives the most accurate measure of relative economic prosperity?

    A) purchasing power parity   B) GDP per capita

    C) GNP per capita   D) national income

Answer: A
Diff: 2

70) In which country are women better off than men according to the United Nations Development Programme's gender empowerment index?

A) United States

B) Canada

C) Sweden

D) Netherlands

E) In no country are women better off.

Answer: E
Diff: 1

71) Which of the following countries has the smallest amount of raw materials and sources of energy?

A) United States

B) Canada

C) Russia

D) Japan

E) Australia

Answer: D
Diff: 1

72) Technology systems

A) contain interrelated transportation, production, and energy technologies.

B) tend to last for several decades.

C) are eventually replaced by more sophisticated systems.

D) all of these

Answer: D
Diff: 1

73) In which time period was the technological system characterized by extensive use of radio and telecommunications?

A) 1790–1840   B) 1840–1890   C) 1890–1950   D) 1950–present

Answer: C
Diff: 1

74) Which of the following is NOT considered an integral part of the current technology system?

    A) nuclear power

    B) biotechnology

    C) robotics

    D) microelectronics

    E) digital telecommunications

Answer: A
Diff: 3

75) Countries with the lowest GDP per capita have work forces engaged for the most part in

    A) primary activities.   B) secondary activities.

    C) tertiary activities.   D) quaternary activities.

Answer: A
Diff: 2

76) In which of the following regions is the smallest percentage of the work force engaged in primary activities?

    A) South America

    B) North America

    C) Africa

    D) Asia

    E) Caribbean

Answer: B
Diff: 2

77) In the United States, the smallest percentage of the labor force is engaged in

    A) primary activities.   B) secondary activities.

    C) tertiary activities.   D) quaternary activities.

Answer: A
Diff: 2

78) During the first half of the Industrial Revolution, geopolitics was dominated by

    A) the United States.

    B) Germany.

    C) France.

    D) Britain.

    E) the Netherlands.

Answer: D
Diff: 2

79) According to W. W. Rostow's model of economic development, in order for a country to be ready for "take-off" it must have

    A) an investment in manufacturing equal or greater than 10 percent of national income.

    B) a physical infrastructure and a social/political elite.

    C) comparative advantages in international trade, which it exploits.

    D) a majority of the population engaged in tertiary activities.

    E) a democratic form of government.

Answer: B
Diff: 3

80) Rostow's model of economic development

    A) is equally applicable to the countries of today as it was to Western countries in the nineteenth century.

    B) holds that all countries can reach high GDP per capita if they follow the right path.

    C) is accepted as valid by most geographers.

    D) takes into account the interdependence of countries.

    E) All of the above are true.

Answer: B
Diff: 2

81) Overall, the most important cultural and institutional factor affecting location decisions for businesses is

    A) the dominant religion.

    B) proximity to necessary material resources.

    C) government policies that affect business.

    D) the availability of skilled labor.

Answer: C
Diff: 2

82) Agglomeration effects

    A) have limited the growth of the computer industry in Silicon Valley.

    B) typically slow down regional economic development.

    C) are one type of external economy.

    D) occur when businesses are located near each other, but are not interdependent with each other.

    E) Both A and B.

Answer: C
Diff: 2

83) External economies can be derived through

    A) economies of scale.

    B) sharing of information between firms in the same industry.

    C) the use of infrastructure in the form of fixed social capital.

    D) External economies can be derived through all of the above.

Answer: D
Diff: 1

84) Economic development is affected significantly by

    A) location.

    B) new technologies.

    C) timing.

    D) all of the above

    E) none of the above

Answer: D
Diff: 1

85) New companies arriving in a region to supply a growing industry with supplies, components, services, and facilities are in the process of

    A) forming forward linkages.

    B) forming backward linkages.

    C) creating ancillary industries.

    D) deindustrialization.

    E) reindustrialization.

Answer: B
Diff: 2

86) The process of cumulative causation

A) was developed by W.W. Rostow.

B) leads to growth in regions affected by the backwash effect.

C) involves a buildup of economic activity based on external economies and localization economies.

D) critiques the core–periphery concept as meaningless in today's economically interdependent world.

Answer: C
Diff: 2

87) The process of regional economic growth through cumulative causation leads to

A) an expansion of taxes the regional government can collect.

B) a drop in the amount of skilled labor in the region.

C) corresponding rapid growth in distant areas with economic difficulties.

D) the increased formation of forward linkages and the eventual ending of backward linkages.

Answer: A
Diff: 3

88) Periphery regions can experience spread effects from core regions when local entrepreneurs in the periphery regions take advantage of

A) local cheap land and labor.

B) the inefficient government bureaucracy of the periphery regions.

C) grants from the United States government.

D) just–in–time production.

E) exploitation of the natural resource base.

Answer: A
Diff: 2

89) Which of the following is NOT an agglomeration diseconomy?

A) higher prices for labor

B) higher prices for land

C) expansion of the tax base

D) the cost of providing city planning and transit systems

E) increased unit costs for disposing of wastes

Answer: C
Diff: 3

90) _____ saw the largest percentage decrease in manufacturing employment from 1960 to 1990.

    A) France

    B) Britain

    C) Germany

    D) Finland

    E) Switzerland

Answer: B
Diff: 2

91) Which of the following is a way that governments can promote economic growth in a region?

    A) invest in infrastructure

    B) provide tax breaks that reduce the cost of labor

    C) provide subsidies for private investment

    D) All of the above can be used to promote regional economic growth.

    E) None of the above, they just create backwash effects.

Answer: D
Diff: 2

92) Growth poles

    A) work best with propulsive industries.

    B) work best without governmental intervention.

    C) seek to thwart the process of cumulative causation.

    D) did not work for the French biotechnology industry.

Answer: A
Diff: 2

93) The World Bank estimates that in 2004 about _____ % of the world labor force was isolated from the global economy.

    A) less than 1

    B) less than 10

    C) around 30

    D) 45

    E) over 50

Answer: B
Diff: 2

94) Transnational corporations

    A) were initially based in Japan and South Korea.

    B) first appeared in the middle of the twentieth century.

    C) are by definition not conglomerate corporations.

    D) have declined in number over the last three decades.

    E) none of these

Answer: E
Diff: 2

95) The growth in the number and scale of transnational corporations

    A) peaked in the 1970s.

    B) has increased over the last three decades.

    C) has retarded the globalization of the economy.

    D) has been independent of changes in the international economy.

    E) all of these

Answer: B
Diff: 2

96) Much of the clothing industry

    A) is concentrated in core cities in Europe.

    B) was concentrated in European colonies in the nineteenth century.

    C) uses cheap labor labor of the periphery.

    D) has not yet been taken over by transnational corporations.

    E) All of above are true about the clothing industry.

Answer: C
Diff: 1

97) High–end apparel (women's fashion, men's suits) is typically manufactured in

    A) semiperipheral countries.

    B) periphery countries with the lowest wages.

    C) a few core countries.

    D) Spain and Canada.

Answer: C
Diff: 1

98) Which of the following is an advantage to a manufacturers operating transnational commodity chains?

    A) economies of scale

    B) able to use world's cheapest labor costs

    C) lack of dependence upon a single supplier

    D) all of these

Answer: D
Diff: 2

99) The increased importance of international banking, finance, and business services was helped by

    A) an increase in the volume of world trade.

    B) the growth in number and scope of transnational corporations.

    C) the globalization of manufacturing.

    D) all of the above

    E) none of the above

Answer: D
Diff: 2

100) Most of the daily international flow of money is due to

    A) trade in goods.

    B) trade in services.

    C) the buying and selling of bonds, securities, currencies, and other financial instruments.

    D) tourism.

Answer: C
Diff: 2

101) Off-shore financial centers

    A) are usually located on the European continent.

    B) often charge taxes on the interest the deposits earn.

    C) have developed a set of international regulations that have prevented most money laundering.

    D) all of these

Answer: B
Diff: 1

102) Overall, _____ has the largest share of the world's carbon based non-renewable energy reserves (coal, natural gas, and crude petroleum, combined).

    A) Saudi Arabia

    B) Russia

    C) the United States

    D) China

    E) Canada

Answer: B
Diff: 2

103) This country has the greatest amount of crude oil reserves:

    A) the United States

    B) Iran

    C) Russia

    D) Iraq

    E) Saudi Arabia

Answer: E
Diff: 2

104) Logging is a _____ sector activity.

    A) primary   B) secondary   C) tertiary   D) quaternary

Answer: A
Diff: 1

105) In 1950, _____ was the world's hegemon.

    A) Soviet Union   B) the United States

    C) China   D) Britain

Answer: B
Diff: 1

7.3 True or False

1) Complementarity and transferability are needed for interdependence between places.

Answer: TRUE
Diff: 1

2) EPZ, GDP, GNP, OPEC and MVA are all measures of economic development.

Answer: FALSE
Diff: 1

3) The beneficial feature of economic development is that it is even across space.

Answer: FALSE
Diff: 1

4) Regional inequalities in economic development occur not only in peripheral and semi–peripheral countries, but in core countries as well.

Answer: TRUE
Diff: 1

5) As the demonstrated by Japan, the resource base of a country determines how well it can do in the world economy.

Answer: FALSE
Diff: 1

6) A country's ecological footprint refers to the types of shoes it wears – a symbolic reference to how it balances environmental concerns with economic development.

Answer: FALSE
Diff: 1

7) The stated goal of the World Trade Organization is to draw semi–peripheral and peripheral countries into the core

Answer: FALSE
Diff: 2

8) Innovations and new technology systems create new opportunities for initial advantage and cumulative causation in peripheral regions.

Answer: TRUE
Diff: 2

9) Once old core regions deindustrialize and suffer the effects of creative destruction, they move to the periphery.

Answer: FALSE
Diff: 3

10) Currently, almost all foreign direct investment goes to the world's core countries.

Answer: FALSE
Diff: 2

11) From high fashion designer wear to clothing sold in large–volume discount stores, the commodity chains for all clothing sold in the United States are nearly identical.

Answer: FALSE
Diff: 2

12) Like Fordism, neo-Fordism relies on mass production and consumption.

Answer: TRUE
Diff: 2

13) In the global office, ancillary services such as banking and customer services are no longer locally oriented but have been decentralized.

Answer: TRUE
Diff: 2

14) In contrast to economies built around natural resources, those based on tourism are not vulnerable to economic or political uncertainties.

Answer: FALSE
Diff: 2

15) Generally, countries with the highest GNIs per capita have the highest HDI scores.

Answer: TRUE
Diff: 3

16) According to the UNDP's gender empowerment index, in no country in the world are women better off than men.

Answer: TRUE
Diff: 1

17) According to the UNDP's gender empowerment index, high GNIs are a prerequisite for empowering women.

Answer: FALSE
Diff: 3

18) Core–periphery inequalities are commonly found *within* core countries.

Answer: TRUE
Diff: 2

19) The debt crisis caught many countries in the debt trap.

Answer: TRUE
Diff: 2

20) International aid is good for jump starting economic development and redressing core–periphery inequities.

Answer: FALSE
Diff: 3

21) From a geographic perspective, economic development is uneven.

Answer: TRUE
Diff: 1

22) The economic gap between rich and poor countries has narrowed over the last two decades.

Answer: FALSE
Diff: 1

23) Changes in technology can change the economic geography of a region.

Answer: TRUE
Diff: 2

24) In peripheral countries, a greater percentage of the labor force is engaged in primary and secondary activities than in tertiary and quaternary activities.

Answer: TRUE
Diff: 1

25) Postindustrial societies have the majority of their work force engaged in tertiary and quaternary activities.

Answer: TRUE
Diff: 2

26) Localization economies occur when many firms in one industry are located in the same area.

Answer: TRUE
Diff: 2

27) External economies are typically found in rural areas.

Answer: FALSE
Diff: 2

28) During the formation of a regional economic core, ancillary industries must be in place before forward linkages are created.

Answer: FALSE
Diff: 3

29) Creative destruction can lead to deindustrialization.

Answer: TRUE
Diff: 2

30) Conglomerate corporations focus on providing one service or product to every potential market in the world.

Answer: FALSE
Diff: 1

31) By 1995 nearly 90 percent of transnational corporations were based in North America.

Answer: FALSE
Diff: 2

32) Greatly increased transnational corporate activity over the last two decades is the primary reason for the globalization of the world economy.

Answer: TRUE
Diff: 3

33) Commodity chains link raw materials and natural resources to finished products.

Answer: TRUE
Diff: 3

34) Banks in OPEC countries are prohibited by the OPEC charter from loaning money to peripheral countries.

Answer: FALSE
Diff: 2

35) The most important banking, finance, and business services are concentrated in a few geographic areas; they are not spread uniformly across core countries.

Answer: TRUE
Diff: 1

36) Off–shore financial centers are strictly regulated by international agencies.

Answer: FALSE
Diff: 1

37) China's Guangdong province hit a prolonged economic slump in the latter part of the 1990s.

Answer: FALSE
Diff: 1

38) In general, the countries with the highest scores on the index of human development are core countries.

Answer: TRUE
Diff: 1

39) A cabinet maker is primarily involved in tertiary activities.

Answer: FALSE
Diff: 2

40) Creative destruction is motivated by a desire for higher profits.

Answer: TRUE
Diff: 2

41) Over the last several decades, foreign direct investment has slowly declined.

Answer: FALSE
Diff: 1

42) Over time, level of knowledge & information have become an important factor in determining level of economic development.

Answer: TRUE
Diff: 1

43) Level of education and availability of educational opportunities have a strong impact on a country's ability to have a strong economy.

Answer: TRUE
Diff: 2

7.4 Matching

CORE-PERIPHERY: Match the description with one or the other group of countries.

1) Developed Regions
   Diff: 2

2) high GDP per capita
   Diff: 2

3) Third World
   Diff: 2

4) large primary sector of
   economy
   Diff: 3

5) high debt service relative to
   GDP
   Diff: 3

6) economically diversified
   Diff: 3

7) high mass consumption
   Diff: 2

8) post-industrial economies
   Diff: 2

9) autarkic regions
   Diff: 3

10) in the "debt trap"
    Diff: 2

11) Establish Export Processing
    Zones (EPZs)
    Diff: 3

12) LDCs
    Diff: 3

A) Core countries

B) Peripheral countries

13) GNP/capita < $5000
   Diff: 3

14) wood for fuel
   Diff: 2

15) smallest share of world MVA
   Diff: 3

16) single resource economies
   Diff: 2

17) small percent of labor force in
   primary sector
   Diff: 2

1) A	2) A	3) B	4) B	5) B	6) A
7) A	8) A	9) B	10) B	11) B	12) B
13) B	14) B	15) B	16) B	17) A	

REGIONAL DEVELOPMENT: Say that a new manufacturing firm moves to town. In the context of regional economic development, match the appropriate term to the set of features/activities/businesses.

18) existing infrastructures, labor
   markets and consumer
   markets
   Diff: 2

19) businesses that emerge to
   serve the new firm (e.g.,
   security, cleaning, financial,
   waste services)
   Diff: 2

20) businesses that buy and use
   products generated by the
   new firm
   Diff: 2

21) businesses that supply the
   new firm with inputs such as
   components, raw materials,
   specialized services
   Diff: 2

A) ancillary industries

B) forward linkages

C) external economies

D) backward linkages

18) C   19) A   20) B   21) D

ACTIVITY & SECTOR: Match the economic activity to its economic sector

22) Tourism in Jamaica
    Diff: 3

23) Dairy farming in the United
    States
    Diff: 3

24) Copper mining in Zambia
    Diff: 3

25) Clothing manufacture in
    Thailand
    Diff: 3

26) Banking in Switzerland
    Diff: 3

27) Pharmaceutical research and
    development in New Jersey
    Diff: 3

28) Coffee growing in Guatemala
    Diff: 3

29) Oil drilling and pumping in
    Indonesia
    Diff: 3

30) Automobile manufacture in
    Germany
    Diff: 3

31) Wal-mart retail store in
    Arkansas
    Diff: 3

A) Secondary sector

B) Quarternary sector

C) Tertiary sector

D) primary sector

E) Primary sector

22) C   23) E   24) E   25) A   26) C   27) B
28) E   29) D   30) A   31) C

7.5 Map Identification

World Map

1) Norway shares a border with which of the following countries?

   A) Romania   B) Finland   C) France   D) Portugal   E) Latvia

   Answer: B
   Diff: 2

2) Which of the following is an island country?

   A) Angola

   B) Cambodia

   C) Norway

   D) Taiwan

   E) Yemen

   Answer: D
   Diff: 2

3) The country of Cambodia is identified by the number

   A) 2.   B) 4.   C) 6.   D) 8.   E) 10.

   Answer: B
   Diff: 1

4) Windhoek is the capital of

    A) Yemen.

    B) Namibia.

    C) Taiwan.

    D) Angola.

    E) Australia.

Answer: B
Diff: 1

5) The capital of country #21 is

    A) Luanda.

    B) Addis Ababa.

    C) Kampala.

    D) Sana.

    E) Taipei.

Answer: A
Diff: 1

6) Sana is the capital of

    A) 5.   B) 14.   C) 21.   D) 46.   E) 55.

Answer: B
Diff: 1

7) The countries of which two capitals share a border?

    A) Helsinki & Oslo

    B) Luanda & Winhoek

    C) Taipei & Sana

    D) Phnom Penh & Taipei

    E) Oslo & Luanda

Answer: A
Diff: 2

8) Which of the following is the capital of #4?

    A) Phnom Penh

    B) Addis Ababa

    C) Port–au–Prince

    D) Ulan Bator

    E) Buenos Aires

Answer: A
Diff: 1

9) Which pair of countries share a continent?

    A) Yemen & Cambodia

    B) Finland & Namibia

    C) Norway & Angola

    D) Taiwan & Namibia

    E) Cambodia & Norway

Answer: A
Diff: 2

10) Which pair of countries does NOT share a continent?

    A) Finland & Norway

    B) Angola & Namibia

    C) Cambodia & Taiwan

    D) Yemen & Angola

    E) Each of the above pairs share the same continent.

Answer: D
Diff: 2

Europe

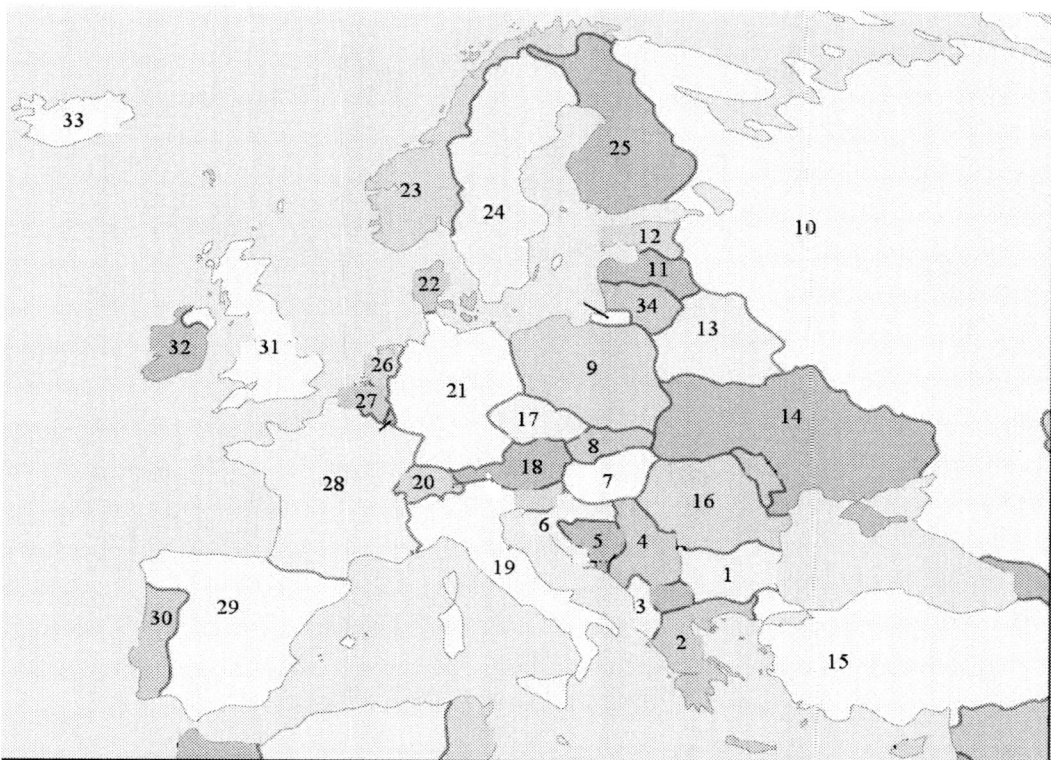

11) Oslo is the capital of the country labeled with which number?

    A) 22   B) 23   C) 24   D) 25   E) 26

Answer: B
Diff: 1

12) Finland is labeled with number

    A) 2.   B) 5.   C) 11.   D) 22.   E) 25.

Answer: E
Diff: 1

13) The capital of Finland is

    A) Moscow.

    B) Copenhagen.

    C) Helsinki.

    D) Bucharest.

    E) Budapest.

Answer: C
Diff: 1

7.6 Chapter 7 Questions with images

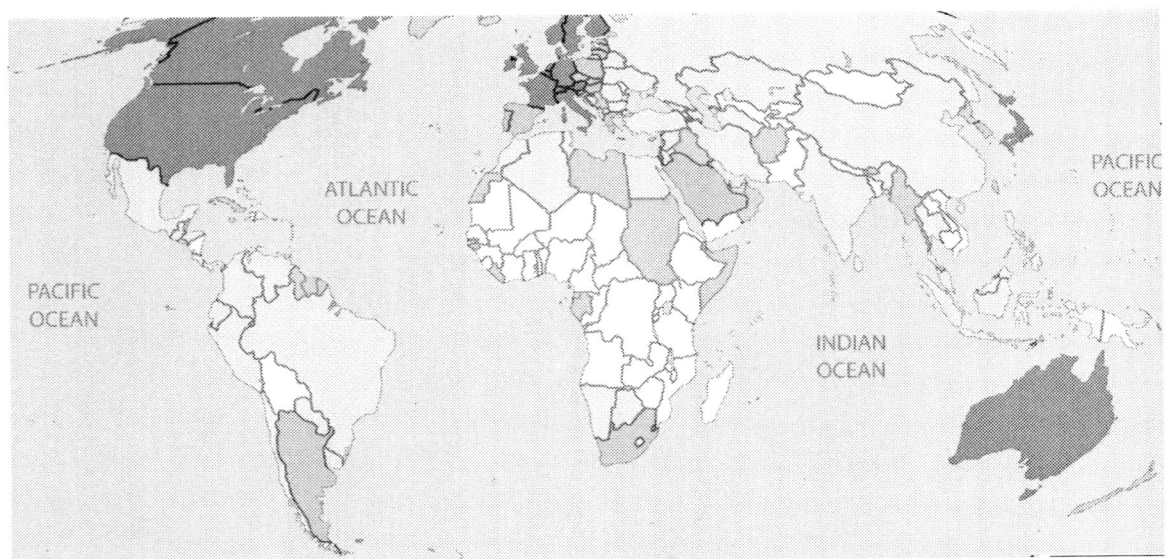

1) The above map of _____ exemplifies the core–periphery nature of today's world system.

    A) gross national income per capita

    B) gross domestic product

    C) total national debt

    D) agricultural cover

    E) percent of workforce in the primary sector

Answer: A
Diff: 3

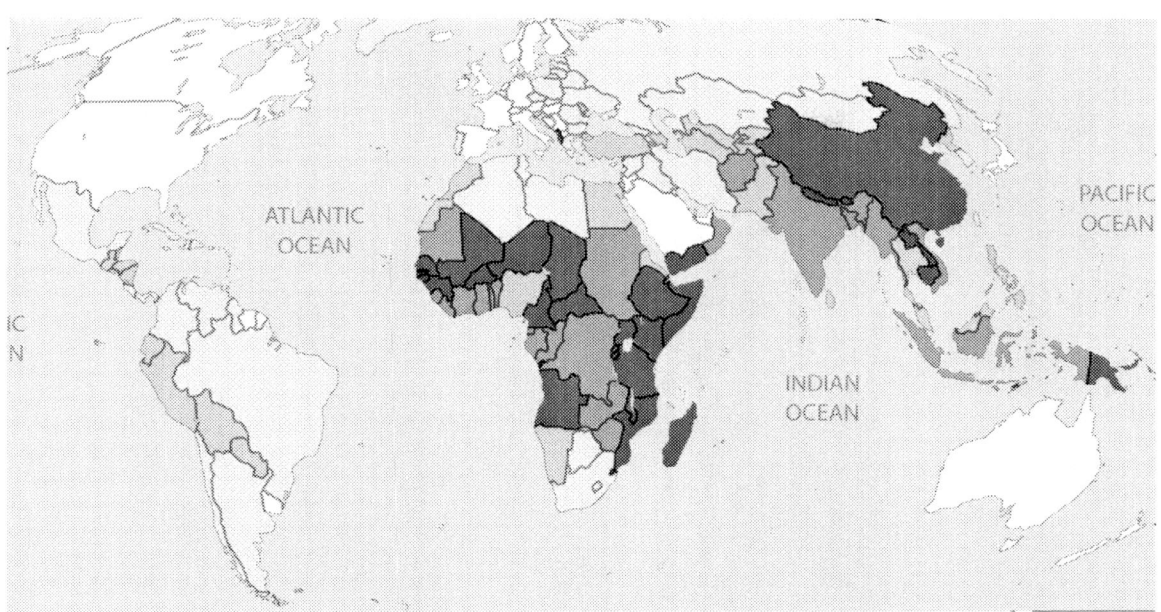

2) The dark shadings in the above map show the distribution of _____ across the world.

    A) primary economic activities

    B) secondary economic activities

    C) tertiary economic activities

    D) localization economies

    E) backwash effects

Answer: A
Diff: 3

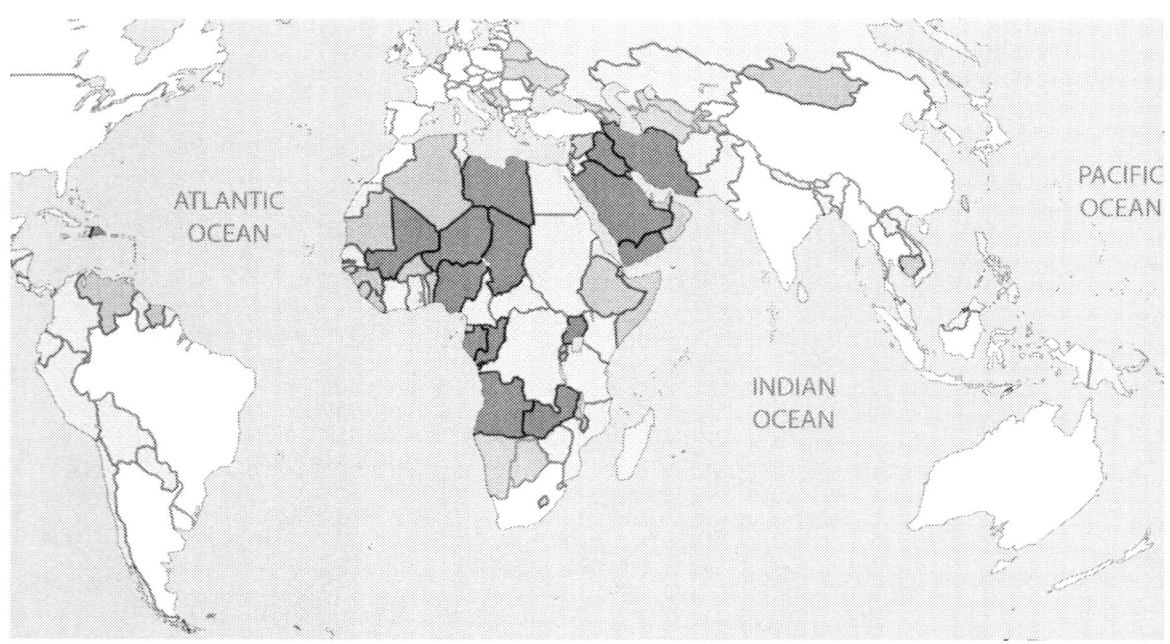

3) The lightly shaded countries have diversified export bases. The darkly shaded countries depend on _____ for foreign exchange (export earnings).

    A) one or two agricultural commodities

    B) one or two mineral resources

    C) energy resources

    D) tourism

    E) both A and B

Answer: E
Diff: 3

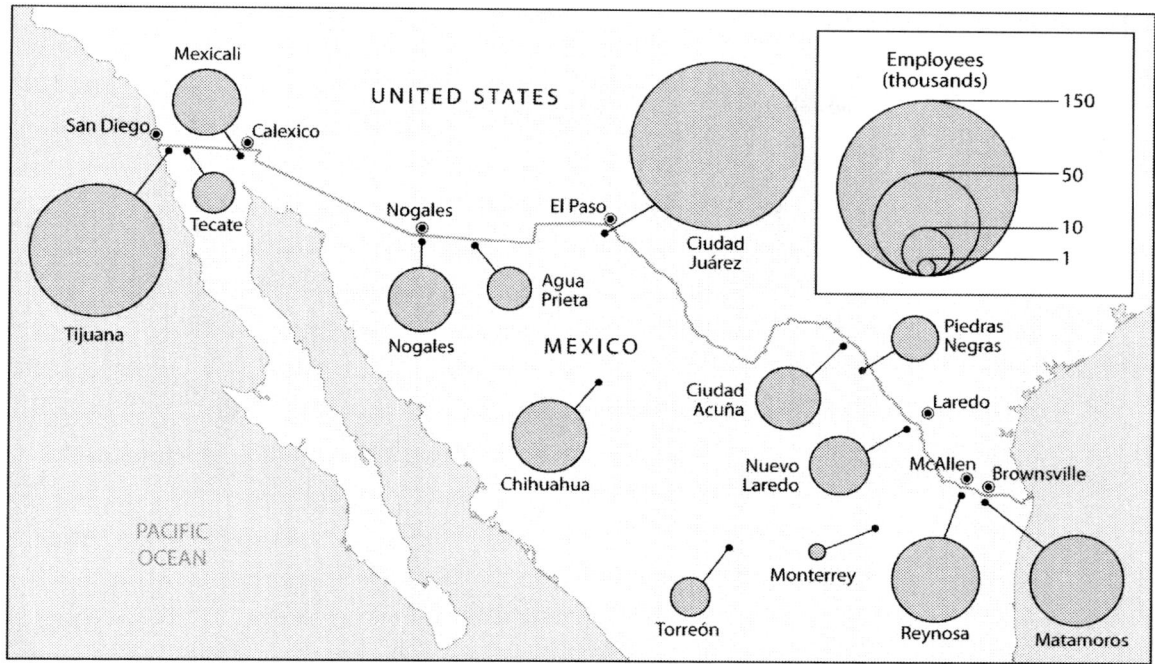

4) The above map shows

    A) principal maquiladora centers.

    B) the world's principal EPZs.

    C) offshore financial centers.

    D) headquarters of principal TNCs.

    E) the world's principal NICs.

    Answer: A
    Diff: 3

Chapter 8 Agriculture and Food Production

8.1 Minimal Choice

1) The average U.S. household spends 40% of its food budget on

    A) food consumed "away from home."   B) chicken.

    Answer: A
    Diff: 1

2) Subsistence agriculture replaced hunting and gathering over the course of the

    A) first agricultural revolution.   B) third agricultural revolution.

    Answer: A
    Diff: 1

3) In places of high population densities, one is more likely to find

    A) intensive subsistence agriculture.   B) shifting cultivation.

    Answer: A
    Diff: 1

4) Intertillage is a form of

    A) polyculture.   B) monoculture.

    Answer: A
    Diff: 3

5) Swiddens are most likely found in

    A) rainforests.   B) plains and prairies.

    Answer: A
    Diff: 1

6) A picture of a landscape in which a man is plowing by machine and the women are thinning or weeding by hand demonstrates

    A) the gender division of labor.   B) land reform.

    Answer: A
    Diff: 2

7) Terraced hillsides in places like Indonesia and Central America strongly suggest

    A) intensive subsistence agriculture.   B) shifting cultivation.

    Answer: A
    Diff: 3

8) Transhumant pastoralists are found in

    A) mountains.   B) deserts.

Answer: A
Diff: 2

9) The second agricultural revolution most importantly coincides with

    A) the Industrial Revolution.   B) the French Revolution.

Answer: A
Diff: 3

10) The third agricultural revolution is characterized as the

    A) industrialization of agriculture.

    B) return to organic agro-food production.

Answer: A
Diff: 2

11) The goal of the Green Revolution was

    A) to feed the world's growing population.

    B) rural and agrarian economic development.

Answer: A
Diff: 2

12) The seed varieties initially developed under the Green Revolution are known as

    A) high yield varieties (HYVs).

    B) genetically modified organisms (GMOs).

Answer: A
Diff: 3

13) Norman Borlaug is said to have saved more lives than any person that ever lived. _____ he was awarded the Nobel Peace prize.

    A) As a founder of the Green Revolution,

    B) For inventing rice and making it available for free,

Answer: A
Diff: 2

14) The crop with the greatest acreage in GMOs is

    A) soybeans.   B) canola.

Answer: A
Diff: 1

15) The country in the world with the greatest percentage of its farmland in GMOs is

A) the USA.   B) Brazil.

Answer: A
Diff: 1

16) Some countries have banned GMOs and the European Union requires strict labeling requirements for foods with GMOs. The USA has

A) no labeling requirements.   B) strict labeling requirements.

Answer: A
Diff: 1

17) The biggest beneficiaries of the Blue Revolution are consumers in the

A) core.   B) periphery.

Answer: A
Diff: 1

8.2 Multiple Choice

1) In comparison to the trend in the United States, average farm size in many areas where intensive subsistence is practiced (Turkey, Bangladesh, China) is

A) remaining constant.

B) increasing.

C) decreasing.

D) fluctuating in response to global crop prices.

Answer: C
Diff: 2

2) A two hectare farm is approximately equivalent in size to a _____ acre farm.

A) 1/2   B) 1   C) 2   D) 5   E) 10

Answer: D
Diff: 3

3) Commercial agricultural systems in the core are especially efficient in terms of food production per unit of

    A) area.

    B) labor.

    C) fuel energy.

    D) water.

    E) all of the above

Answer: B
Diff: 3

4) Plantations -- from coffee, cocoa and tea to rubber, palm oil and bananas -- typically practice

    A) monoculture.

    B) polyculture.

    C) silviculture.

    D) aquaculture.

    E) multiculture.

Answer: A
Diff: 2

5) After petroleum, the second most important (by value) legally traded commodity in the world is

    A) coffee.

    B) bananas.

    C) water.

    D) chocolate.

    E) salt.

Answer: A
Diff: 1

6) Which of the following is *not* one of the major changes occurring globally in agriculture?

    A) increase in the use of chemicals

    B) increase in the use of machinery

    C) increased integration into wider economic systems

    D) increase in the number of people employed

    E) all of the above

Answer: D
Diff: 3

7) An *agrarian* culture is one (in) which

    A) agricultural production is predominant in daily life.

    B) is reliant on food imports.

    C) agricultural production results in plentiful food exports.

    D) has gone through First, Second and Third Agricultural Revolutions.

    E) benefited from the Green Revolution.

Answer: A
Diff: 2

8) Subsistence agriculture is characterized by agriculturalists who

    A) consume what they produce.

    B) farm on swiddens.

    C) practice transhumance.

    D) reject globalization and monoculture.

    E) live on their farms.

Answer: A
Diff: 2

9) Shifting cultivation is characterized by the practice of rotating _____ to maintain soil fertility.

    A) crops

    B) fields

    C) chemicals

    D) farm animals

    E) ownership

Answer: B
Diff: 1

10) The benefits of intertillage include all *except*

    A) reduced risk of crop failure.

    B) spreading out food production over the farming season.

    C) increased ability to replace people with equipment, like tractors.

    D) soil erosion control.

    E) soil moisture retention and maximization.

Answer: C
Diff: 2

11) Characteristic of intensive subsistence agriculture is the great amount of _____ required for attaining high yields.

    A) labor

    B) fertilizers

    C) land

    D) all of the above

    E) both A and B

Answer: E
Diff: 2

12) Compared to large, industrial farms, traditional intensive subsistence farms tend to

    A) have very high yields per acre.

    B) rely more on sophisticated forms of mechanization.

    C) use chemical fertilizers rather than manure and compost.

    D) less sustainable forms of production.

    E) lack agricultural and environmental understanding.

Answer: A
Diff: 2

13) Pastoral nomads

    A) wander around harsh environments in search of water and forage for their animals.

    B) are increasing in number as the nomadic life-style appeals to people tired of the city.

    C) are found only in the Middle East and North Africa.

    D) depend on animals rather than crops for their livelihood.

    E) all of the above

Answer: D
Diff: 3

14) The dramatic increase in yields associated with the second agricultural revolution coincided with

    A) a commercial market for food created by the growing urban labor force.

    B) the advent of communism and the emergence of communal farming systems.

    C) the arrival of crops (potatoes, tomatoes, peppers, chocolate) from the New World.

    D) the introduction of hybrid seeds and GMOs (genetically modified organisms).

    E) the large influx of migrants from peripheral to core countries.

Answer: A
Diff: 1

15) In contrast to the first two agricultural revolutions, the third one originated in the

A) New World.

B) Old World.

C) core.

D) periphery.

E) laboratory.

Answer: A
Diff: 1

16) Which of the following is not characteristic of the Third Agricultural Revolution?

A) mechanized inputs – replacement of human farm labor with machines

B) chemical inputs – use of inorganic fertilizers and pesticides

C) occurred in the twentieth century and continues through today

D) ended with the arrival of the Green Revolution

E) turned agricultural outputs into secondary sector inputs

Answer: D
Diff: 3

17) The industrialization of agriculture has made the farm

A) the center of agricultural production.

B) the center of the service sector of the economy.

C) the cutting edge of new technology.

D) a component in the agro–commodity production system.

E) an unnecessary part of food production.

Answer: D
Diff: 2

18) The industrialization of agriculture involves all of the following *except*

A) the replacement of labor with machines.

B) technological changes in inputs that affect the biological outputs.

C) the replacement of agricultural products with manufactured (synthetic/artificial) products.

D) the globalization of the food chain.

E) the replacement of chemically–oriented agriculture with organic production.

Answer: E
Diff: 2

19) The Green Revolution innovations in agriculture based on a package of inputs including all of the following *except*

    A) high yielding seed varieties.

    B) synthetic fertilizers.

    C) chemical pesticides.

    D) irrigation.

    E) natural fertilizers (compost, green manure, animal manure).

Answer: E
Diff: 2

20) The primary worldwide benefit of the Green Revolution has been an increase in

    A) food production.

    B) environmental benefits.

    C) land reform.

    D) wages for farmers.

    E) conflicts between the primary and secondary sectors.

Answer: A
Diff: 2

21) For the most part, at least in its first decades, the Green Revolution targeted _____ for improvements.

    A) grains like rice, corn and wheat

    B) agricultural production in Africa

    C) export luxury crops like coffee, tea, and cocoa

    D) nontraditional agricultural exports (NTAEs) like fruit, flowers and vegetables

    E) all of the above

Answer: A
Diff: 2

22) In the early and mid-twentieth century, land reform in Mexico returned land to landless peasants in the form of *ejidos*, which are

    A) communally owned lands.

    B) government subsidized lands.

    C) lands designate for export crops.

    D) lands designated for food production.

    E) the agricultural equivalent of *maquiladoras*.

Answer: A
Diff: 1

23) At various times in the twentieth century, numerous countries in Latin America attempted to increase agricultural productivity and reduce social unrest among rural populations through

    A) land reform programs.

    B) the first agricultural revolution.

    C) land privatization.

    D) structural adjustment programs.

    E) industrialization.

    Answer: A
    Diff: 2

24) In the context of agribusiness and the globalization of agriculture, the food chain is a way of understanding complex connections between

    A) agricultural producers and food consumers.

    B) foods in the major food groups.

    C) governments and transnational food corporations.

    D) monoculture and polyculture.

    E) consumption, behavior and health.

    Answer: A
    Diff: 2

25) A food regime is the specific set of links that exists among food production, consumption, capital investment and accumulation opportunities. Since the 1960s, global agriculture has changed from a wheat and livestock food regime to a

    A) fast food regime.

    B) fish regime.

    C) fresh fruits and vegetables regime.

    D) poultry regime.

    E) hot dish and casserole regime.

    Answer: C
    Diff: 2

26) The great thing about biotechnology is that

   A) environmental impacts are completely understood.

   B) it has increased the number of agricultural jobs in the core.

   C) it has saved the family farm.

   D) all of the above

   E) none of the above

   Answer: E
   Diff: 2

27) An organism that has had its DNA modified in a laboratory rather than through cross–pollination or other forms of evolution is known as a

   A) GMO.   B) HMO.   C) HBO.   D) GOP.   E) WTO.

   Answer: A
   Diff: 2

28) Because the health and environmental impacts of GMOS are not well–understood,

   A) the United States allows GMOs to be used only in research.

   B) Europe severely limits GMO food imports.

   C) farmers in the United States refuse to use them.

   D) they are not widely used and were just another passing fad.

   E) all of the above

   Answer: B
   Diff: 2

29) Globally, 24,000 people per day die from complications associated with undernutrition. Ultimately, the core cause of undernutrition is

   A) poverty.

   B) famine.

   C) the green revolution.

   D) food security.

   E) GMOs.

   Answer: A
   Diff: 2

30) For a person, household or country to be food secure means that

    A) access to enough food is assured.

    B) enough food is available.

    C) the person, household or country is self–reliant.

    D) all of the above

Answer: A
Diff: 2

31) In many metropolitan areas around the world, _____ is/are critical in supporting household food security.

    A) urban agriculture

    B) U.S. food aid

    C) GMOs

    D) the food chain

    E) NTAEs

Answer: A
Diff: 2

32) In 1991, per capita chicken consumption surpassed beef consumption in the U.S.. Which of the following is *not* among the reason U.S. consumers eat more chicken than ever?

    A) chicken is inexpensive.

    B) chicken comes in a wide variety of forms.

    C) chicken (white) meat is perceived to be healthier than red meat.

    D) the U.S. is the world's biggest importer, with suppliers all around the world.

    E) the poultry processing industry relies on underpaid, imported labor.

Answer: D
Diff: 2

33) The biorevolution is expected to lead to more

    A) monoculture.

    B) agricultural jobs.

    C) widely accessible seed varieties.

    D) organic foods.

    E) environmental protection.

Answer: A
Diff: 1

34) From the following, the most characteristic product of the Blue Revolution is

  A) shrimp.

  B) poultry.

  C) dairy products.

  D) berries.

  E) wine.

Answer: A
Diff: 1

35) Agriculture is a(an)

  A) science.   B) art.   C) business.   D) all of these

Answer: D
Diff: 1

36) Which of the following is in proper historical sequence?

  A) subsistence agriculture, commercial agriculture, hunting and gathering

  B) hunting and gathering, subsistence agriculture, commercial agriculture

  C) hunting and gathering, commercial agriculture, subsistence agriculture

  D) commercial agriculture, subsistence agriculture, hunting and gathering

Answer: B
Diff: 1

37) Which of the following has dominated food-gathering practices in the twentieth century?

  A) hunting and gathering

  B) commercial agriculture

  C) subsistence agriculture

  D) pastoralism

  E) swidden agriculture

Answer: B
Diff: 1

38) Subsistence agriculture

  A) produces food for the direct consumption of the growers and their families.

  B) is designed to produce a surplus for sale.

  C) does not include the raising of livestock.

  D) has grown in importance over the course of the twentieth century.

Answer: A
Diff: 1

39) Shifting cultivation is most commonly practiced in

A) core countries.   B) tropical and subtropical regions.

C) southern Africa and Australia.   D) Siberia.

Answer: B
Diff: 1

40) Subsistence agriculture is most common in

A) Asia.

B) the Caribbean.

C) Australia.

D) North America.

E) the Middle East.

Answer: A
Diff: 2

41) Shifting cultivation

A) technology and practice has changed dramatically over the last three centuries.

B) requires more expenditure of energy than modern farming methods.

C) works best with low population densities.

D) is experiencing a revival among organic agriculturalists.

Answer: C
Diff: 2

42) In shifting cultivation, fields are generally worked for about

A) 1 year.

B) 2 years.

C) 5-7 years.

D) 10 to 15 years.

E) 20-50 years.

Answer: C
Diff: 2

43) Practitioners of shifting cultivation usually begin the process of clearing a new field when

A) the government tells them to do so.

B) they are certain the last frost is past.

C) the soil of the old field is depleted of nutrients.

D) the women vote to do so.

E) seasonal and annual rainfall patterns shift.

Answer: C
Diff: 1

44) Intensive subsistence agriculture

A) is used primarily in parts of the world with small populations.

B) involves more human labor than swidden agriculture.

C) usually achieves only low productivity.

D) is most commonly practiced in areas with little rainfall.

E) relies on chickens and geese as draft animals.

Answer: B
Diff: 2

45) _____ dominate subsistence agriculture.

A) Lettuces and other leafy vegetables

B) Various varieties of squash

C) Potatoes, yams, and other tubers

D) Rice and other grains

E) Pigs and chickens

Answer: D
Diff: 1

46) Pastoralism

A) requires elaborate fencing networks and patterns to manage herds.

B) is most commonly practiced in drier climates unsuitable for subsistence agriculture.

C) is increasing in important in most parts of the world.

D) has largely replaced intensive subsistence agriculture in Southeast Asia.

Answer: B
Diff: 1

47) Which agricultural revolution is characterized by the creation of a significant surplus of production that could be sold?

A) first   B) second   C) third   D) fourth

Answer: B
Diff: 1

48) In which agricultural revolution was the family farm considered "ideal" for making a living and living a good life?

A) first

B) second

C) third

D) It was considered ideal in all three revolutions.

Answer: B
Diff: 2

49) The height of the second agricultural revolution coincided with

A) the Renaissance.

B) the Reformation.

C) the reign of Louis XIV of France.

D) the Industrial Revolution.

E) the use of nonorganic fertilizers and synthetic herbicides and pesticides.

Answer: D
Diff: 1

50) In the middle of the eighteenth century in Europe, peasant agriculture was characterized by

A) communal farming practices borrowed from Russia.

B) an ever–tightening grip by feudal landlords on the peasants.

C) crop rotation that increased yields and soil fertility.

D) the first use of the tractor.

Answer: C
Diff: 2

51) The third agricultural revolution occurred

    A) about 2,000 years ago.

    B) about 1,000 years ago.

    C) in the eighteenth century.

    D) in the twentieth century.

    E) with the introduction of GMOs.

Answer: D
Diff: 1

52) Which of the following does not characterized one of the three phases of the third agricultural revolution?

    A) significant surplus production   B) food manufacturing

    C) chemical farming   D) mechanization

Answer: A
Diff: 1

53) Which phase of the third agricultural revolution affected agricultural outputs rather than inputs?

    A) food manufacturing   B) chemical farming

    C) mechanization   D) surplus production

Answer: A
Diff: 2

54) Which of the following is not one of the three important developments in the industrialization of agriculture?

    A) the development of industrial substitutes for agricultural products

    B) the introduction of agrochemicals, biotechnologies, fertilizers, and hybrid seeds

    C) increased focus on the family farm as the centerpiece of agricultural production

    D) changes in rural labor activities

Answer: C
Diff: 2

55) Which of the following had had significant impacts on commercialized agriculture?

    A) recessions

    B) inflation

    C) fluctuations in the value of international currency

    D) changes in the price of oil

    E) all of the above

Answer: E
Diff: 1

56) The Green Revolution

    A) has been an unqualified success.

    B) began with the peace and environmental movement of the 1960s.

    C) has led to only slight increases in crop yields.

    D) has been most successful in Africa.

    E) none of the above

Answer: E
Diff: 2

57) The goal of Green Revolution scientists was to develop improved and better

    A) irrigation systems.

    B) fertilizers.

    C) high-yield seeds.

    D) non-toxic pesticides.

    E) training manuals.

Answer: C
Diff: 1

58) Which region or country has benefited the least from the green revolution?

    A) Africa

    B) India

    C) East Asia

    D) Latin America

    E) Mexico

Answer: A
Diff: 2

59) During recent years Green Revolution scientists have

A) focused attention on developing colorful and snazzly looking strains of wheat and corn.

B) engaged in little activity since their funding has dwindled to nothing.

C) entered the political arena to seek more hands–on control of agriculture in developing countries.

D) produced seeds for a widening variety of crops.

Answer: D
Diff: 1

60) Agricultural subsidies

A) are no longer used by the U.S. government.

B) are often achieved without spending money.

C) distort the true market value of the agricultural products being subsidized.

D) leave farmers, not consumers with the government money.

Answer: C
Diff: 2

61) The most successful international efforts to aid agricultural development in peripheral countries have been

A) those directed by the United States government.

B) small projects at the local level.

C) large projects aimed at grand–scale transformation.

D) those in which the aid money is given to the governments of the peripheral countries.

Answer: B
Diff: 2

62) In core countries, which of the following dominates the food production process?

A) consumers
B) transnational corporations
C) government officials
D) agricultural workers

Answer: B
Diff: 2

63) Which of the following is NOT one of the five central and connected sectors of the food web?

    A) governmental farm policies

    B) food distribution

    C) agricultural inputs

    D) food consumption

    E) agricultural product processing

Answer: A
Diff: 2

64) Rachel Carson's *Silent Spring*

    A) focused on the negative effects of chemical fertilizers.

    B) led to the banning of DDT and other harmful chemicals in the United States.

    C) led to international rules prohibiting the use of harmful pesticides in developing countries.

    D) did major damage to the environmental movement in the United States.

Answer: B
Diff: 2

65) In a dry climate with cold winters, this grain would least likely be cultivated:

    A) rice   B) wheat   C) barley   D) oats   E) corn

Answer: A
Diff: 2

66) Transhumance is least common in

    A) Turkey.

    B) northern France.

    C) northern Spain.

    D) Greece.

    E) North Africa.

Answer: B
Diff: 2

67) Synthetic fertilizer use is least common in

    A) Africa.   B) the United States.

    C) Europe.   D) Asia.

Answer: A
Diff: 1

68) The "postmodern diet" is centered on

   A) wheat and livestock.

   B) fresh fruits and vegetables.

   C) homeopathic herbs.

   D) free-range chicken and hormone-free beef.

   Answer: B
   Diff: 1

69) This grain was NOT a major focus of the green revolution:

   A) maize   B) wheat   C) rice   D) millet

   Answer: D
   Diff: 2

8.3 True or False

1) Hunting and gathering is typically associated with non-commercial, primitive subsistence agricultural systems.

   Answer: TRUE
   Diff: 2

2) The Green Revolution is so named because it is environmentally sustainable.

   Answer: FALSE
   Diff: 1

3) Subsistence agriculture began to replace hunting and gathering with the advent of the the first agricultural revolution.

   Answer: TRUE
   Diff: 1

4) The last subsistence agriculturalists disappeared with the third agricultural revolution.

   Answer: FALSE
   Diff: 2

5) Intertillage involves growing many different agricultural crops together in the same plot.

   Answer: TRUE
   Diff: 1

6) Pastoral nomads know their environments intimately.

   Answer: TRUE
   Diff: 1

7) Among the important benefits of the Green Revolution is reduced reliance on oil and other non–renewable resources.

Answer: FALSE
Diff: 2

8) Agribusiness in the core economies has helped the small, family farmer remain competitive in the food chain.

Answer: FALSE
Diff: 2

9) Negative impacts from the globalization of agriculture are confined to the world's core.

Answer: FALSE
Diff: 2

10) Though agriculture in New Zealand produces fruits and vegetables for the current global food regime, its economy still relies significantly on wool and lamb.

Answer: TRUE
Diff: 1

11) The Green Revolution was directed toward the needs of the world's core countries.

Answer: FALSE
Diff: 2

12) The the great thing about biotechnology and the biorevolution is that both positive and negative impacts are spread evenly across core and peripheral regions.

Answer: FALSE
Diff: 2

13) In the biorevolution, control over food production is moving from the farmer to the biotechnological firm.

Answer: TRUE
Diff: 2

14) Despite the fact that impacts from GMOs and GMO foods on human health and the environment are not well–understood, they are permitted in foods in the United States.

Answer: TRUE
Diff: 1

15) Famines can occur when overall levels of food availability are adequate.

Answer: TRUE
Diff: 3

16) Farmers are the primary players in the global food system.

   Answer: FALSE
   Diff: 2

17) Consistent with its pro-trade position, the United States no longer subsidizes agriculture.

   Answer: FALSE
   Diff: 1

18) Agriculture in the core is characterized by its integration into the manufacturing, service, finance and trade sectors.

   Answer: TRUE
   Diff: 2

19) The WTO has determined that prohibiting GMO food from entering a country is an illegal barrier to trade.

   Answer: TRUE
   Diff: 1

20) Many of the pesticides currently sprayed on crops in peripheral countries have been banned in core countries.

   Answer: TRUE
   Diff: 2

21) Subsistence agriculture replaced hunting and gathering.

   Answer: TRUE
   Diff: 1

22) Crop rotation is most commonly practiced in tropical forests.

   Answer: FALSE
   Diff: 1

23) Practitioners of swidden typically plant only one crop per field.

   Answer: FALSE
   Diff: 2

24) Intensive subsistence agriculture is capable of supporting large rural populations.

   Answer: TRUE
   Diff: 2

25) The practice of transhumance involves changing pastoral locations as the seasons change.

Answer: TRUE
Diff: 1

26) The history of world agriculture is characterized by long periods of no change interrupted with short periods of major change.

Answer: FALSE
Diff: 3

27) The Industrial Revolution spurred the first agricultural revolution.

Answer: FALSE
Diff: 1

28) The third agricultural revolution had its roots in North America.

Answer: TRUE
Diff: 2

29) Some have criticized the green revolution for increasing social inequalities in targeted countries.

Answer: TRUE
Diff: 2

30) Political leaders sometimes subsidize the cost of food in order to keep themselves in power.

Answer: TRUE
Diff: 2

31) Most agricultural researchers think that global agriculture is now characterized by a grain–and–meat food regime.

Answer: FALSE
Diff: 1

32) Despite the development of modern techniques in agriculture, the environment still has a significant effect on food production.

Answer: TRUE
Diff: 1

33) The global loss of topsoil each year is greater than the amount that is created each year.

Answer: TRUE
Diff: 1

34) Desertification can include more than just the loss of topsoil.

Answer: TRUE
Diff: 2

35) As a sign of cultural change, the French welcome every opportunity to eat at McDonald's and other American-based fast-food franchises.

Answer: FALSE
Diff: 1

36) Subsistence agriculture has been growing in importance in the last few decades.

Answer: FALSE
Diff: 1

37) Shifting cultivation is more commonly practiced by small groups than by larger groups.

Answer: TRUE
Diff: 2

38) Transhumance is still practiced in North Africa.

Answer: TRUE
Diff: 1

39) Communal farming declined after the Industrial Revolution.

Answer: TRUE
Diff: 2

40) The Green Revolution began as a League of Nations program in the early 1920s.

Answer: FALSE
Diff: 1

41) High yield seed varieties were the first major product of the Green Revolution.

Answer: TRUE
Diff: 1

42) Hybrid and cloned plants are generally more disease-resistant than naturally-developed ones.

Answer: FALSE
Diff: 2

43) Most forms of modern agriculture have led to a net increase in soil on farmlands.

Answer: FALSE
Diff: 2

8.4 Matching

AGRICULTURE: Match the characteristic to the agricultural activity.

1) found in areas of high
population density
   Diff: 3

2) found in rainforest climate
   Diff: 3

3) found in harsh, typically arid,
environments
   Diff: 3

4) transhumance
   Diff: 3

5) involves modifications of the
environment (like terraces)
   Diff: 3

6) swidden (slash and burn)
   Diff: 3

7) livestock oriented
   Diff: 3

8) high yields per unit of land
   Diff: 3

A) shifting cultivation

B) intensive subsistence

C) pastoral nomadism

1) B	2) A	3) C	4) C	5) B	6) A
7) C	8) B				

REVOLUTIONS: Match the agricultural revolution to its defining characteristic.

9) first agricultural revolution
   Diff: 2

A) domestication of plants and
   animals

10) second agricultural revolution
    Diff: 2

B) food manufacturing

C) package of high–yielding crops,
   irrigation, pesticides, fertilizers

11) third agricultural revolution
    Diff: 2

D) Industrial Revolution

12) Green Revolution
    Diff: 2

9) A   10) D   11) B   12) C

8.5 Map Identification

World Map

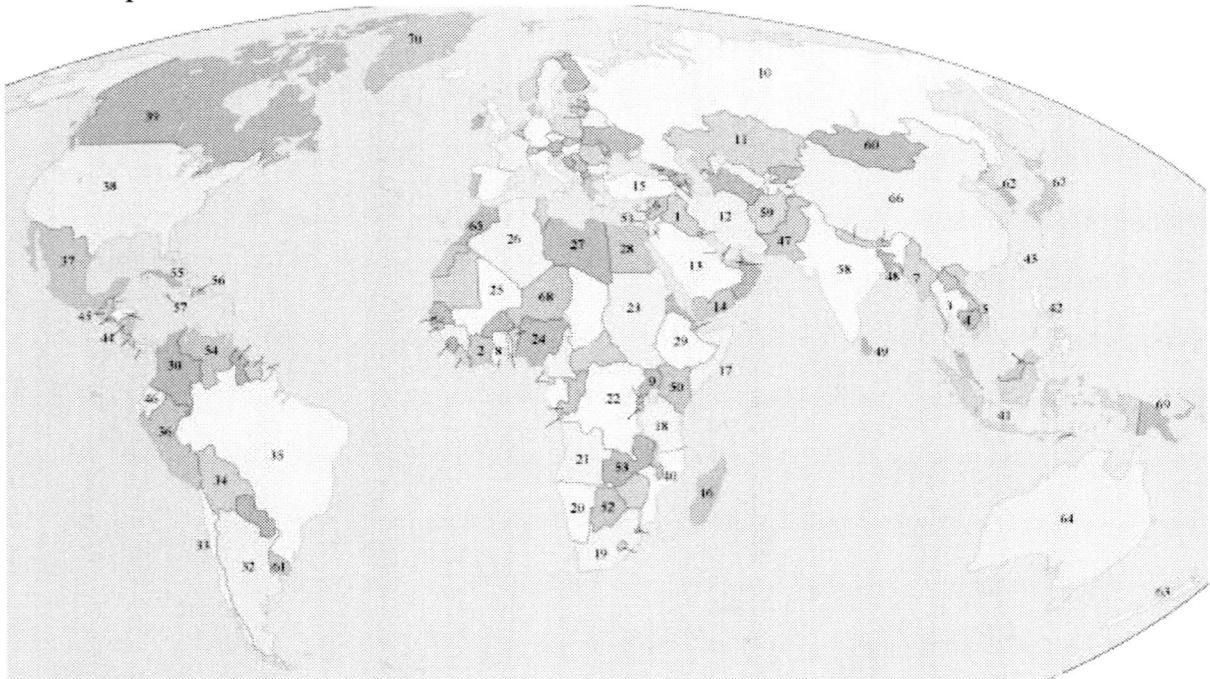

1) Which of the following countries is not in Southeast Asia?

A) Myanmar

B) New Zealand

C) Vietnam

D) Thailand

E) All of the above are in the world region of Southeast Asia.

Answer: B
Diff: 2

2) Myanmar shares a border with which of the following countries?

A) Vietnam

B) Niger

C) Nicaragua

D) Chile

E) Thailand

Answer: E
Diff: 2

3) Which of the following is an island country?

   A) Nicaragua

   B) Chile

   C) Thailand

   D) New Zealand

   E) Niger

Answer: D
Diff: 2

4) The country of Vietnam is identified by the number

   A) 3.   B) 5.   C) 7.   D) 9.   E) 11.

Answer: B
Diff: 1

5) Santiago is the capital of

   A) 22.   B) 33.   C) 44.   D) 55.   E) 66.

Answer: B
Diff: 1

6) The capital of country #7 is

   A) Yangon (Rangoon).

   B) Bangkok.

   C) Managua.

   D) Wellington.

   E) Niamey.

Answer: A
Diff: 1

7) Hanoi is the capital of

   A) 3.   B) 4.   C) 5.   D) 6.   E) 7.

Answer: C
Diff: 1

8) The countries of which two capitals share a border?

    A) Bangok & Yangon

    B) Niamey & Wellington

    C) Santiago & Managua

    D) Hanoi & Yangon

    E) Niamey & Managua

Answer: A
Diff: 2

9) Which of the following is the capital of #44?

    A) Managua

    B) Santiago

    C) Port-au-Prince

    D) Guatemala City

    E) Buenos Aires

Answer: A
Diff: 2

10) Which country is landlocked?

    A) Niger

    B) Chile

    C) Nicaragua

    D) Vietnam

    E) New Zealand

Answer: A
Diff: 2

11) Which country is in the Southern Hemisphere?

    A) Nicaragua

    B) Niger

    C) Vietnam

    D) Chile

    E) Thailand

Answer: D
Diff: 2

12) Niamey is the capital of the country labeled with which number?

A) 23   B) 30   C) 59   D) 60   E) 68

Answer: E
Diff: 1

Chapter 9 Politics of Territory and Space

9.1 Minimal Choice

1) The state boundary between Wisconsin and Minnesota -- as between all 50 U.S. states -- is

    A) inclusionary.   B) exclusionary.

Answer: A
Diff: 2

2) *De jure* spaces are delimited by _____ boundaries.

    A) formal   B) informal

Answer: A
Diff: 1

3) Straight-line boundaries between territories suggest

    A) frontier regions.   B) natural barriers.

Answer: A
Diff: 1

4) Choropleth maps are based on

    A) *de jure* spaces.   B) territorial organization.

Answer: A
Diff: 3

5) The concept of citizen and citizenship developed with the emergence of

    A) republics   B) monarchies.

Answer: A
Diff: 1

6) The United States is a

    A) multinational state.   B) nation state.

Answer: A
Diff: 1

7) For most of its existence, the USSR -- like the czarist Russian state from which it emerged -- operated as a

    A) unitary state.   B) federal state.

Answer: A
Diff: 1

8) Generally, minority nationalist movements are

    A) centrifugal.   B) centripetal.

Answer: A
Diff: 2

9) The first phases of imperialism is based on the exploitation of the periphery for

    A) raw materials.   B) labor.

Answer: A
Diff: 1

10) Despite Algeria's independence from _____ in the 1960s, the violence that began under colonialism continued to the end of the twentieth century.

    A) France   B) England

Answer: A
Diff: 1

11) Despite 200 years of British colonialism the caste system remains much a part of _____ social life.

    A) India's   B) Rwanda's

Answer: A
Diff: 1

12) In the political geographic division of the world into North and South (the North/South Divide), Australia and New Zealand are part of the

    A) North.   B) South.

Answer: A
Diff: 1

13) In the political geographic division of the world into North and South (the North/South Divide), the North is generally the

    A) core.   B) periphery.

Answer: A
Diff: 1

14) In the political geographic division of the world into North and South (the North/South Divide), the South is generally considered

    A) politically independent.   B) economically independent.

Answer: A
Diff: 3

15) For the most part, the countries of South America received their independence by the middle of the

   A) nineteenth century.   B) twentieth century.

   Answer: A
   Diff: 1

16) With few exceptions, the countries of _____ did not gain independence until the second half of the twentieth century.

   A) Africa   B) Latin America

   Answer: A
   Diff: 2

17) One of the first international organizations ever formed had international peace and security as its goal; known as the _____, it attempted to assist in the independence of colonies.

   A) League of Nations   B) United Nations

   Answer: A
   Diff: 1

18) According to the geographer _____, Eurasia (Central Asia) is the geographical pivot from which a world empire could be controlled.

   A) Halford Mackinder   B) Friecrich Ratzel

   Answer: A
   Diff: 1

19) In the context of Cold War terminology, _____ is on the eastern side of the East/West divide.

   A) Cuba   B) Turkey

   Answer: A
   Diff: 3

20) During the Cold War, some policy makers strongly believed that if one country became communist, neighboring countries would follow. This theory is known as the

   A) Domino theory.   B) Heartland theory.

   Answer: A
   Diff: 1

21) Belief in the _____ drew the USA into numerous twentieth century conflicts (Vietnam, most notably).

   A) Domino theory   B) Heartland theory

   Answer: A
   Diff: 1

22) Most people would agree that, by the end of the twentieth century, _____ had ended.

    A) the Cold War   B) neocolonialism

Answer: A
Diff: 2

23) The territorial divisions of Antarctica are based on

    A) lines of longitude.   B) natural features.

Answer: A
Diff: 3

24) The original use of the term *terrorism* -- in the eighteenth century -- was to describe the violent actions of a

    A) state.   B) a separatist group.

Answer: A
Diff: 2

25) Austria, Spain, Estonia, and the Netherlands are members of

    A) the EU.   B) ASEAN.

Answer: A
Diff: 1

26) Southeast Asian countries like Indonesia, Vietnam and Thailand are members of

    A) ASEAN.   B) OPEC.

Answer: A
Diff: 2

27) The International Criminal Court (ICC) was established by the United Nations in 1998 to

    A) protect human rights.   B) promote free trade.

Answer: A
Diff: 1

28) Which was among seven United Nation member countries that voted against the treaty to establish the International Criminal Court?

    A) United States   B) Canada

Answer: A
Diff: 1

29) The Basque collective identity and commitment to place is a good example of

    A) regionalism.   B) sectionalism.

Answer: A
Diff: 2

30) The separation wall Israel is erecting around the West Bank exemplifies an

    A) exclusionary boundary.   B) inclusionary boundary.

Answer: A
Diff: 3

31) The United States is a

    A) federation.   B) unitary state.

Answer: A
Diff: 1

32) The United States has 50 states and over _____ counties, parishes & boroughs.

    A) 3,000   B) 30,000

Answer: A
Diff: 1

9.2 Multiple Choice

1) According to our text, imperialism begins with

    A) exploration and exploitation of raw materials.

    B) advertising.

    C) colonization.

    D) military expansion.

    E) settlement–building.

Answer: A
Diff: 1

2) Prior to Belgian colonialism in Rwanda, the Hutus and Tutsis lived together quite peacefully. According to our text, conflicts between the groups emerged after the Belgians introduced the concept of

   A) money.

   B) borders.

   C) ethnic difference.

   D) slavery.

   E) cash crops.

Answer: C
Diff: 2

3) Patriotism is place identity based on _____ territoriality.

   A) class   B) ethnic   C) state   D) racial   E) religious

Answer: C
Diff: 1

4) The people of Kurdistan will have a difficult time attaining _____ because the region spans the territory of four other states.

   A) nationalism

   B) sovereignty

   C) irredentism

   D) territoriality

   E) reapportionment

Answer: B
Diff: 2

5) The predominately Kurdish homeland (sometimes referred to as Kurdistan) does not lie in part of which state?

   A) Pakistan   B) Iran   C) Iraq   D) Syria   E) Turkey

Answer: A
Diff: 2

6) Contributing to the conflicts and tensions in Africa is the colonial legacy of borders that

 A) divided nations that had been united.

 B) united nations that had been separate.

 C) separated people from traditional resources.

 D) cut spatial relationships, like migration and trade patterns.

 E) all of the above

Answer: E
Diff: 2

7) On 30 October 1995, in a vote related to sovereignty, the people of Quebec chose

 A) to become part of Canada.

 B) to not join Canada.

 C) to secede from Canada.

 D) to not secede from Canada.

 E) to become part of the United States.

Answer: D
Diff: 2

8) Which is the most inclusive organization (has most members) and has as a primary goal the maintenance of international peace and security?

 A) OPEC

 B) United Nations

 C) Organization of Economic Cooperation and Development

 D) North Atlantic Treaty Organization

 E) NAFTA

Answer: B
Diff: 1

9) Which two countries are not members of the European Union?

 A) Finland and Sweden

 B) Germany and Denmark

 C) Norway and Switzerland

 D) Portugal and Austria

 E) Spain and France

Answer: C
Diff: 2

10) A federal state (or federation) is one in which

    A) government power and control is centralized.

    B) government power is disbursed to local units.

    C) countries unite toward a common economic, or sometimes military, goal.

    D) local units of government work to adopt uniform rules and regulations.

    E) administered by the Federal government, like Washington, DC.

Answer: B
Diff: 1

11) Nationalists that want an independent state of Quebec are properly thought of as

    A) secessionists.

    B) irredentists.

    C) orthodontists.

    D) provincialists.

    E) statists.

Answer: A
Diff: 1

12) The Zapatista rebellion in Chiapas (Mexico), that coincided with the beginning of NAFTA, was over the issue of

    A) corn & coffee.

    B) autonomy.

    C) globalization.

    D) exploitation.

    E) all of the above

Answer: E
Diff: 2

13) Drawing from social Darwinism, Friedrich Ratzel's model of the state -- in which state growth and change were "natural" and inevitable -- portrayed the state as a

    A) snowball.

    B) biological organism.

    C) soldier.

    D) religion.

    E) volcano.

Answer: B
Diff: 1

14) Ratzel's belief that geopolitics stems from the interaction of _____ is still popular today.

    A) power and territory

    B) nature and society

    C) men and women

    D) the rich and the poor

    E) space and place

Answer: A
Diff: 1

15) The Berlin Wall and the Mexican border are good examples of _____ boundaries.

    A) exclusionary

    B) inclusionary

    C) unitary

    D) monetary

    E) illusionary

Answer: A
Diff: 1

16) Among the following, the best example of an inclusionary boundary is the boundary between

    A) North and South Korea.

    B) Wisconsin and Minnesota.

    C) East and West Berlin during the Cold war.

    D) the U.S. and Mexico.

    E) Israel and the West Bank.

Answer: B
Diff: 3

17) Frontier regions, where territoriality is underdeveloped, are known for their

    A) marginality.

    B) belonging.

    C) rapid growth.

    D) conflicts.

    E) untapped resources.

Answer: A
Diff: 1

18) Only _____ currently exists as a frontier region where territoriality is undeveloped.

   A) Antarctica

   B) Australia

   C) sub-Saharan Africa

   D) Siberia

   E) Northern Canada

Answer: A
Diff: 1

19) Territories like Canada, Michigan, and Washtenaw County that are delimited by formal boundaries are known as _____ spaces or regions.

   A) *du jure*   B) *de facto*   C) *de limito*   D) *de rigeur*

Answer: A
Diff: 3

20) As used in our text, the term state is closest in meaning to

   A) nation.   B) territory.   C) country.   D) province.   E) colony.

Answer: C
Diff: 1

21) In the context of the course and text, _____ is the best example of a state.

   A) Minnesota

   B) Quebec

   C) Kurdistan

   D) Egypt

   E) Chechnya or Kosovo

Answer: D
Diff: 3

22) Which of the following pairs best represent nation-states?

   A) the Basque Region and Kurdistan   B) Japan and Iceland

   C) United States and Canada   D) India and Russia

Answer: B
Diff: 2

23) A cultural group with a territorial identity is known as a

   A) nation.   B) province.   C) state.   D) race.   E) class.

   Answer: A
   Diff: 1

24) Of the following, the United States is best characterized as a

   A) republic.

   B) confederation.

   C) nation–state.

   D) monarchy.

   E) supranational organization.

   Answer: A
   Diff: 1

25) To be considered a nation, a group of people must

   A) share cultural elements like religion, language, history, politics.

   B) have their own country.

   C) reside in the same territory.

   D) share a sense of nationalism.

   E) be sovereign and self–determined.

   Answer: A
   Diff: 1

26) The township and range system west of the Mississippi was designed to

   A) facilitate opening and settling the west.

   B) preserve natural features on the landscape.

   C) set aside prime reservation lands for Native Americans.

   D) identify opportunities for resource exploration and exploitation.

   E) equitably distribute land to all that wanted it.

   Answer: A
   Diff: 2

27) In the context of political geography, centripetal forces

    A) bind the people and places of a state together.

    B) highlight differences between the people of a state.

    C) promote self-rule among the people of a state.

    D) contributed to the break-up of the Soviet Union.

    E) encourage secession.

    Answer: A
    Diff: 2

28) Attempts by existing states to annex the territory of another state which their co-nationals inhabit is known as

    A) nationalism.

    B) reapportionment.

    C) secessionism.

    D) irredentism.

    E) separatism.

    Answer: D
    Diff: 1

29) In the transition of the USSR to the CIS, Russia went from being the core of a unitary state to being the most powerful member of a

    A) confederation.

    B) coalition.

    C) nation-state.

    D) supranational organization.

    E) zionist state.

    Answer: A
    Diff: 2

30) Which of the following have been tried by 20th-century states to eliminate or minimize the impact of centrifugal forces?

    A) decentralization of power

    B) consolidation or centralization of power

    C) destruction of ethnic minorities

    D) increased autonomy to ethnic minorities

    E) All of the above have been used.

    Answer: E
    Diff: 2

31) From the following, the best example of a supranational organization is (are) the

    A) Commonwealth of Independent States.

    B) NAFTA.

    C) Canadian provinces.

    D) United Nations.

    E) European Union.

Answer: E
Diff: 1

32) According to Ratzel's theory of the state, imperialism emerges from the need for territorial expansion tied to

    A) population growth.

    B) centrifugal forces.

    C) low rates of natural increase.

    D) irredentism.

    E) a new world order.

Answer: A
Diff: 2

33) In the relationship between imperialism and colonialism, which of the following is not true?

    A) imperialism generally precedes colonialism

    B) imperialism ends with independence

    C) colonialism ends with independence

    D) colonialism is a form of imperialism

    E) None of the above are true.

Answer: B
Diff: 2

34) Despite independence, the continuing effects of colonialism in India, Rwanda and Algeria are still seen in

    A) English as the official language or *lingua franca*.

    B) their incorporation into the world system core.

    C) violent conflicts involving territory and power.

    D) the large secondary (manufacturing) sector of the economy.

    E) the loss of all cultural identity.

Answer: C
Diff: 2

35) The North/South Divide is used in our text to distinguish

    A) North African states from Sub-Saharan states.

    B) anti-slavery from pro-slavery states.

    C) former colonizers from formerly colonized states.

    D) (former) communist from non-communist states.

Answer: C
Diff: 1

36) Contract farming -- whereby production in the periphery is for consumption in the core -- is one example of

    A) neocolonialism.

    B) regionalism.

    C) self-determination.

    D) the end of colonialism.

    E) independence.

Answer: A
Diff: 2

37) The reacquisition of sovereignty and territorial integrity following colonization is known as

    A) decolonization.

    B) post-colonialism.

    C) neocolonialism.

    D) protocolonialism.

    E) quasicolonialism.

Answer: A
Diff: 1

38) Of the following, the most prominent theory supporting U.S. involvement in the Vietnam War was

    A) domino theory.

    B) zionism.

    C) theory of the state.

    D) heartland theory.

    E) anti-terrorism.

Answer: A
Diff: 2

39) According to Halford Mackinder's Heartland Theory, the "geographical pivot" from which world conquest could be controlled includes the area of

    A) Eurasia, including Iran, Afghanistan and Central Asia.

    B) Europe from Italy to Holland.

    C) North America from Chicago to Montreal to Washington, DC.

    D) the Arabian peninsula.

    E) Southeast Asia, including Indonesia.

Answer: A
Diff: 2

40) The East/West divide refers to the divide between

    A) the New and Old Worlds.

    B) the core and the periphery.

    C) Indo-European language speakers and Sino-Tibetan/Afro-Asiatic language speakers.

    D) the Christian and Islamic spheres of belief.

    E) none of the above -- the East/West divide disappeared with the end of the Cold War.

Answer: E
Diff: 3

41) The fall of the Berlin Wall symbolizes the

    A) end of the Cold War.

    B) beginning of the "new world order."

    C) triumph of capitalism over communism.

    D) all of the above

Answer: D
Diff: 2

42) The new world order is characterized by all of the following except

    A) U.S. hegemony.

    B) transnational corporate growth.

    C) globalized capitalism.

    D) regional instabilities.

    E) reduction in world terrorism.

Answer: E
Diff: 2

43) OPEC has member countries from all of the following regions except

A) Europe.

B) South America.

C) Sub-Saharan Africa.

D) Southeast Asia.

E) Middle East.

Answer: A
Diff: 2

44) The recent experience of the Chechens and Kosovar Albanians is similar in that both

A) recently received independence after a long and bloody struggle.

B) have struggled unsuccessfully for independence.

C) have occupied Palestine for centuries before being driven out by Zionists.

D) are the newest members of the European Union.

E) are oil-rich members of the Commonwealth of Independent States.

Answer: B
Diff: 3

45) With globalization and the increasing importance of trade-facilitating organizations, states are

A) disappearing.

B) growing as containers of political and economic power.

C) becoming sites of flows and connections.

D) becoming irrelevant.

E) trying to spread the benefits of globalization.

Answer: C
Diff: 2

46) The territorially based sense of identity in groups like the Basques, Kurds and Quebec's French-speaking population is referred to as

A) regionalism.

B) sectionalism.

C) nationalism.

D) multinationalism.

E) territorialism.

Answer: A
Diff: 2

47) _____ is the strong devotion to local interests and customs and has been used to explain the Civil War as the Union's effort to make sure that the strong attachment to the institution of slavery would not take priority over the unity of the whole.

    A) Regionalism

    B) Sectionalism

    C) Nationalism

    D) Multinationalism

    E) Territorialism

Answer: B
Diff: 1

48) Whereas reapportionment adjusts the amount of political representation give to a certain area, redistricting adjusts

    A) territorial boundaries.

    B) population size.

    C) Federal lands.

    D) country, state and/or county boundaries.

    E) term limits.

Answer: A
Diff: 2

49) Antarctica has been colonized by

    A) the core countries.

    B) countries of the periphery.

    C) no country.

    D) the United Nations.

    E) a handful of countries from both the North and the South.

Answer: E
Diff: 3

50) According to a map in your book, _____ claim the largest portions of Antarctica.

    A) Australia & Norway

    B) Chile and Argentina

    C) the United States and Russia

    D) New Zealand and France

    E) none of the above -- Antarctica remains unclaimed by individual states.

Answer: A
Diff: 2

51) Of the five sovereign states that emerged from the ruins of Yugoslavia, all but one are a mix of nationalities. Only _____ comes close to being a nation-state.

    A) Slovenia

    B) Croatia

    C) Bosnia and Herzegovina

    D) Macedonia

    E) Serbia and Montenegro

Answer: A
Diff: 3

52) Political geography

    A) began with Socrates, Plato and Strabo.

    B) has generally ignored the people-land tradition.

    C) was influenced by environmental determinism in the late nineteenth-early twentieth centuries.

    D) places little importance on globalization.

Answer: C
Diff: 2

53) The geopolitics of Friedrich Ratzel

    A) held that a state grows by absorbing larger units.

    B) saw a definite relationship between power and territory.

    C) was an attack on the Social Darwinism in fashion at the end of the nineteenth century.

    D) was focused on the domestic policies of states, not their foreign policy.

    E) all of these

Answer: B
Diff: 2

54) Which of the following can best be considered a modern frontier?

    A) Antarctica

    B) the Australian interior

    C) sub-Saharan Africa

    D) the Andean highlands

    E) the Yukon

Answer: A
Diff: 2

55) For political geographers, _____ is at the center of most inquiry.

    A) the state

    B) the nation

    C) sovereignty

    D) democracy

    E) natural rights

Answer: A
Diff: 1

56) The nation–state

    A) often contains two or more sizable nations within it.

    B) gives sovereignty to each nation within its borders.

    C) is relatively uncommon.

    D) is best exemplified by France.

    E) is best exemplified by the United States.

Answer: C
Diff: 1

57) The expansion of the Russian Empire

    A) began at the beginning of the third century, A.D.

    B) was mostly westward and northward.

    C) was primarily designed to increase national pride.

    D) stopped in the eighteenth century.

    E) none of these

Answer: E
Diff: 2

58) What distinguished the Russian Empire from other empires existing in the nineteenth century was that it

    A) was not motivated by a desire for economic gain.

    B) incorporated conquered territories into the state.

    C) already had several warm–water ports.

    D) did not have to deal with centripetal forces.

    E) experienced all of the above.

Answer: B
Diff: 2

59) Lenin's solution to the "national problem" was

    A) brutal suppression of nationalism.

    B) a federalist system of government.

    C) the granting of independence to areas with less than 25% ethnic Russian population.

    D) multiparty democracy and an independent judiciary.

Answer: B
Diff: 2

60) In which form of government is significant power given to smaller units of government within the State?

    A) unitary State

    B) confederate State

    C) federal State

    D) organic State

    E) democratic State

Answer: C
Diff: 1

61) Under Mikhail Gorbechev, the USSR

    A) expanded its territory farther into eastern Europe.

    B) changed from a confederation to a unitary state.

    C) suppressed *glasnost* (openness).

    D) introduced *perestroika* (economic and government restructuring).

    E) experienced no nationalist uprisings.

Answer: D
Diff: 1

62) The relatively peaceful breakup of the USSR

    A) was facilitated in part by the fact that the USSR had a federal structure.

    B) occurred in the mid–1980s.

    C) would not have occurred without the brilliant statesmanship of President Bush.

    D) left many of the Soviet Republics without independence.

Answer: A
Diff: 2

63) Which of the following is NOT one of the states that formed from the former Soviet Union after its breakup?

A) Ukraine

B) Russia

C) Kazakhstan

D) Chechnya

E) Estonia

Answer: D
Diff: 2

64) The Baltic Republics

A) were independent between World Wars I and II.

B) have a relatively well–developed economic base compared to other former Soviet republics.

C) have population majorities that are non–Russian.

D) All of the above are true fo the Baltics.

Answer: D
Diff: 1

65) The state

A) is a set of institutions.

B) controls territory.

C) is active, not static.

D) All of the above are true for the state.

Answer: D
Diff: 2

66) In the first phases of imperialism, a core state

A) extracts raw materials from the periphery.

B) sets up formal government in the periphery.

C) sends colonists to the periphery.

D) arranges for the eventual transition to independence for the periphery.

Answer: A
Diff: 2

67) The British presence in India

    A) started with the interjection of the British military around 1700.

    B) did not formally end until just after World War II.

    C) was welcomed by the indigenous ruling elites.

    D) had little lasting effect on Indian society.

    E) All of the above are true about the British presence in India.

Answer: B
Diff: 1

68) The postcolonial history of India included

    A) partition.

    B) regional conflicts.

    C) ethnic conflicts.

    D) All of the above are part of India's postcolonical history.

Answer: D
Diff: 1

69) The main cause of civil strife in Rwanda stems from

    A) antidemocratic values learned from the Germans.

    B) interference by South Africa.

    C) the Belgian colonial practice of favoring Tutsis.

    D) the legacy of superpower competition left over from the Cold War.

Answer: C
Diff: 2

70) The League of Nations

    A) was formed in the middle of the nineteenth century.

    B) established the colonial mandate system.

    C) had no significant successes.

    D) never allowed the Soviet Union to join.

Answer: B
Diff: 2

71) Neocolonialism

    A) peaked near the end of the nineteenth century.

    B) allows core states to continue exploiting periphery states.

    C) is still relevant in Africa, but not in other parts of the Southern Hemisphere.

    D) has in general been anticapitalist.

Answer: B
Diff: 2

72) Antarctica

    A) is owned by the United Nations.

    B) has a small but thriving native population.

    C) is the coldest place in the Northern Hemisphere.

    D) has been carved like a territorial pie into claims by various states.

Answer: D
Diff: 1

73) The heartland theory held that

    A) North America was the best place from which to launch a campaign for world domination.

    B) sea power was the dominant form of military advantage.

    C) Britain should give its colonies independence.

    D) all of these

    E) none of these

Answer: E
Diff: 2

74) Halford Mackinder, developer of the heartland theory, thought that this country was most likely to make a bid for world domination:

    A) Russia

    B) Britain

    C) France

    D) the United States

    E) Japan

Answer: A
Diff: 1

75) Fidel Castro

    A) was quickly removed from power by the United States.

    B) was initially hostile to the United States and the West.

    C) still receives large amounts of foreign aid from Russia.

    D) has spent more years in power than any four American presidents put together.

    E) was briefly a professional football player in the United States.

    Answer: D
    Diff: 2

76) The domino theory

    A) was rejected by President Eisenhower, a former general.

    B) was the rationale behind stopping the spread of communism.

    C) was applied to Greece and Turkey, but not to Berlin.

    D) was confined to the Eurasian landmass.

    E) The domino theory was all of the above.

    Answer: B
    Diff: 1

77) Which of the following countries is NOT a member of the United Nations Security Council?

    A) Japan   B) Britain   C) China   D) Russia   E) France

    Answer: A
    Diff: 2

78) Which of the following organizations demphasizes the importance of individual states?

    A) North American Free Trade Agreement

    B) Organization of Petroleum Exporting Countries

    C) European Union

    D) Organization for Economic Cooperation and Development

    E) Association of Southeast Asian Nations

    Answer: C
    Diff: 2

79) The process of determining the boundaries of districts for the purpose of electing political officials is called

    A) reapportionment.   B) gerrymandering.

    C) redistricting.   D) confabulation.

    Answer: C
    Diff: 1

80) This was NOT an independent country in 1989:

    A) Poland   B) Hungary   C) Slovakia   D) Bulgaria   E) Austria

Answer: C
Diff: 2

81) The Alps form Italy's boundary with all of the following countries, except

    A) Greece.   B) France.   C) Austria.   D) Switzerland.

Answer: A
Diff: 1

82) In 2005, this was still formally a part of Yugoslavia along with Serbia:

    A) Macedonia

    B) Slovenia

    C) Croatia

    D) Bosnia

    E) Montenegro

Answer: E
Diff: 2

83) This part of the former Yugoslavia has seen the least amount of fighting:

    A) Kosovo   B) Bosnia   C) Croatia   D) Slovenia

Answer: D
Diff: 2

84) Which country was most involved in the colonization of South America?

    A) Portugal

    B) Britain

    C) Holland

    D) Spain

    E) the United States

Answer: D
Diff: 1

9.3 True or False

1) Borders between countries are always exclusionary.

Answer: FALSE
Diff: 2

2) Decolonization marks the end of core domination of the periphery.

Answer: FALSE
Diff: 2

3) Among other things, boundaries help eliminate stereotypes.

Answer: FALSE
Diff: 3

4) Straight–line boundaries between states suggest that the boundary was based on natural features, such as rivers or mountains.

Answer: FALSE
Diff: 2

5) The basic area units of analysis in human geography for comparing statistics are *de jure* territories.

Answer: TRUE
Diff: 1

6) The boundaries of most countries of the world describe *de jure* spaces.

Answer: TRUE
Diff: 1

7) Kurds living outside of Kurdistan are still part of the Kurdish nation.

Answer: TRUE
Diff: 3

8) Nationalists believe that the nation to which they belong has a right to determine its own affairs.

Answer: TRUE
Diff: 2

9) Most countries of the world are simultaneously multinational and nation–states.

Answer: FALSE
Diff: 2

10) The township and range system underlies the shape of counties and states west of the Mississippi.

Answer: TRUE
Diff: 2

11) In both federal and unitary states, power is dispersed throughout the country.

Answer: FALSE
Diff: 1

12) To hold multinational states together, governments search for centripetal policies to counter centrifugal forces.

Answer: TRUE
Diff: 2

13) Historically, geographers have played a significant role in imperialism and colonialism by aiding in exploration and resource development.

Answer: TRUE
Diff: 1

14) The United States was an influential member of the League of Nations.

Answer: FALSE
Diff: 2

15) The Arab–Israeli conflict goes back to the time of Jesus and the Romans.

Answer: FALSE
Diff: 2

16) The root cause of the Arab–Israeli conflict is the fundamental differences between Islam and Judaism.

Answer: FALSE
Diff: 2

17) Gerrymandering is a political tool for ensuring an equitable balance between territory and political representation.

Answer: FALSE
Diff: 2

18) Despite efforts to end the practice, gerrymandering in the U.S. continues through the present.

Answer: TRUE
Diff: 2

19) Inclusionary boundaries tend to be more permeable than exclusionary boundaries.

Answer: TRUE
Diff: 3

20) People of different nations can be citizens of the same state, but citizens of different states cannot be of the same nation.

Answer: FALSE
Diff: 3

21) Neocolonial relationships exist only between former colonies and their former colonizers.

Answer: FALSE
Diff: 3

22) Early geographical expeditions from Europe were used to evaluate the potential for imperialism and colonialism.

Answer: TRUE
Diff: 2

23) Ratzel's model of geopolitics has the State acting like a biological organism.

Answer: TRUE
Diff: 2

24) Boundaries tend to eliminate spatial differentiation.

Answer: FALSE
Diff: 2

25) Nationalism is currently confined to a relatively small area of the globe.

Answer: FALSE
Diff: 1

26) Stalin extended Lenin's policy of federal government in the USSR.

Answer: FALSE
Diff: 2

27) The Commonwealth of Independent States formed primarily for economic reasons.

Answer: TRUE
Diff: 2

28) Ironically, India's violent war of independence has been followed by a peaceful postcolonial history.

Answer: FALSE
Diff: 1

29) When partitioning Africa, the European colonial powers generally attempted to respect pre-existing political affiliations and alliances.

Answer: FALSE
Diff: 1

30) The heartland theory recognizes North America as the world's "heartland."

Answer: FALSE
Diff: 1

31) The Bay of Pigs invasion helped turn Castro toward the Soviet Union.

Answer: TRUE
Diff: 1

32) The European Union retains economic barriers between member countries.

Answer: FALSE
Diff: 3

33) Most citizens of the United States are affected by three or more levels of government.

Answer: TRUE
Diff: 2

34) Gerrymandering, while common prior to 1900, is no longer an issue today.

Answer: FALSE
Diff: 1

35) Natural barriers are often based on formal boundaries.

Answer: FALSE
Diff: 2

36) By definition, *de jure* spaces do not have formal boundaries.

Answer: FALSE
Diff: 1

37) The United Nations currently recognizes over 65 nearly "pure" nation-states.

Answer: FALSE
Diff: 1

38) Russian expansion did not become significant until the seventeenth century.

Answer: FALSE
Diff: 2

39) Lenin sought to suppress all nationalist feelings within the Soviet Union.

Answer: FALSE
Diff: 2

40) Once colonization has begun, the periphery becomes a market for goods from the core.

Answer: TRUE
Diff: 2

41) The domino theory held that a certain amount of communist expansion was tolerable, but it should not be allowed to go too far.

Answer: FALSE
Diff: 1

9.4 Matching

ACRONYMS: Match the acronym to its organization or the example.

1) group of 11 energy rich developing countries
   Diff: 2

2) United States and its major trade partners
   Diff: 2

3) organization of former Soviet countries
   Diff: 2

4) rebel group from the Mexican state of Chiapas
   Diff: 2

5) Military alliance emerging from Cold War tensions
   Diff: 2

6) 15 member supranational organization established with the Maastricht Treaty, 1993
   Diff: 2

7) The unitary state of 15 Soviet republics ruled from Moscow
   Diff: 2

8) group trying to free Northern Ireland of British Rule
   Diff: 2

9) organized in 1964 to resist Israeli occupation of Palestine
   Diff: 2

10) action of neighborhood residents to unwanted land uses in their vicinity
   Diff: 2

A) NIMBY

B) EZLN

C) EU

D) PLO

E) USSR

F) IRA

G) CIS

H) UN

I) OPEC

J) NAFTA

K) NATO

11) League of Nations served as
   its model
   Diff: 2

1) I	2) J	3) G	4) B	5) K	6) C
7) E	8) F	9) D	10) A	11) H	

POLITICS OF GEOGRAPHY: Match the term to the example.

12) dedication of Texans to Texas
   (over the rest of the country)
   Diff: 3

    A) regionalism

    B) sectionalism

13) devotion of U.S. westerners to
   ranching as a way of life
   Diff: 3

14) strong commitment to
   suburban needs over urban
   problems
   Diff: 3

15) NIMBYism
   Diff: 3

16) Frency Quebecois and
   Scottish separatism
   Diff: 3

17) place competition to attract
   corporate investment
   Diff: 3

12) A	13) B	14) B	15) B	16) A	17) A

9.5 Map Identification

World Map

1) Israel shares a border with

    A) Russia.

    B) Pakistan.

    C) Afghanistan.

    D) Algeria.

    E) Syria.

Answer: E
Diff: 2

2) The Baltics include all the following except

    A) Estonia.

    B) Norway.

    C) Latvia.

    D) Lithuania.

    E) The Baltic states include all of the above.

Answer: B
Diff: 2

3) Which of the following is the largest country in terms of area?

    A) Lithuania   B) Latvia   C) Estonia   D) Algeria   E) Israel

Answer: D
Diff: 2

4) The country of Algeria is identified by the number

    A) 26.   B) 27.   C) 28.   D) 23.   E) 65.

Answer: A
Diff: 1

5) Damascus is the capital of

    A) Afghanistan.

    B) Syria.

    C) Lebanon.

    D) Jordan.

    E) Egypt.

Answer: B
Diff: 1

6) The capital of country #59 is

    A) Kabul.

    B) Baghdad.

    C) Riyadh.

    D) Kampala.

    E) Kathmandu.

Answer: A
Diff: 1

7) Which of the following is the capital of #51?

    A) Tel Aviv   B) Tehran   C) Tallinn   D) Taipei   E) Algiers

Answer: A
Diff: 1

8) Which pair of countries share a continent?

   A) Latvia & Lithuania

   B) Afghanistan & Algeria

   C) Norway & Nicaragua

   D) Taiwan & Tanazania

   E) Israel & England

Answer: A
Diff: 2

9) Which pair of countries does NOT share a continent?

   A) Estonia & Lithuania

   B) Afghanistan & Syria

   C) Israel & Afghanistan

   D) Afghanistan & Algeria

   E) Each of the above pairs share the same continent.

Answer: D
Diff: 2

Europe

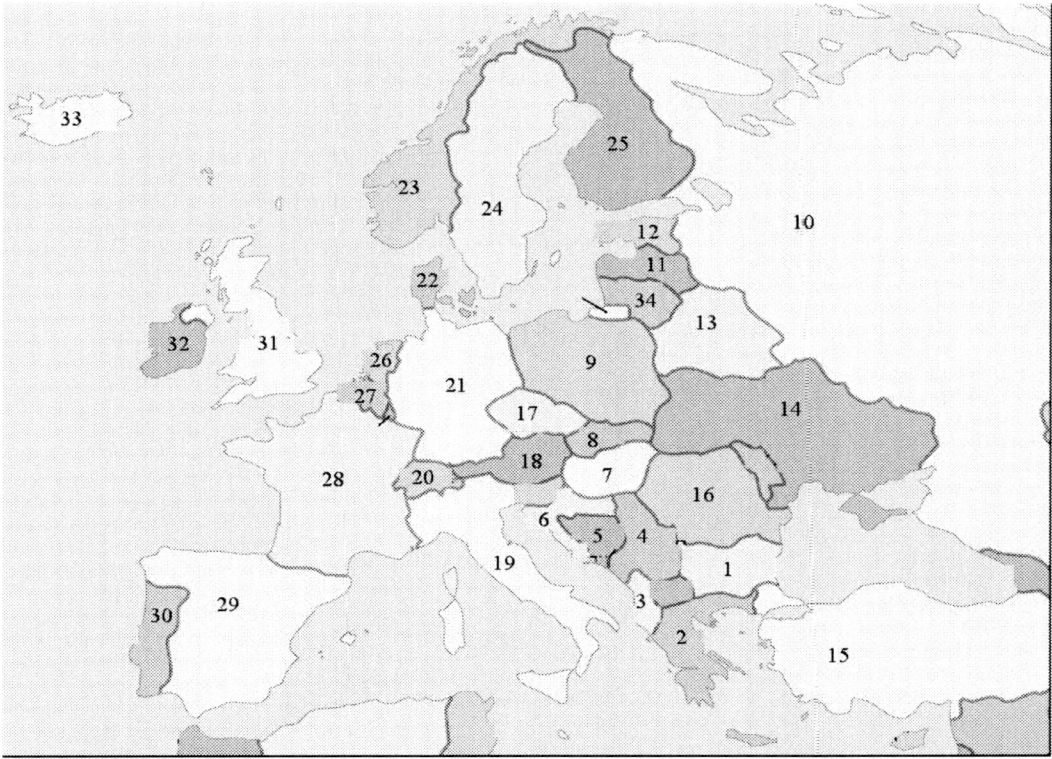

10) Vilnius is the capital of the country labeled with which number?

    A) 9   B) 11   C) 12   D) 13   E) 34

Answer: E
Diff: 1

11) The countries of which two capitals share a border?

    A) Riga & Vilnius

    B) Vilnius & Tallinn

    C) Tallinn & Tel Aviv

    D) Vilnius & Moscow

    E) Oslo & Vilnius

Answer: C
Diff: 2

12) The capital of Latvia is

   A) Tallinn.

   B) Vilnius.

   C) Riga.

   D) Helsinki.

   E) Budapest.

Answer: C
Diff: 1

Chapter 10 Urbanization

10.1 Minimal Choice

1) The world's oldest cities are in today's

    A) periphery countries.   B) core countries.

    Answer: A
    Diff: 3

2) Manchester, England and Chicago, USA are both examples of

    A) shock cities.   B) ecclesiastical cities.

    Answer: A
    Diff: 2

3) Shock cities emerged with

    A) industrialization.   B) colonialism.

    Answer: A
    Diff: 3

4) Istanbul (and Constantinople before that) is situated on a relatively narrow land bridge connecting Europe and Asia. Thus, it seems most likely to be a

    A) gateway city.   B) colonial city

    Answer: A
    Diff: 3

5) According to central place theory,

    A) small settlements are closely spaced.

    B) people travel far for inexpensive things.

    Answer: A
    Diff: 2

6) The urban system of the United States is best characterized as a

    A) functional hierarchy.   B) primate system.

    Answer: A
    Diff: 2

7) _____ are good examples of primate cities.

   A) Paris and London
          B) New York City and Toronto

Answer: A
Diff: 2

8) The most urbanized continent in the world is

   A) North America.
          B) Asia.

Answer: A
Diff: 1

9) Which country has more people living in urban areas?

   A) China
          B) United States

Answer: A
Diff: 2

10) A country with a high level of urbanization means that

   A) many people live in cities.
          B) much of the area is urban.

Answer: A
Diff: 1

11) Many of the largest cities in the world's periphery will double in the next _____ years.

   A) 10-20
          B) 1-2

Answer: A
Diff: 2

12) _____ is generally considered a first-tier World City.

   A) Brussels, Belgium
          B) Miami, USA

Answer: A
Diff: 1

13) Natural disasters, environmental degradation and civil war have made Malawi (in East Africa) the world's

   A) fastest-urbanizing country.
          B) least-urbanized country.

Answer: A
Diff: 1

14) About 60% of the urban population in the world's periphery is attributable to

   A) natural increase.
          B) net in-migration.

Answer: A
Diff: 1

15) Squatter settlements are an outcome of

    A) overurbanization.   B) counterurbanization.

Answer: A
Diff: 2

16) In the United States, new immigrants and baby boomers are driving

    A) reurbanization.   B) splintering urbanism.

Answer: A
Diff: 2

17) According to the rank size rule, the largest city in an urban system should have _____ people if the fourth largest city had 1 million.

    A) 4 million   B) 2 million

Answer: A
Diff: 3

10.2 Multiple Choice

1) By the mid–nineteenth century, Manchester, England was one of the world's leading industrial centers, built around the manufacture and export of

    A) cotton textiles.

    B) steel and trains.

    C) luxury food items like sugar and tea.

    D) steam and diesel engines.

    E) kitchen ware.

Answer: A
Diff: 1

2) Primate cities are found in the world's

    A) core countries.

    B) peripheral countries.

    C) core and peripheral countries, both.

    D) North.

    E) South.

Answer: C
Diff: 2

3) The urban system of which country is NOT centered around a primate city?

    A) United States

    B) England

    C) France

    D) Mexico

    E) Argentina

Answer: A
Diff: 2

4) According to statistics compiled by the United Nations, about _____ of the world's population today lives in cities.

    A) 25%   B) 50%   C) 75%   D) 100%

Answer: B
Diff: 1

5) North America is about 75% urbanized. This mean that about 75% of North American

    A) cities contain 1 million or more people.

    B) people live in cities.

    C) territory is covered with urban structures like streets and commercial buildings.

    D) resources are used in cities.

    E) places are cities.

Answer: B
Diff: 2

6) The very first region of independent urbanism was in

    A) the Middle East.

    B) the Baltics.

    C) the Andes.

    D) the Pearl River Delta.

    E) Europe's industrial core.

Answer: A
Diff: 2

7) The urbanized economies of a number of a number of early empires (Mesopotamian, Mayan, Roman) collapsed because of

   A) labor shortages.

   B) mismanagement.

   C) changing trade routes.

   D) imperialism.

   E) technological innovations.

   Answer: A
   Diff: 2

8) The specific roles of prominent urban settlements of medieval Europe include all of the following *except* the role of

   A) ecclesiastical center.

   B) administrative center.

   C) center of eduction.

   D) defensive stronghold.

   E) agricultural center.

   Answer: E
   Diff: 1

9) In contrast to sixteenth century Spanish colonizers that established military and administrative centers in the New World, Portuguese colonizers situated cities to

   A) facilitate trade and commerce.

   B) convert locals to Christianity.

   C) replicate European lifestyles.

   D) promote industrial development in the New World.

   E) blend in as well as possible with the local environment and lifestyles.

   Answer: A
   Diff: 2

10) The European cities growing the fastest by the year 1700 were

   A) Atlantic coast cities through which resources from the colonies came.

   B) Mediterranean cities through which Silk Road products flowed.

   C) Southern European cities which retained the Roman trade networks.

   D) Scandinavian cities because of their humane social programs.

   E) country capitals, due to migrant labor from the Middle East & North Africa.

   Answer: A
   Diff: 2

11) Which of the following is not true? Gateway cities

    A) tend to be port cities.

    B) were typically established by Europeans in their colonies.

    C) are control centers providing access into and out of particular countries or regions.

    D) have become the urban centers of the world's core.

    E) funneled mineral and agricultural resources from continental interiors to Europe.

Answer: D
Diff: 2

12) Geographers are interested in urbanism as a

    A) form of religion drawing people to urban settlements.

    B) way of life that emerges in urban settings.

    C) way of distinguishing refined and polite society from people of popular culture.

    D) taxonomy by which cities in urban systems are categorized.

    E) form of counter urbanization.

Answer: B
Diff: 2

13) Manchester, England and Chicago, USA are both good examples of

    A) shock cities.

    B) gateway cities.

    C) megacities.

    D) colonial cities.

    E) informal cities.

Answer: A
Diff: 1

14) By the late eighteenth century and the Industrial Revolution, cities of Europe began to grow with rural to urban migration and

    A) rising birth rates.

    B) falling death rates.

    C) importation of slaves.

    D) migration from Asia.

    E) all of the above

Answer: B
Diff: 2

15) Chicago's explosive population growth of the late nineteenth century was due to industrialization and its excellent

    A) geographic situation.

    B) natural resources.

    C) educational system.

    D) political leadership.

    E) social programs.

Answer: A
Diff: 2

16) Urbanization in the world's core was stimulated by increased agricultural productivity that

    A) provided surplus rural labor for urban industrialization.

    B) provided food for the growing urban populations.

    C) benefitted from improved tools and machinery manufactured in industrial areas.

    D) contributed all of the above.

Answer: D
Diff: 2

17) Colonial planning and construction of colonial cities was based on

    A) European concepts and practices.

    B) local environments and climate.

    C) local cultures and preferences.

    D) capitalist democratic principles.

    E) building up local political and economic capacities.

Answer: A
Diff: 2

18) The interdependent relationship between cities and settlements of different sizes and functions within a given region is known as (an)

    A) urbanization.

    B) urbanism.

    C) urban ecology.

    D) urban system.

    E) urban form.

Answer: D
Diff: 1

19) Central place theory explains the relative size and spacing of urban centers based on

   A) markets & consumer behavior.

   B) government planning.

   C) cultural differences.

   D) natural resources.

   E) urban ecology.

Answer: A
Diff: 1

20) In the context of urban systems, basic tenets of central place theory include all of the following *except*

   A) people will travel farther for more expensive, less frequently purchased goods.

   B) the smallest settlements provide goods and services that meet everyday needs.

   C) the larger the settlement, the greater the variety of specialized goods and services.

   D) settlements of similar population sizes are grouped together.

   E) the larger the settlement, the farther apart it will be from others of a similar size.

Answer: D
Diff: 2

21) The Spanish urban system is dominated by

   A) two cities of national scope (Madrid and Barcelona).

   B) coastal cities (Bilbao, Valencia, Malaga).

   C) the European Union.

   D) Basque nationalists.

   E) cities built around tourism and leisure activities.

Answer: A
Diff: 2

22) The two largest cities in the U.S. are New York City and Los Angeles. The 2000 Census provides evidence to suggest that cities in the United States tend to follow the rank–size rule. Thus, the actual populations for NYC and LA are, in order,

   A) 8 and 12.3 million.

   B) 8 and 8 million.

   C) 8 and 7.2 million.

   D) 8 and 3.7 million.

   E) 8 and 1 million.

Answer: D
Diff: 3

23) The functional dominance (cultural, economic, political) of a city within an urban system is known as

    A) centrality.

    B) primacy.

    C) overurbanization.

    D) reurbanization.

    E) urban imperialism.

Answer: A
Diff: 1

24) Today's world cities are distinguished by being centers of all of the following *except*

    A) international NGO and IGO headquarters.

    B) major corporate headquarters.

    C) world's most powerful media organizations.

    D) specialized and advanced business services.

    E) industrial production for global mass consumption.

Answer: E
Diff: 2

25) The definition of urban used by the United Nations

    A) is 1,000 people.

    B) is 2,000 people.

    C) is 10,000 people.

    D) is 50,000 people.

    E) varies by country.

Answer: E
Diff: 2

26) According to our text, urban growth in peripheral countries is a consequence of migration to cities, stimulated, largely, by the onset of

    A) war.

    B) drought and famine.

    C) the demographic transition.

    D) pollution and disease.

    E) structural adjustment programs.

Answer: C
Diff: 2

27) The doubling time of some of the world periphery's largest, fastest growing cities is

   A) 6 months.   B) 10 years.   C) 50 years.   D) 100 years.

   Answer: B
   Diff: 2

28) *Gecekondus* (Turkey), *favelas* (Brazil), *gourbevilles* (North Africa) and *bustees* (India) all refer to urban

   A) squatter settlements.

   B) market places.

   C) open spaces.

   D) high rent neighborhoods.

   E) transportation networks.

   Answer: A
   Diff: 1

29) _____ is when cities grow faster than their ability to provide jobs, housing and other basic needs.

   A) Overurbanization

   B) Decentralization

   C) Megacities

   D) Deindustrialization

   E) Counterurbanization

   Answer: A
   Diff: 1

30) Squatter settlements refer to residential housing

   A) serving as transitional housing for recent immigrants to the city.

   B) that takes place beyond the city limits.

   C) on land neither owned or rented by its occupants.

   D) in massive, multi-story, government-supported apartment blocks.

   E) that emerges with reurbanization.

   Answer: A
   Diff: 1

31) Megacities are determined by all of the following except their

A) primacy.   B) centrality.

C) size.   D) status as world city.

Answer: D
Diff: 1

32) In the 1970s and 1980s, the United States entered a period of _____, during which time there was a net loss of population from big cities to smaller towns and rural areas.

A) counterurbanization

B) reurbanization

C) overurbanization

D) splintering urbanism

E) urbanism

Answer: A
Diff: 2

33) Splintering urbanism refers to the increasing separation of the fast and slow worlds, where

A) enclaves of the rich and super connected have more in common with each other across the globe than with the majority of people in their own cities.

B) the informal and formal sectors of the economy fragment and realign.

C) urban systems begin to reflect a hierarchy based on wealth rather than size.

D) central place theory is replaced by peripheral place theory.

E) primate cities break up into smaller cities and adhere to the rank size rule.

Answer: A
Diff: 2

34) Given that urban populations are growing at twice the general population growth-rate, it is likely that

A) urban areas have low unemployment.

B) urban areas have adequate housing.

C) there is a net movement of people from rural areas to urban areas.

D) people live better lives in urban areas than in rural areas.

Answer: C
Diff: 3

35) The world's megacities are

  A) hold half of the world's population.

  B) are declining in population.

  C) more populated than half of the nearly 200 hundred countries in the United Nations.

  D) follow the rank–size rule.

  E) are gateway cities.

Answer: C
Diff: 3

36) Urban settlements

  A) facilitate decision–making by public policymakers and private institutions.

  B) increase the efficiency of economic activities.

  C) increase the range of lifestyle choices of inhabitants.

  D) generate innovation and the development of new knowledge.

  E) do all of the above.

Answer: E
Diff: 1

37) Urban geographers are quite interested in

  A) how the identities of urban areas evolve.

  B) relationships between urban areas and surrounding territory.

  C) land–use within urban areas.

  D) all of the above.

Answer: D
Diff: 1

38) An _____ is an interdependent group of urban settlements in a given region.

  A) urban system   B) urban form   C) urban ecology   D) urbanism

Answer: A
Diff: 1

39) The physical structure and organization of cities is termed

  A) urbanism.   B) urban form.   C) urban ecology.   D) urban system.

Answer: B
Diff: 1

40) Greek colonization was centered around

    A) the Aegean Sea.

    B) the Mediterranean Sea.

    C) the Black Sea.

    D) the Red Sea.

    E) the mouth of the Nile River.

Answer: A
Diff: 1

41) The feudal system in early medieval Europe was characterized by

    A) estates that were relatively self-sufficient.

    B) highly developed and widely distributed urban areas.

    C) a general lack of warfare.

    D) strong central governments that ruled large areas.

Answer: A
Diff: 2

42) By 1400, long-distance trading in Europe

    A) dealt primarily with luxury goods.

    B) dealt primarily with energy resources.

    C) was dominated by Paris.

    D) centered on port cities.

    E) was minimal compared to trade with China and Spanish colonies.

Answer: D
Diff: 2

43) Which of the following changes occurred between the fifteenth and seventeenth centuries that eventually led to the growth of urban areas in Europe and its colonies?

    A) the Protestant Reformation   B) the Scientific Revolution

    C) an increase in merchant capitalism   D) all of these

Answer: D
Diff: 1

44) Spanish colonial towns were established primarily to

    A) spread Catholicism to the natives.

    B) serve as administrative and military centers.

    C) provide education to the natives.

    D) exploit nearby natural resources.

Answer: B
Diff: 2

45) During the Renaissance in Europe, these urban areas grew the fastest:

    A) towns where French was the dominant language

    B) port cities

    C) cities in the interior of France and the German states

    D) cities in Russia

Answer: B
Diff: 2

46) Most gateway cities were

    A) ports.

    B) located primarily in northern Germany and Scandinavia.

    C) controlled by native elites.

    D) in existence for at least a millennium.

Answer: A
Diff: 2

47) The growth of cities in the nineteenth century was most closely linked with the

    A) increased power of states.

    B) increased size of states.

    C) increased importance of industrialization.

    D) decreased output of agriculture in rural areas.

    E) increased amount of social services available in cities.

Answer: C
Diff: 2

48) Which of these factors was a significant cause of nineteenth-century urbanization in Europe?

    A) drops in death rates   B) increase in labor supply

    C) higher wages in urban areas   D) all of these

Answer: D
Diff: 1

49) This city was the shock city of European industrialization in the nineteenth century:

    A) Venice, Italy

    B) Manchester, England

    C) Paris

    D) Berlin

    E) London

Answer: B
Diff: 1

50) The most important reason for Chicago's emergence and large size is

    A) religious.   B) military.   C) political.   D) industrial.

Answer: D
Diff: 1

51) Which region has the largest percentage of its population living in urban regions?

    A) North America

    B) Latin America

    C) Europe

    D) Asia

    E) Africa

Answer: A
Diff: 1

52) Rapid urbanization is greatest in which of the following areas?

    A) Africa

    B) western Europe

    C) China

    D) South America

    E) India

Answer: C
Diff: 2

53) For decades since the middle of the twentieth century, rural Chinese stayed in rural areas primarily because

    A) of religious reasons.

    B) they needed to stay there to take care of their elders.

    C) they were obligated to stay under a centuries–old feudal system.

    D) the government forced them to stay.

Answer: D
Diff: 2

54) Reasons for urban growth in peripheral countries include

    A) population shifts caused by war.   B) deforestation in rural areas.

    C) desertification in rural areas.   D) all of these

Answer: D
Diff: 1

55) Central place theory holds that the size and spacing of urban areas is a function of

    A) government planning.

    B) historical development of religious centers.

    C) where people go to purchase goods and services.

    D) the specific types of economic activity in the overall area studied.

Answer: C
Diff: 1

56) People would most likely travel the farthest to

    A) buy bread and milk.

    B) see a professional sports event.

    C) get a haircut.

    D) get the car's engine oil changed.

    E) purchase a New York Times bestseller.

Answer: B
Diff: 2

57) Which of the following goods and services has the highest threshold?

    A) hospital

    B) beauty salon

    C) supermarket

    D) restaurant

    E) drug store

Answer: A
Diff: 1

58) Which of the following American cities is NOT a world city?

    A) Los Angeles   B) Boston

    C) Chicago   D) New York City

Answer: B
Diff: 1

59) Following the rank-size rule, if the population of the largest city in a country or region is 1 million, the fourth-largest city should contain about this many people:

    A) 500,000   B) 400,000   C) 250,000   D) 133,000   E) 100,000

Answer: C
Diff: 3

60) Primacy

    A) occurs only in core countries.

    B) occurs only in peripheral countries.

    C) occurs in both core and peripheral countries.

    D) occurs only in semi-peripheral countries.

Answer: C
Diff: 1

61) World cities

    A) did not exist until the twentieth century.

    B) were initially intimately involved with imperialism and colonialism.

    C) typically do not change in influence over time.

    D) are none of the above

Answer: B
Diff: 1

62) The most important functions of world cities have to do with

    A) economic functions.

    B) dissemination of global culture.

    C) international politics and diplomacy.

    D) the influential media they host.

    E) the nongovernmental organizations headquartered in them.

Answer: A
Diff: 2

63) Which of the following is NOT a top-tier world city?

    A) Los Angeles   B) New York   C) London   D) Tokyo

Answer: A
Diff: 1

64) Increased agricultural productivity in the nineteenth century

    A) freed up rural labor for urban factories.

    B) provided the food to feed the swelling urban population.

    C) was fueled in part by tools and machinery provided by urban factories.

    D) all of the above

Answer: D
Diff: 1

65) Counterurbanization

    A) results in a much slower increase in population growth for cities.

    B) is due in part to agglomeration economies.

    C) is due in part to the increased accessibility of smaller towns and rural areas.

    D) has been successful at shrinking the size of the world's megacities.

Answer: C
Diff: 1

66) Urban growth in peripheral countries

    A) often occurs at a rapid rate.

    B) can lead to overurbanization.

    C) usually is far in advance of industrial development in urban areas.

    D) Urban growth involves all of the above

Answer: D
Diff: 1

67) By A.D. 1000, a city-based world empire had not yet occurred in

    A) Europe.   B) North America.

    C) the Middle East.   D) China.

    Answer: B
    Diff: 1

68) Of the following regions, which is least urbanized?

    A) Africa

    B) Asia

    C) Latin America

    D) Europe

    E) North America

    Answer: A
    Diff: 1

69) In 2010 it is projected that the largest city will be in

    A) North America.

    B) Europe.

    C) Latin America.

    D) Africa.

    E) Asia.

    Answer: E
    Diff: 2

10.3 True or False

1) According to the UNCHS, technological and industrial innovations now make the urbanization process reversible.

    Answer: FALSE
    Diff: 2

2) The Gross Domestic Product of some cities is so big that they exceed the GDP of the countries in which they are located.

    Answer: FALSE
    Diff: 2

3) While the urban system of medieval and feudal Europe was struggling to avoid collapse, Baghdad was known as the intellectual center of the world.

    Answer: TRUE
    Diff: 2

4) The new phase of urbanization (fourteenth century) that emerged with the regional trade networks of Northern Italy and the Hanseatic League was based on merchant capitalism.

Answer: TRUE
Diff: 1

5) Gateway cities are thus named because of their function as centers of computer and technology production.

Answer: FALSE
Diff: 1

6) Pure colonial cities are located where colonial administrators can easily keep colonizers separate from the local population.

Answer: FALSE
Diff: 2

7) A basic assumption of central place theory is that people are spread evenly over space.

Answer: TRUE
Diff: 2

8) Primate cities are only found in the core.

Answer: FALSE
Diff: 1

9) The original urban hearths are today's world cities.

Answer: FALSE
Diff: 2

10) The majority of urban population growth in peripheral countries is due to natural increase.

Answer: TRUE
Diff: 1

11) It is not uncommon for well over 50% of the population of major peripheral cities to live in squatter settlements.

Answer: TRUE
Diff: 1

12) A country can be highly urbanized and have a low rate of urbanization.

Answer: TRUE
Diff: 3

13) United Nations reports state that the continued growth of urban populations is essentially irreversible.

Answer: TRUE
Diff: 1

14) For the urban geographer, urban areas are part of both an economy and a society.

Answer: TRUE
Diff: 1

15) After the 11th century, towns grew in size and importance in part because landlords raised taxes on peasants.

Answer: TRUE
Diff: 2

16) Long-distance trading did not become significant until the late eighteenth century.

Answer: FALSE
Diff: 1

17) By definition, a gateway city is located in a core country.

Answer: FALSE
Diff: 1

18) Most urbanization has taken place during the last hundred years.

Answer: TRUE
Diff: 3

19) For the purpose of gathering comparable data, the United Nations has imposed a precise definition of the meaning of urban upon the world's states.

Answer: FALSE
Diff: 2

20) Typically, peripheral countries have a more rapid rate of urbanization than do core countries.

Answer: TRUE
Diff: 1

21) The density of world cities in the United States is lowest in the Southwest and Rocky Mountains area.

Answer: TRUE
Diff: 2

22) The rank-size rule worked well for nineteenth century towns and cities, but it has limited applicability to modern towns and cities.

Answer: FALSE
Diff: 2

23) New York City is a primate city.

Answer: FALSE
Diff: 2

24) World cities appeared at the same time that imperialism and colonialism became significant.

Answer: TRUE
Diff: 2

25) World cities attract businesses in part because of agglomeration effects.

Answer: TRUE
Diff: 2

26) Chicago is a top-tier world city.

Answer: FALSE
Diff: 1

27) An increase in the production of basic functions of a city will typically lead to growth in the city's population.

Answer: TRUE
Diff: 2

28) Most migrants to urban centers in the periphery are drawn by plentiful job opportunities and adequate housing.

Answer: FALSE
Diff: 2

29) Poor migrants make up the bulk of the population growth of frontier towns in the periphery.

Answer: TRUE
Diff: 1

30) Urbanization has made the plight of poor children worse in less-developed countries.

Answer: TRUE
Diff: 1

31) Urbanization first occurred in the Middle East, which triggered urbanization in the other hearth areas of the world.

Answer: FALSE
Diff: 2

32) Urbanization is commonly found in areas where subsistence agriculture is the primary source of food.

Answer: FALSE
Diff: 2

33) Although its economic importance increased during the course of the nineteenth century, Manchester's population size remained relatively constant.

Answer: FALSE
Diff: 1

34) In 1950 seven of the world's ten largest cities were located in core countries. In 2010, eight will be located in the periphery.

Answer: TRUE
Diff: 2

10.4 Matching

URBANIZATION: Match the world region to the characteristic city.

1) counterurbanization
   Diff: 1

2) highest rates of urbanization
   Diff: 1

3) highest levels of urbanization
   Diff: 1

4) site of original urban hearths
   Diff: 1

5) pan regional world cities
   Diff: 1

6) megacities
   Diff: 1

7) gateway cities
   Diff: 1

8) economic urban growth
   Diff: 1

9) demographic urban growth
   Diff: 1

A) peripheral countries

B) core countries

1) B	2) A	3) B	4) A	5) B	6) A
7) A	8) B	9) A			

FUNDAMENTAL URBAN ROLES: Match the description to the function it describes.

10) mobilizing function
Diff: 1

11) decision–making capacity
Diff: 1

12) generative functions
Diff: 1

13) transformative capacity
Diff: 1

A) cities as sites of innovation, knowledge and information

B) sites of social change and alternatives to tradition

C) cities as site of organizing resources, producing and distributing finished products

D) cities as concentrations of political and economic power

10) C   11) D   12) A   13) B

CITY TYPES: Match the type of city to the examples.

14) current world cities
Diff: 2

15) gateway cities
Diff: 2

16) pure colonial cities
Diff: 2

17) shock cities
Diff: 2

18) primate cities
Diff: 2

19) megacities
Diff: 2

20) former world cities
Diff: 2

A) Rio de Janeiro, Accra, Kolkata, Sao Paolo

B) Bombay, Saigon, Jakarta, Manila, Nairobi

C) Beijing, Cairo, Teheran, Lagos, Mexico City

D) New York, London, Hong Kong, Miami, Singapore

E) Manchester, Chicago, Lagos

F) Venice, Antwerp, Lisbon, St. Petersburg

G) London, Paris, Buenos Aires

14) D   15) A   16) B   17) E   18) G   19) C
20) F

10.5 Map Identification

World Map

1) Which of the following is not at least partially in the geographic region of Europe?

    A) Sweden

    B) Belgium

    C) Turkey

    D) Poland

    E) Philippines

Answer: E
Diff: 2

2) Sweden lies only 120 miles -- directly across the Baltic Sea -- from

    A) Belgium.

    B) Poland.

    C) Turkey.

    D) South Korea.

    E) Guatemala.

Answer: B
Diff: 2

3) Which of the following is located entirely on a peninsula?

    A) Guatemala

    B) Belgium

    C) Poland

    D) South Korea

    E) Sweden

Answer: D
Diff: 2

4) The Philippines is identified by the number

    A) 42.   B) 55.   C) 56.   D) 63.   E) 69.

Answer: A
Diff: 1

5) Seoul is the capital of

    A) Sweden.

    B) South Korea.

    C) Belgium.

    D) Turkey.

    E) Philippines.

Answer: B
Diff: 1

6) The capital of country #62 is

    A) Seoul.

    B) Ping Pong.

    C) Ankara.

    D) Guatemala City.

    E) Bangkok.

Answer: A
Diff: 1

7) Ankara is the capital of

    A) 12.   B) 15.   C) 37.   D) 58.   E) 65.

Answer: B
Diff: 1

8) Guatemala and the Philippines have which of the following in common? They both

   A) border the Pacific Ocean.

   B) are islands.

   C) border Mexico.

   D) sit south of the Equator.

   E) belong to the European Union.

   Answer: A
   Diff: 2

9) The capital of country #45 is

   A) Guatemala City.

   B) Manila.

   C) Portabella.

   D) Nutella.

   E) New Della.

   Answer: A
   Diff: 1

10) Which pair of countries share a continent?

   A) Belgium & Poland

   B) South Korea & Sweden

   C) Sweden & the Philippines

   D) Turkey & Guatemala

   E) Guatemala & the Philippines

   Answer: A
   Diff: 2

Europe

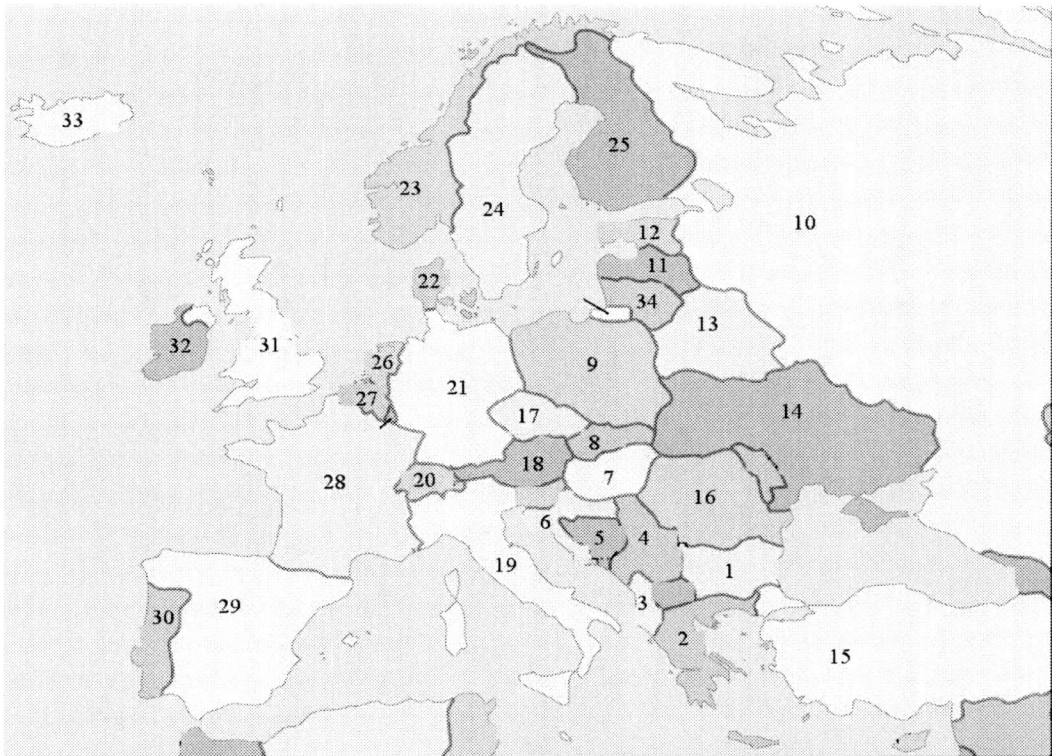

11) Brussels is the capital of the European Union and of the country labeled by number

    A) 23.   B) 24.   C) 25.   D) 26.   E) 27.

Answer: E
Diff: 1

12) Poland is labeled with number

    A) 9.   B) 16.   C) 21.   D) 28.   E) 29.

Answer: A
Diff: 1

13) The capital of country #15 is

    A) Istanbul.

    B) Constantinople.

    C) Ankara.

    D) Manila.

    E) Guatemala City.

Answer: C
Diff: 1

10.6 Chapter 10 Questions with images

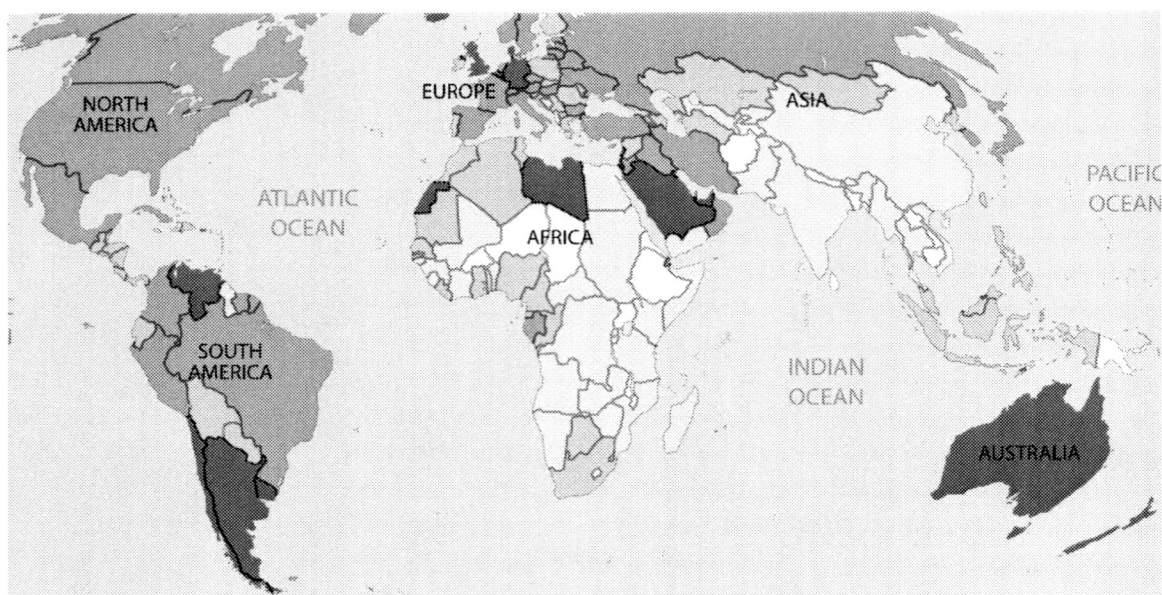

1) The above map shows the percentage of each country's

    A) population that lives in urban settlements.

    B) population that lives in the primate city.

    C) area that is urban.

    D) cities that are shock cities.

    E) cities that are central places.

Answer: A
Diff: 3

Chapter 11 Urban Structure

11.1 Minimal Choice

1) The cost of accessibility is reflected in urban land use patterns. Thus, most _____ are found far from the CBD.

    A) homes and residences   B) big retailers and factories

Answer: A
Diff: 1

2) Discrimination combined with _____ results in segregation.

    A) congregation   B) gentrification

Answer: A
Diff: 1

3) Urban enclaves, ghettos and colonies suggest

    A) segregation.   B) congregation.

Answer: A
Diff: 1

4) Gentrification can be part of the process of

    A) invasion and succession.   B) urban sprawl.

Answer: A
Diff: 3

5) Exploring the internal organization of cities, understanding urban spatial patterns and how & why they emerge, is what it means to examine

    A) urban structure.   B) urban systems.

Answer: A
Diff: 3

6) A city's infrastructure would include its

    A) sewer system.   B) system of government.

Answer: A
Diff: 2

7) _____ occurs when tax revenues aren't able to keep up with increasing costs of urban infrastructure and city services.

    A) A fiscal squeeze   B) Redlining

Answer: A
Diff: 1

8) The low skylines, lively downtowns and neighborhood stability of major European cities can all be linked to the fact that they

    A) are old cities.   B) had to be rebuilt after World War II.

Answer: A
Diff: 3

9) The most dominant feature of the Islamic City is its

    A) principal mosque (*Jami*).   B) citadel (*Kasbah*).

Answer: A
Diff: 1

10) Covered markets, a fortress, narrow & twisting streets, a city wall and a central mosque are features of a classic

    A) Islamic city.   B) peripheral city.

Answer: A
Diff: 1

11) It is estimated that 30–50% of the employed workforce in peripheral cities are actually

    A) underemployed.   B) unemployed.

Answer: A
Diff: 2

12) Which of the following -- according to International Labor Office estimates -- is growing 10 times faster than the other?

    A) informal–sector employment   B) formal–sector employment

Answer: A
Diff: 2

13) Increasingly, city authorities in the periphery are viewing informal housing (eg., squatter settlements) with

    A) tolerance & as rational responses to poverty.

    B) animosity and are eradicating them.

Answer: A
Diff: 2

14) Internal, external and outermost edge cities, traditional downtown and newer business centers, and specialized subcenters are

A) nodes within the polycentric metropolis.

B) slums within unintended metropolises.

Answer: A
Diff: 2

15) Generally, smart growth is designed to

A) curb urban & suburban sprawl.

B) break the cycle of poverty.

Answer: A
Diff: 2

16) Megapolitan regions are

A) functional regions.

B) perceptual regions.

Answer: A
Diff: 2

17) The USA's 10 megapolitan regions cover 20% of the land area and include _____ of the population.

A) 70%

B) 40%

Answer: A
Diff: 2

18) Chateau Regalia, Sydney Coast, Upper East Side, Napa Valley and Vancouver Forest are neighborhoods in the sprawling suburbs of _____ biggest cities.

A) China's

B) Canada's

Answer: A
Diff: 3

19) Many European cities have street plans that date as far back as

A) Roman times.

B) the ancient Greeks.

Answer: A
Diff: 2

11.2 Multiple Choice

1) U.S. suburbanization is associated with all of the following except
   A) high use of automobiles for commuting.
   B) efficient use of space.
   C) white flight.
   D) taking the tax base out of inner cities.
   E) loss of prime agricultural land.

   Answer: B
   Diff: 2

2) On maps like the Washington, DC metro map, the region where most of the subway lines intersect is most probably the
   A) CBD.
   B) zone of transition.
   C) suburbs.
   D) exurbs.
   E) edge cities.

   Answer: A
   Diff: 3

3) As accessibility and utility decline in a concentric zone model of the the city, land use generally changes from
   A) high-volume retailing to residential.   B) residential to warehousing.
   C) factories to high-voluming retailing.   D) warehousing to factories.

   Answer: A
   Diff: 2

4) The urban land use model is sometimes referred to as the trade-off model because all people make a trade-off between accessibility and
   A) living space.
   B) crime.
   C) jobs.
   D) leisure activities.
   E) public transportation.

   Answer: A
   Diff: 2

5) A critical assumption behind the concentric zone model of a city is that it has an isotropic surface, meaning that the city

A) is flat, uniform and barrier free.

B) does not have motorized transportation.

C) only has streets that are parallel and perpendicular to each other.

D) has high buildings in the center which get lower with distance outward.

E) is located on a slope, like a mountain side.

Answer: A
Diff: 2

6) Which of the following is not a specific advantage of congregation to urban minority groups?

A) It helps the minority groups merge with other minority groups.

B) It helps maintain and preserve the culture of the minority groups.

C) It provides mutual support networks for members of the minority group.

D) It helps preserve minority group membership and identity.

E) It provides a power base and a defense in relation to the host society.

Answer: A
Diff: 2

7) Though congregation can be voluntary, segregation is when congregation is combined with

A) discrimination.

B) counterurbanization.

C) immigration.

D) redlining.

E) the fiscal squeeze.

Answer: A
Diff: 2

8) The characteristics by which urban minority groups are typically defined and congregate typically include any of the following *except*

A) race.

B) langauge and religion.

C) nationality.

D) sexual orientation or lifestyle.

E) The characteristics can be any of the above.

Answer: E
Diff: 2

9) In the concentric zone model of cities, the zone of transition typically begins at the dynamic outer edge of a city's

   A) central business district.

   B) factory area.

   C) warehouse district.

   D) residential neighborhoods.

   E) suburban neighborhoods.

   Answer: A
   Diff: 2

10) The classic case study of urban ecology and the example of concentric zones of dynamic neighborhoods of different ethnicity and social status was

   A) Chicago.

   B) London.

   C) New York.

   D) Los Angeles.

   E) Detroit.

   Answer: A
   Diff: 1

11) The rippling process of change throughout a city, whereby displaced social or ethnic groups displace others in residential areas, is known as

   A) invasion and succession.

   B) congregation and segregation.

   C) the cycle of poverty.

   D) smart growth.

   E) socio–spatial formation.

   Answer: A
   Diff: 1

12) Until the last quarter of the twentieth century, the direction of invasion and succession was

   A) outward from the center.

   B) along the various concentric zones or rings.

   C) outward from the suburban districts.

   D) inward from the CBD.

   E) inward from the suburbs.

   Answer: A
   Diff: 2

13) The invasion of older, centrally-located working-class neighborhoods by higher-income professionals in search of character and convenience is called

    A) gentrification.

    B) congregation.

    C) smart growth.

    D) urban ecology.

    E) the fiscal squeeze.

Answer: A
Diff: 2

14) When increased demand for urban services combines with a shrinking tax base (where businesses and and affluent people move out to the suburbs and beyond), central cities around the country struggle with

    A) the fiscal squeeze.

    B) urban sprawl.

    C) invasion and succession.

    D) isotopic surfaces.

    E) how to fill ecological niches.

Answer: A
Diff: 1

15) The fiscal squeeze has made it extremely difficult for central cities to address a wide variety of urban problems. Which of the following is not directly one of such problems faced by central cities?

    A) urban sprawl

    B) poverty

    C) neighborhood decay

    D) infrastructure decay

    E) overcrowding

Answer: A
Diff: 3

16) By making loans unattainable to people in certain neighborhoods, the practice of _____ compounds the difficulty in achieving inner city improvements.

   A) microlending

   B) gentrification

   C) redlining

   D) postmodernism

   E) fiscal squeezing

Answer: C
Diff: 1

17) Redlining is, most specifically, a form of

   A) gender poverty.

   B) housing discrimination.

   C) gentrification.

   D) ethnic succession.

   E) fiscal squeezing.

Answer: B
Diff: 2

18) In the summer of 2001, the President of the United States signed tax cuts totalling $1.35 trillion. According to figures provided by the American Society of Civil Engineers in 2005, this was nearly enough to

   A) bring the country's infrastructure up to acceptable standards.

   B) eliminate homelessness.

   C) eliminate smog.

   D) create 20 new cities in in the American heartland.

   E) establish new subway systems in San Francisco, Detroit and New Orleans.

Answer: A
Diff: 3

19) European cities are different from North American cities largely because European cities

   A) have long histories of numerous periods of urban development.

   B) did not grow according to competitive land markets.

   C) do not suffer from problems of infrastructure decay and poverty.

   D) have almost no ethnic congregation and segregation.

   E) European cities differ from North American cities according to all of the above.

Answer: A
Diff: 2

20) Which of the following is not true? Compared to U.S. cities, European cities

    A) are more compact.

    B) have lower skylines.

    C) usually have central squares and marketplaces.

    D) have lower population densities.

    E) are more socioeconomically stable.

Answer: D
Diff: 2

21) The Bueax Arts style of architecture was

    A) used in the urban redevelopment and planning of Paris in the nineteenth century.

    B) the name given by European orientalists for the architecture of the Islamic city.

    C) the unique style of construction used in New Orleans to withstand flooding.

    D) what has made Quebec City a UNESCO World Heritage site.

    E) a replication of classical Greek and Roman styles of architecture.

Answer: A
Diff: 2

22) The Modern movement of the early twentieth century was based on the idea that cities should be designed and run like

    A) machines.

    B) biological organisms.

    C) corporations.

    D) ant colonies.

    E) democracies.

Answer: A
Diff: 2

23) The most compelling feature of the International Style of urban design and architecture was that it was quite

    A) inexpensive.

    B) artistic.

    C) environmental.

    D) energy efficient.

    E) culturally sensitive.

Answer: A
Diff: 2

24) The tradition of urban design that has imposed more uniformity on the big cities of the world than any other is

  A) the Beaux Arts style.

  B) the Modern movement.

  C) the International Style.

  D) the Global Village style.

  E) McDonaldization.

Answer: C
Diff: 1

25) The best example of where environmental responses and social and cultural values are integrated into urban form and design is found in the

  A) Modern movement.

  B) Islamic city.

  C) North American city.

  D) International Stye.

  E) boomburbs.

Answer: B
Diff: 2

26) Of the following, which is not among the fundamentals of urban layout and design that stem from the Holy Qur'an and that guide development of traditional Islamic cities?

  A) emphasis on personal privacy and virtue

  B) communal well–being

  C) the inner essence of things

  D) the outer appearance of things

Answer: D
Diff: 2

27) *Suqs, kasbahs, jamis* and *medinas* are typically found in

  A) Islamic cities.

  B) West European cities.

  C) East European cities.

  D) cities designed by Le Corbusier.

  E) Postmodern cities.

Answer: A
Diff: 1

28) The stark contrast of high-rise modern office buildings and luxury housing with the slums and shantytowns of unintended metropolises is visual evidence of their

    A) dualism.

    B) multiculturalism.

    C) gentrification.

    D) economic development.

    E) isotropism.

Answer: A
Diff: 1

29) The informal economies of peripheral cities

    A) often benefit consumers in the core.

    B) mainly involved illegal activities such as drug and gun smuggling, prostitution and gambling.

    C) rarely involved children.

    D) is quite small compared to the formal economy of peripheral cities.

    E) has significantly declined over the last couple of decades.

Answer: A
Diff: 2

30) Contributing to the unprecedented population growth that has made Lagos, Nigeria a shock city are all of the following *except*

    A) replacement of informal economic activities with high-paying, formal jobs.

    B) the discovery of oil.

    C) the demographic transition.

    D) political independence.

Answer: A
Diff: 2

31) Shantytowns and squatter housing are growing in the unintended metropolises of the periphery due to

    A) poverty and the lack of affordable housing.

    B) the lack of engineers and developers with the skills to build homes.

    C) environmental conditions that make permanent housing difficult to build.

    D) misleading advertising.

    E) inavailability of construction materials.

Answer: A
Diff: 2

32) Environmental degradation in peripheral cities is largely the result of

   A) inadequate infrastructure to handle sewage.

   B) the accumulation of human wastes.

   C) the dumping of industrial wastes.

   D) industrial and automobile air emissions.

   E) all of the above

Answer: E
Diff: 2

33) The decentralized commercial and office districts that have emerged on the fringes of metropolitan areas near such features as freeway interchanges and airports have been called

   A) edge cities.

   B) 100-mile cities.

   C) polycentric metropolises.

   D) boomburbs.

   E) all of the above

Answer: A
Diff: 1

34) Splintering urbanism is linked to

   A) the galactic metropolis.

   B) edge cities.

   C) polycentric metropolises.

   D) suburban sprawl.

   E) all of the above

Answer: E
Diff: 1

35) Attempts to limit suburban sprawl through smart growth are based on efforts to

   A) preserve open spaces on the fringe and redevelop the inner metropolitan regions.

   B) stop all economic development.

   C) package landscapes.

   D) encourage out-migration to other metropolitan regions.

   E) expand the highway system and increase reliance on private automobiles.

Answer: A
Diff: 2

36) Suburbs are no longer just bedroom neighborhoods of workers commuting to traditional downtowns. They now include _____, the sprawling, fast-growing, low density, auto-dependent suburban cities found mostly in California and the U.S. Southwest.

A) boomburbs

B) sonic cities

C) 100-mile cities

D) generica

E) repliburbs

Answer: A
Diff: 2

37) As a deliberate reaction to Modernism, Postmodern urban design emphasizes

A) diversity and consumption.

B) the future.

C) smart growth.

D) functionality and practicality.

E) conservation and sustainability.

Answer: A
Diff: 2

38) Globalization and the increasing financial distance between the rich and the poor has resulted in the quartering of urban spaces into

A) compartmentalized residential enclaves.

B) CBDs, inner edge cities and outer edge cities.

C) suburbs, exurbs and boomburbs.

D) a loose coalition of urban realms (economic subregions).

E) Modern and Postmodern neighborhoods.

Answer: A
Diff: 2

39) Packaged landscapes are most strongly associated with

A) Postmodern urban design.   B) the Modern movement.

C) the Beaux Arts style.   D) the International Style.

Answer: A
Diff: 2

40) Gated communities exemplify the quartering of urban space into

    A) security zones.

    B) leisure zones

    C) ethnic enclaves.

    D) smart growth communities.

    E) edge communities.

Answer: A
Diff: 1

41) The central business district

    A) contains the zone in transition.

    B) is usually the headquarters for national government.

    C) typically has the tallest buildings.

    D) contains many factories but few shops or offices.

Answer: C
Diff: 1

42) The zone in transition

    A) contains apartment buildings, public housing and old neighborhoods.

    B) is outside the area of gentrification.

    C) is where railway terminals and the intersection of transportation networks are found.

    D) typically contains edge cities.

Answer: A
Diff: 2

43) Gentrification typically

    A) leads to the renovation of older buildings.

    B) raises property values.

    C) displaces original occupants.

    D) Gentrification is associated with all of the above.

Answer: D
Diff: 1

44) Which of the following is a specific advantage of congregation for a minority group?

    A) minimization of conflict with "outsiders"

    B) easy establishment of mutual support networks and institutions

    C) easier means of cultural preservation

    D) all of the above

    E) none of the above

Answer: D
Diff: 1

45) Jewish districts in the cities of the eastern United States are best considered

    A) colonies.

    B) enclaves.

    C) ghettos.

    D) neighborhoods.

    E) edge cities.

Answer: B
Diff: 1

46) The area of maximum accessibility in an idealized city located on an isotropic surface is

    A) the zone in transition.   B) an edge city.

    C) the CBD.   D) the upper–scale suburbs.

Answer: C
Diff: 2

47) According to our understanding of urban accessibility and land use, which of the following is located farthest from the city center?

    A) factories   B) warehouses

    C) high–volume retail stores   D) residences

Answer: D
Diff: 2

48) The cores of older European cities have complex street patterns because

    A) the streets were the product of slow growth.

    B) the patterns were developed before the introduction of automobiles and trucks.

    C) they reflected ancient patterns of ownership and boundary formation.

    D) of all of the above.

Answer: D
Diff: 2

49) Which of the following is generally NOT a characteristic of European cities?

    A) plazas and squares

    B) relatively low skylines

    C) lively downtowns

    D) rapid neighborhood change

    E) scars of war

Answer: D
Diff: 2

50) Which of the following was generally NOT a major influence on the shaping of European cities?

    A) Roman influence on town layout   B) careful long–range urban planning

    C) the presence of defensive walls   D) the value of land prices in the city

Answer: B
Diff: 3

51) Why do Western European cities typically have low skylines compared to American cities?

    A) The economy was not advanced enough to finance tall skyscrapers.

    B) Soviet planners preferred thick and massive buildings over tall ones.

    C) Much urban growth occurred before technology made skyscrapers possible.

    D) Buildings were poorly constructed and did not last long.

Answer: C
Diff: 2

52) In the larger cities of Britain, France, and Germany, roughly _____% of all housing is public housing.

    A) less than 1

    B) 1–5

    C) 5–20

    D) 20–40

    E) over 50

Answer: D
Diff: 2

53) _____ was one characteristic of socialist government policy in the cities of Eastern Europe.

    A) Large public housing projects in outlying districts

    B) Industrial zones in city centers

    C) Massive restructuring of city centers

    D) Destruction of all buildings closely related to capitalist activities

Answer: A
Diff: 2

54) Which of the following is NOT a common and important element of cities in the periphery?

    A) a zone of elite residential neighborhoods

    B) squatter zones or shantytowns

    C) a zone devoted to tourism

    D) a central zone with a concentration of commerce, industry, and retailing

    E) All of these are common and important elements of peripheral cities.

Answer: C
Diff: 2

55) It is least likely you would find an Islamic city in this region:

    A) North Africa

    B) southern Africa

    C) the Middle East

    D) South-central Asia

    E) Indonesia

Answer: B
Diff: 2

56) The values that shape the layout and design of Islamic cities derive from

    A) Greek culture.

    B) Roman culture.

    C) the Qur'an.

    D) the various peoples conquered by Muslims in the eighth and ninth centuries.

    E) Islamic fundamentalists.

Answer: C
Diff: 1

57) The dominant feature of a traditional Islamic city is

A) the sultan's palace.

B) the principal mosque, the *Jami*.

C) the main marketplace, the *suq*.

D) the Kasbah.

E) the cemetery.

Answer: B
Diff: 2

58) The traditional Islamic city typically contains all of the following *except*

A) a citadel.

B) *suqs*.

C) *cul-de-sacs*.

D) multiple *jamis*.

E) a monastery.

Answer: E
Diff: 3

59) Deliberate urban design began as early as

A) the height of the Roman Empire.   B) the early medieval period.

C) the Renaissance.   D) the Baroque period.

Answer: A
Diff: 1

60) The Beaux Arts style of urban design

A) flourished in the eighteenth century.

B) fell out of favor during the rule of Napoleon III.

C) synthesized earlier styles to fit the Industrial Age.

D) had its greatest influence in America.

E) emerged in London from the ideas of Baron Haussmann.

Answer: C
Diff: 2

61) The Modern movement

    A) was inspired by the ideals of nineteenth-century Romanticism.

    B) stressed an unadorned, functional type of architecture.

    C) opposed high-rise buildings.

    D) paved the way for the Beaux Arts style.

Answer: B
Diff: 2

62) The International style drew primarily from the _____ tradition of urban design.

    A) Modern

    B) Beaux Arts

    C) City Beautiful

    D) Postmodern

    E) Greek

Answer: A
Diff: 2

63) Postmodern urban design

    A) is a slight refinement of Modern urban design.

    B) has yet to have significant influence.

    C) stresses diversity in architectural styles and elements.

    D) tends towards unobtrusive structures painted in mute colors.

Answer: C
Diff: 2

64) Urban change in core regions has been influenced the most by

    A) higher levels of education.

    B) Postmodern architectural styles.

    C) the economic transformation to a postindustrial economy.

    D) increased racial tensions.

    E) higher levels of spending on urban renewal by national governments.

Answer: C
Diff: 3

65) The inability of central city areas to generate sufficient tax revenue is due to all of the following *except*

A) decentralization of cities.

B) loss of residential taxpayers.

C) increased demands for social services.

D) increased demands for infrastructure repairs.

E) inadequate collection mechanisms.

Answer: E
Diff: 1

66) Maintenance and repair on housing in poor, inner–city neighborhoods is inadequate because

A) renters cannot afford to do it.

B) landlords have no incentive to do it.

C) government officials choose not to do it, or are unable to do it.

D) of all of the above.

Answer: D
Diff: 1

67) The cycle of poverty

A) is of little consequence in core countries.

B) results in the middle class dropping down into poverty.

C) transmits poverty from one generation to the next.

D) occurs primarily in rural areas of peripheral countries.

E) is found only in the periphery.

Answer: C
Diff: 2

68) _____ is a characteristic of the cycle of poverty?

A) School absenteeism

B) Improper nutrition

C) Psychological stress from crowding

D) Unemployment

E) All of these above are found in the cycle of poverty.

Answer: E
Diff: 1

69) Redlining

   A) targets the underclass.

   B) is legal.

   C) gives government-subsidized loans to low-income families.

   D) helps break the cycle of poverty.

   E) promotes geographic literacy.

Answer: A
Diff: 2

70) In most peripheral cities, it is true that, of the people who would like full-time work,

   A) nearly all have it.

   B) a majority have it.

   C) the majority is either unemployed or underemployed.

   D) none really want it.

Answer: C
Diff: 1

71) Slum eradication

   A) is most commonly tried in core countries.

   B) usually results in the quick construction of another slum in another part of the city.

   C) was banned by the South Korean government in the early 1980s.

   D) could affect up to 1 billion people world-wide if it were applied to all slums.

Answer: B
Diff: 2

72) In some instances squatter settlements in peripheral cities can be considered "slums of hope" because

   A) governments sometimes provide help to squatters.

   B) settlements provide affordable shelter for the poor.

   C) settlements provide a supportive environment for newly arrived migrants.

   D) all of the above

Answer: D
Diff: 1

73) According to the World Bank, approximately what percentage of urban residents in peripheral cities have access to a satisfactory water source?

A) 95 percent

B) 65 percent

C) 35 percent

D) 15 percent

E) 0 percent

Answer: B
Diff: 2

74) Typically, city governments in peripheral countries are

A) quite powerful compared with the national government.

B) rife with corruption.

C) as efficient as their core counterparts.

D) well financed.

Answer: B
Diff: 2

75) Which of the following is a typical responsibility of urban governments in peripheral countries?

A) protection of the environment

B) protection of public health

C) management of public transportation

D) all of the above

E) none of the above

Answer: D
Diff: 1

76) The typical African–American neighborhood in an American city can best be termed a(n)

A) ghetto.   B) enclave.   C) congregation.   D) colony.

Answer: A
Diff: 2

11.3 True or False

1) Generally, as the accessibility of a location increases, its utility decreases.

Answer: FALSE
Diff: 2

2) In an idealized city, the center is the point of maximum utility where bid–rents are highest.

Answer: TRUE
Diff: 2

3) As one travels outward from the center in a concentric zone model of the the city, accessibility, utility and bid–rents decrease.

Answer: TRUE
Diff: 2

4) The territorial and residential clustering of Arabs in Dearborn, MI (metropolitan Detroit) is an example of congregation.

Answer: TRUE
Diff: 3

5) Enclaves, ghettos and colonies are spatial forms of segregation.

Answer: TRUE
Diff: 2

6) Segregation is involuntary congregation.

Answer: TRUE
Diff: 2

7) In the last 2–3 decades of the twentieth century, gentrification reversed the traditional direction of invasion and succession.

Answer: TRUE
Diff: 3

8) Gentrification has helped long–term residents of centrally–located working class neighborhoods save and renew their neighborhoods.

Answer: FALSE
Diff: 2

9) In contrast to cities of the world's periphery, U.S. cities have been able to maintain spending and repairs on infrastructures, making them the world's best functioning cities.

Answer: FALSE
Diff: 3

10) Globalization and economic restructuring have helped break the cycle of poverty and reduce homelessness in U.S. cities.

Answer: FALSE
Diff: 2

11) In contrast to Baron George Haussman, Le Corbusier had no intention of making his buildings and architecture blend into the preexisting urban landscape.

Answer: TRUE
Diff: 2

12) Islamic cities can be found throughout the Islamic world, not just on the Arabian Peninsula.

Answer: TRUE
Diff: 2

13) Because of their high population densities and compact structure, it is difficult to maintain any sense of personal privacy in Islamic cities.

Answer: FALSE
Diff: 2

14) Informal sector employment, housing and transportation is, increasingly, acknowledged to be a rational response to poverty.

Answer: TRUE
Diff: 2

15) Shanty and squatter neighborhoods can be viewed as "slums of hope" for the opportunities, support and community they provide new immigrants.

Answer: TRUE
Diff: 2

16) Edge cities are a peculiarly North American phenomena.

Answer: FALSE
Diff: 2

17) One positive side to urban sprawl is that suburban and exurban development has become less generic, and is resulting in more creative, unique and individual landscapes.

Answer: FALSE
Diff: 2

18) Gated communities are unique to North America.

Answer: FALSE
Diff: 1

19) Zoomers are early retiring baby boomers.

Answer: TRUE
Diff: 1

20) Edge cities are typically situated near major highway intersections.

Answer: TRUE
Diff: 1

21) Segregation can occur through congregation, discrimination, or both.

Answer: TRUE
Diff: 2

22) The corridors–and–sectors model is best used in urban areas that have seen large numbers of migrants for many decades.

Answer: FALSE
Diff: 2

23) The shape of most European cities is almost entirely due to building and planning activity in the twentieth century.

Answer: FALSE
Diff: 2

24) Compared to their American counterparts, European neighborhoods are more stable in terms of how long people tend to live there.

Answer: TRUE
Diff: 2

25) The shape and nature of an urban landscape reflect the values and intentions of the people associated with it.

Answer: TRUE
Diff: 2

26) When geographers speak of the Islamic city, they refer to the few cities left in the world that still reflect the important principles of historical Islamic urban development.

Answer: FALSE
Diff: 2

27) The residential areas of traditional Islamic cities were designed to minimize the likelihood that a woman would be seen by strangers.

Answer: TRUE
Diff: 2

28) The most serious problems faced by postindustrial cities are usually found in the central city areas.

Answer: TRUE
Diff: 2

29) The infrastructure in most large American cities is currently in good shape, but will need major repairs or replacement in about 25 to 50 years.

Answer: FALSE
Diff: 1

30) In core countries the vast majority of the homeless are white, adult males.

Answer: FALSE
Diff: 1

31) In peripheral cities, the informal sector often makes a significant con tribution to the formal sector.

Answer: TRUE
Diff: 2

32) Throughout much of the periphery, less than 5% of the sewage is treated before it is released into the environment.

Answer: TRUE
Diff: 2

33) "Colonies" as a form of urban structure are found only in Europe and North America.

Answer: FALSE
Diff: 1

34) An isotropic surface has the same topography everywhere.

Answer: TRUE
Diff: 2

35) Most European cities are densely populated.

Answer: TRUE
Diff: 1

36) Most European cities have downtowns that are losing their economic vitality.

Answer: FALSE
Diff: 1

37) Islamic cities have no underlying urban forms that unify them.

Answer: FALSE
Diff: 2

38) You would expect to find narrow, twisting streets in a *medina*.

Answer: TRUE
Diff: 2

39) Neighborhood decay has been increasing in American cities since the 1960s.

Answer: TRUE
Diff: 1

40) Substandard educational facilities are usually an important factor in the cycle of neighborhood poverty.

Answer: TRUE
Diff: 1

41) Most members of the underclass quickly rise in economic status.

Answer: FALSE
Diff: 1

42) Homelessness in core cities rose significantly in the mid–1970s.

Answer: TRUE
Diff: 1

43) In peripheral countries, unemployment is usually higher in urban areas than in rural areas.

Answer: TRUE
Diff: 1

11.4 Matching

WORLD CITIES: Match the characteristics to the region in which it is most likely to be found.

1) boomburbs and generica
   Diff: 3

2) covered bazaars, street
   markets, citadel and central
   mosque
   Diff: 3

3) low skylines, lively
   downtowns, stable
   neighborhoods & municipal
   socialism
   Diff: 3

4) CBDs, concentric zones, zones
   of transition, and the fiscal
   squeeze
   Diff: 3

5) huge public housing estates
   and government built
   industrial zones in outlying
   areas
   Diff: 3

6) very high rates of growth due
   to push factors in the
   countryside
   Diff: 3

7) large informal sectors and
   high underemployment
   Diff: 3

A) North American cities

B) peripheral cities

C) East–Central European city

D) Islamic city

E) U.S. city

F) Western European city

1) E   2) D   3) F   4) A   5) C   6) B
7) B

11.5 Map Identification

World Map

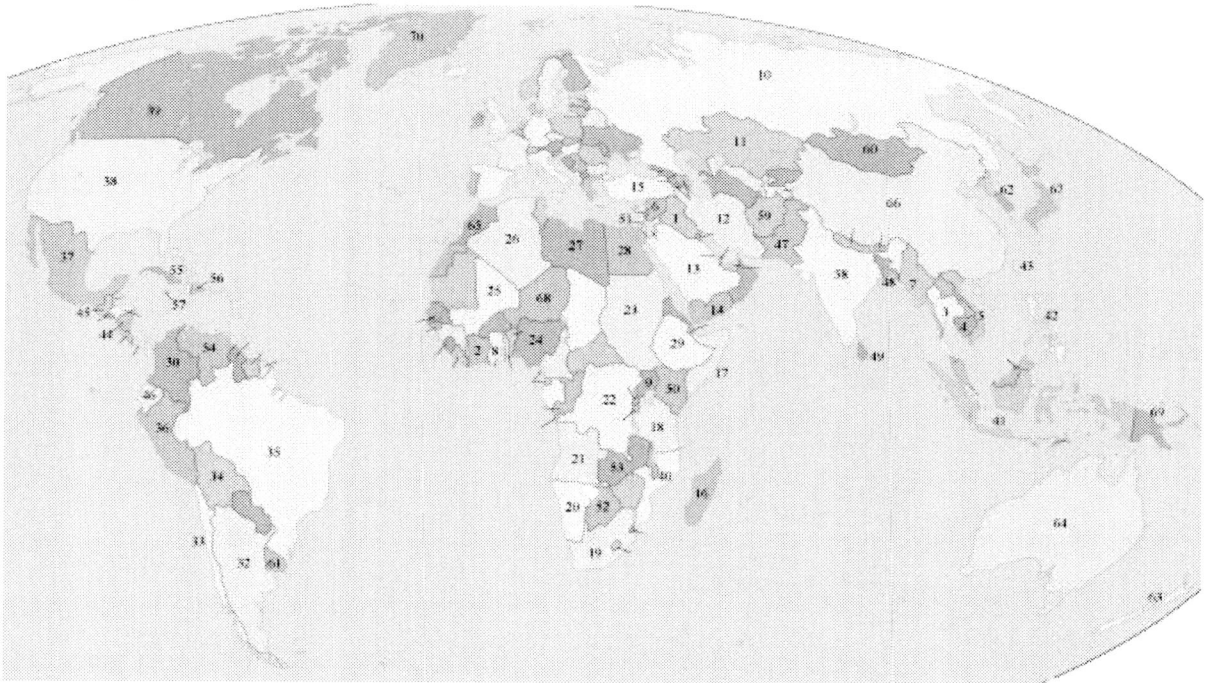

1) Which of the following is the European country?

    A) Libya

    B) Morocco

    C) Ecuador

    D) Kazakhstan

    E) Croatia

Answer: E
Diff: 2

2) Which of the following is landlocked (does not have a sea coast)?

    A) Libya

    B) Croatia

    C) Ecuador

    D) Kazakhstan

    E) Morocco

Answer: D
Diff: 2

3) Ecuador is identified by the number

    A) 30.   B) 36.   C) 46.   D) 54.   E) 61

    Answer: A
    Diff: 1

4) Bogota is the capital of

    A) Croatia.

    B) Ecuador.

    C) Hungary.

    D) Kazakhstan.

    E) Morocco.

    Answer: B
    Diff: 1

5) The capital of country #11 is

    A) Astana (Aqmola).

    B) Tashkent.

    C) Ankara.

    D) Ashgabat.

    E) Budapest.

    Answer: A
    Diff: 1

6) Tripoli is the capital of

    A) 11.   B) 27.   C) 48.   D) 58.   E) 65.

    Answer: B
    Diff: 1

7) The capital of country #65 is

    A) Budapest.

    B) Casablanca.

    C) Rabat.

    D) Quito.

    E) Zagreb.

    Answer: C
    Diff: 1

8) Morocco and Libya have which of the following in common? They both

A) border the Indian Ocean.

B) are in North Africa.

C) border Mexico.

D) sit south of the Equator.

E) belong to the European Union.

Answer: B
Diff: 2

9) Which pair of countries share a border?

A) Ecuador & Colombia

B) Kazakhstan & Morocco

C) Libya & Morocco

D) Hungary & Kazakhstan

E) Ecuador & Croatia

Answer: A
Diff: 2

Europe

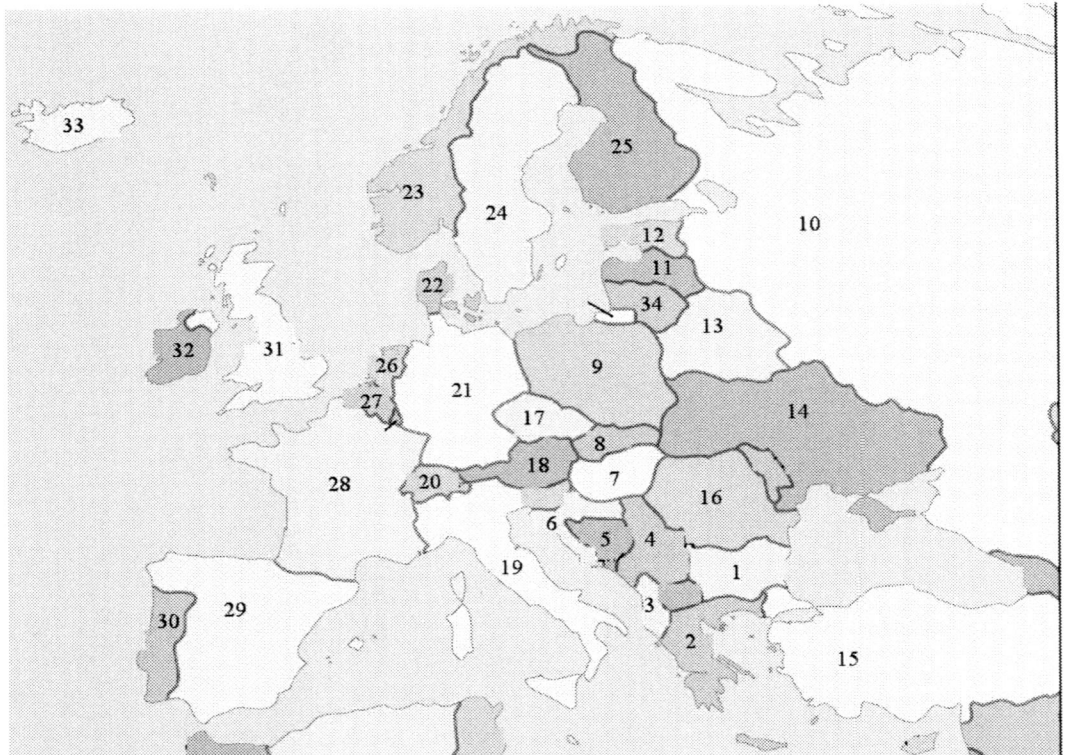

10) Zagreb is the capital of the country labeled by number

    A) 2.   B) 3.   C) 4.   D) 5.   E) 6.

    Answer: E
    Diff: 1

11) Hungary is labeled with number

    A) 7.   B) 8.   C) 13.   D) 17.   E) 18.

    Answer: B
    Diff: 1

12) The capital of country #7 is

    A) Bratislava.

    B) Prague.

    C) Budapest.

    D) Zagreb.

    E) Bucharest.

    Answer: C
    Diff: 1

Chapter 12 Future Geographies

12.1 Minimal Choice

1) The "short twentieth century" can be defined largely in terms of the beginning and end of

    A) the Cold War.   B) U.S. hegemony.

    Answer: A
    Diff: 1

2) Geo-economics in the "short twentieth century" was based on a

    A) North–South divide.   B) East–West divide.

    Answer: A
    Diff: 2

3) Which of the following dimensions of human geography are most uncertain looking into the future, most likely to bear the most surprises?

    A) politics and technology

    B) demography, environmental resources & regional economies

    Answer: A
    Diff: 1

4) According to Knox and Marston, peripheral and semi–peripheral countries will consume over half the world's _____ by the year 2020.

    A) energy   B) water

    Answer: A
    Diff: 1

5) In the future, we are likely to hear more and more about impacts to human geography from TEN, QSAT, ICE and ITS -- these refer to advances in _____ technologies

    A) transporation   B) information

    Answer: A
    Diff: 3

6) In 2005, with current telecommunications, about 8 % of the core workforce was "distributed." By 2020, as many as 20% may be

    A) working at home.   B) outsourced overseas.

    Answer: A
    Diff: 2

7) With the stratification of the world economy through contemporary globalization, the elite people and places in peripheral countries have more in common with

    A) elite people and places in the core.

    B) the poorer people and places in their own country.

Answer: A
Diff: 2

8) With recent globalization, the economic disparity between the core and periphery continues to

    A) grow.   B) shrink.

Answer: A
Diff: 1

9) China's competitive advantage in the world economy is in wages kept low by its

    A) huge labor force.   B) "open door" policy.

Answer: A
Diff: 2

10) According to Knox and Marston, the main challenger to U.S. hegemony is

    A) the European Union.   B) India.

Answer: A
Diff: 1

11) After the European Union, the United States and Japan, _____ has the world's 4th largest economy.

    A) China   B) Australia

Answer: A
Diff: 1

12) Nigeria's Sani Abacha, DRC's Mobut Sese Seko, Haiti's Jean–Claude Duvalier and Peru's Alberto Fujimori are notable for having recently

    A) established kleptocracies.

    B) won Nobel prizes in peace, literature, chemistry and economics, respectively.

Answer: A
Diff: 1

13) Regarding information technologies, General Electric's biggest research facility outside the United States is in

    A) India.   B) Europe.

Answer: A
Diff: 2

12.2 Multiple Choice

1) For human geographers, the greatest areas of future uncertainty and surprise are in

A) politics.

B) politics and technology.

C) demography & technology.

D) natural resources.

E) technology and natural resources.

Answer: B
Diff: 2

2) The "short century" in which the contemporary, modern world was developed refers to

A) the period between World War I and World War II.

B) the period between World War I and the fall of the Soviet Union.

C) the era of the United Nations, World Bank and the European Union.

D) the period since the end of the Cold War.

E) the 1990s and the emergence of the Internet and cyberspace.

Answer: B
Diff: 1

3) Optimist futurists maintain a vision of the future in which

A) technological innovation will solve the world's problems.

B) a return to traditional cultures (including family values and agricultural practices) will overcome violence and poverty.

C) poverty, population pressures and environmental degradation will be limited to the periphery.

D) what happens in this world doesn't matter because of belief in an afterlife.

E) the Detroit Tigers will again win the World Series.

Answer: A
Diff: 1

4) Hyperglobalists, skeptics and transformationalists are participants in debates over

A) globalization.

B) democracy.

C) migration.

D) free trade.

E) population control.

Answer: A
Diff: 2

5) The argument that the world was more interconnected and globalized 100 years ago than today is supported largely by statistics documenting

A) the flow of capital among the core countries.

B) the flow of information between the core countries.

C) the speed and frequency of transportation between the core countries.

D) tourist exchanges between the core and periphery.

E) the flow of ideas between the core and periphery.

Answer: A
Diff: 2

6) Kleptocries refer to corrupt

A) dictatorships that steal national wealth.

B) politicians that steal votes.

C) companies that steal ideas and intellectual property.

D) populations that steal from their governments.

E) companies that violate copywrite laws.

Answer: A
Diff: 1

7) Despite independence, marginalized countries must to compete in the world economy with increasing amounts of all of the following *except*

A) foreign investment.

B) external debt.

C) people.

D) poor health.

E) civil strife.

Answer: A
Diff: 2

8) According to your text, the main resource issue in the near future will revolve around

   A) raw materials.

   B) energy.

   C) food.

   D) labor.

   E) water.

   Answer: B
   Diff: 1

9) According to numerous national and international agencies, the most critical areas for future economic development include all of the following *except*

   A) military technology.   B) biotechnology.

   C) materials technology.   D) information technology.

   Answer: A
   Diff: 1

10) Emerging technologies show the least promise for future innovations in transportation

   A) on land.   B) at sea.   C) in the air.   D) in space.

   Answer: B
   Diff: 1

11) As presented in our text, potential, anticipated long–term benefits of biotechnology include all of the following except

   A) increased natural biodiversity.

   B) reduced toxics in the environment.

   C) increased food production in the periphery.

   D) increased water quality.

   E) reduced infrastructural requirements.

   Answer: A
   Diff: 1

12) In 2000, almost the entire area planted in genetically engineered crops worldwide were in

    A) North and South America.

    B) the European Union.

    C) Scandinavia and New Zealand.

    D) Africa.

    E) China and India.

Answer: A
Diff: 1

13) The hope for budding innovations in materials technology is that they

    A) replace scarce natural resources.

    B) provide new opportunities for the economies of the world's periphery.

    C) lead to a whole new wave of environmental problems.

    D) increase energy demands world-wide.

    E) replace biotechnology as a potential solution for regional food shortages.

Answer: A
Diff: 1

14) Colletta di Castelbianco in Italy, Arabianranta in Finland and Blacksburg, Virginia are all examples of

    A) super connected cybervillages.

    B) super technological new materials villages.

    C) biotechnological villages.

    D) commuterless, new transportation technology suburbs.

    E) super biotech communities in which all restaurant food has been genetically engineered.

Answer: A
Diff: 2

15) With the post-Cold War homogenization of culture, new cultural fault lines are emerging as

    A) people attempt to reestablish distinctive cultural identities.

    B) governments impose new cultural requirements on their populations.

    C) transnational corporations search for new markets for their products.

    D) the gap between the core and the periphery widens.

    E) sports becomes the new arena for international conflict.

Answer: A
Diff: 2

16) The biggest obstacles impeding regional integration lie in the desire of countries to remain culturally distinct and

    A) reluctance to give up control over their own affairs.

    B) from fundamental differences in language and religion.

    C) in the competition over the same export markets.

    D) a general unwillingness to resolve differences diplomatically.

    E) the difficulties in bridging the North–South divide.

Answer: A
Diff: 2

17) The Asian Brown Cloud affecting temperature, rainfall and, ultimately, agricultural productivity, is the result of

    A) burning wood and fossil fuels.

    B) dust storms combined with volcanic ash.

    C) a rise in nuclear power generation and use.

    D) pollution blown eastward from Europe.

    E) unexplained natural causes.

Answer: A
Diff: 1

18) Geography is particularly relevant to the ideal of sustainable development because

    A) of its emphases on scale, place and nature–society relationships.

    B) it is on the cutting edge of space.

    C) maps are the solution to all problems.

    D) geographers have long participated in the highest levels of global decisionmaking.

    E) geography is the only social science interested in what is happening worldwide.

Answer: A
Diff: 2

19) According to Knox and Marston, _____ earn the least from illegal trafficking around the globe.

    A) weapons   B) drugs

    C) trafficked humans   D) environmental products

Answer: A
Diff: 2

20) According to some, the USA is slipping toward a "Dark Age" due to the

    A) deterioration of the stabilizing forces of society.

    B) steady rise in terrorism.

    C) environmental degradation.

    D) the rise of Chinese and Indian economic power.

    E) the impending shortage of petroleum.

Answer: A
Diff: 2

21) Optimistic futurists ultimately rest their hopes on

    A) the spiritual advancement of humankind.

    B) technological advances.

    C) the United Nations.

    D) help from benevolent extraterrestrials.

    E) the spread of democracy.

Answer: B
Diff: 2

22) Pessimistic futurists feel that

    A) the environment is very resilient.

    B) there will be a strengthening of law and order on a global scale.

    C) social class will become relatively unimportant.

    D) gourmet dinners will no longer be served.

    E) there will be an increased polarization between haves and have–nots.

Answer: E
Diff: 1

23) About which of the following do we know the least regarding its future trends?

    A) distribution of environmental resources

    B) changes in technology

    C) characteristics of regional economies

    D) demographic characteristics

24) United Nations and World Bank projections for the future of the world economy are based on

   A) macroeconomic variables.

   B) economic growth in the 1940s and 1950s.

   C) microeconomic variables.

   D) hunches of the World Bank's president.

Answer: A
Diff: 2

25) The United Nations predicts that in the future the gap between the world's rich and poor will

   A) alternate unpredictably.   B) widen.

   C) stay about the same.   D) narrow.

Answer: B
Diff: 1

26) This region is forecast to have a decline in GDP per capita through the year 2010:

   A) sub–Saharan Africa

   B) Latin America

   C) South Asia

   D) China

   E) East Asia

Answer: A
Diff: 2

27) In the same way that the twentieth century was called the American Century, some are beginning to forecast the twenty–first century as the _____ Century.

   A) Latino   B) Asian   C) European   D) Asian   E) Islamic

Answer: D
Diff: 2

28) Of the following regions, which has exploited the greatest percentage of its raw materials?

   A) Africa   B) Europe   C) Eurasia   D) East Asia

Answer: B
Diff: 3

29) According to our text, which is the leading contender to be the world leader in the coming years?

   A) the United States

   B) European Union

   C) China

   D) India

   E) ASEAN

Answer: B
Diff: 1

30) The European Union has a greater _____ than the United States.

   A) GDP   B) sense of community

   C) population   D) all of the above

Answer: A
Diff: 2

31) The United States has the second largest _____ in the world after the European Union.

   A) GDP

   B) purchasing power

   C) population

   D) growth in demand for oil by 2020

   E) all of the above

Answer: A
Diff: 2

32) The U.S. government, the European Union, the United Nations and the OECD have argued that all of the following are critical for future economic development, *except*

   A) materials technology.   B) biotechnology.

   C) information technology.   D) alternative–energy technology.

Answer: D
Diff: 1

33) The region, state, or country with the most advanced scheme for high–speed trains is

A) California.

B) New York.

C) Japan.

D) Canada.

E) Europe.

Answer: E
Diff: 1

34) This mode of transport will see the smallest change from technology in the near future:

A) air travel   B) sea travel   C) car travel   D) train travel

Answer: B
Diff: 1

35) In 2004, 75% of the annual increase in world agricultural production was from

A) the core.

B) the world's periphery.

C) applications of biotechnology.

D) improvements in irrigation technologies.

E) the United States.

Answer: C
Diff: 2

36) Advances in materials technologies will

A) produce large amounts of waste.

B) increase the weight and size of most products.

C) lead to a cycle of creative destruction destructive to the world's periphery.

D) reduce the demand for traditional raw materials.

Answer: D
Diff: 2

37) Regarding information technologies, it appears that

    A) less than half the potential benefits have been realized.

    B) the necessary research and development occurs primarily in China.

    C) manufacturing and application occurs primarily in core countries.

    D) it will have little effect on the geographical divisions between the slow world and the fast world.

Answer: A
Diff: 2

38) Information technologies

    A) will increase the digital divide separating the world's core and periphery.

    B) have had the smallest impact on cities.

    C) have yet to reach the peripheral countries.

    D) have already brought nearly 90% of the world on-line.

    E) include both soft- and hardware.

Answer: A
Diff: 2

39) Globalization of the economy is affecting states by

    A) increasing their power in international organizations.

    B) leading to the demise of NAFTA and the European Union.

    C) increasing the flow of capital and information across their borders.

    D) creating more revenue for governments to spend on social welfare.

Answer: C
Diff: 3

40) Global consumer trends that transcend traditional national and cultural differences are most apparent among the world's

    A) upper class.   B) middle class.

    C) lower-middle class.   D) impoverished.

Answer: A
Diff: 2

41) The "short twentieth century"

 A) refers to the boom years of the 1990s.

 B) ended with the Bolshevik Revolution in Russia.

 C) refers to the glory years of the baby boom.

 D) ended with the end of the Cold War.

 E) was still longer than the "tedious fourteenth century."

Answer: D
Diff: 2

42) This country or region dominated the "short twentieth century":

 A) the United States

 B) the European Union

 C) Asia

 D) the Soviet Union

 E) Britain

Answer: A
Diff: 1

12.3 True or False

1) In the "short twentieth" century, geoeconomics was based on the North–South divide and geopolitics on the East–West divide.

Answer: TRUE
Diff: 2

2) According to our text, pessimistic futurists believe that world stabilization and homogenization will be achieved through supranational or "world" governments.

Answer: FALSE
Diff: 1

3) Economic forecasting can now predict 25 years into the future with a high degree of reliability.

Answer: FALSE
Diff: 1

4) Hope for the future of the world economy lies in the fact that, since the 1970s, the gap between the GDPs/capita of the core and periphery has decreased.

Answer: FALSE
Diff: 1

5) The most marginalized countries of the world are found in Central America, on the doorstep of the United States.

Answer: FALSE
Diff: 1

6) As with the marginalized countries of the world, socioeconomic prospects for the world's core regions are dismal.

Answer: FALSE
Diff: 1

7) The elite regions and social groups within a country have more in common with the elite of other countries than with the embattled and marginalized in their own country.

Answer: TRUE
Diff: 1

8) The fundamental problem behind the global inequitable distribution of wealth is that there is, simply, not sufficient wealth to provide for the basic needs of the world's people.

Answer: FALSE
Diff: 3

9) According to our text, the emerging transportation technologies currently under design are being developed to assist people of the periphery.

Answer: FALSE
Diff: 2

10) Economically, producers and exporters of traditional raw materials will be big losers as innovations in materials technology evolve.

Answer: TRUE
Diff: 1

11) With the Information Revolution and ongoing advances in information technologies, it is expected that the divide between the Fast and Slow Worlds will narrow.

Answer: FALSE
Diff: 2

12) Global metropolitanism is a form of cultural homogenization among the affluent.

Answer: TRUE
Diff: 2

13) To predict future geographies it is necessary to have a solid understanding of past geographies.

Answer: TRUE
Diff: 2

14) It's easier to predict the future of technology than the future of demographic trends.

Answer: FALSE
Diff: 2

15) According to our text, future prospects for the world's periphery and marginalized peoples are extremely bleak.

Answer: TRUE
Diff: 1

16) Income inequality in the United States is similar to that found in Russia, China, Bolivia, and Senegal.

Answer: TRUE
Diff: 1

17) The goal of Intelligent Transportation Systems is fully automated transportation, where drivers do not actively drive.

Answer: TRUE
Diff: 1

18) Information technology employment is usually found in areas with highly localized agglomerations of information technology firms.

Answer: TRUE
Diff: 1

19) The end of the Cold War has increased geopolitical uncertainty.

Answer: TRUE
Diff: 2

20) In terms of political instability and domestic violence, globalization will probably have a more pronounced effect on peripheral countries than on core countries.

Answer: TRUE
Diff: 2

21) Cultural fault lines are becoming increasingly apparent and important as globalization progresses.

Answer: TRUE
Diff: 2

22) The fact that environmental problems often go beyond national borders makes these problems significant international issues.

Answer: TRUE
Diff: 1

23) China is gaining ground economically on the core countries.

Answer: TRUE
Diff: 2

24) The population of the EU is greater than that of the United States.

Answer: TRUE
Diff: 1

25) The hegemony of the United States is in relative decline.

Answer: TRUE
Diff: 1

26) Genetic engineering has had a significant impact on animal husbandry.

Answer: TRUE
Diff: 1

12.4 Matching

DEBATING THE FUTURE: Match the statement to the category of people most likely to have made it.

1) Technological innovation will solve the problems of the future.
Diff: 2

2) The technological fix for future global problems is "globaloney."
Diff: 2

3) The Earth's resources are finite and very susceptible to the the Malthusian spectre.
Diff: 2

4) The world will become borderless as economies transcend traditional state boundaries.
Diff: 2

5) National governments are essential to a world economy that is regionalizing around each of the world's three core regions.
Diff: 2

6) All this talk of globalization is overblown -- the world is actually less integrated than it once was.
Diff: 2

7) Current globalization -- though unprecedented -- is part of a long-term historical process of socioeconomic change.
Diff: 2

A) pessimistic futurists

B) the transformationalists

C) hyperglobalists

D) the skeptics

E) pessimistic futurists

F) optimistic futurists

1) F   2) E   3) A   4) C   5) D   6) D
7) B

12.5 Map Identification

World Map

1) Which of the following is not a sub–Saharan country?

   A) Botswana

   B) Bulgaria

   C) Zambia

   D) Mozambique

   E) Democratic Republic of the Congo

   Answer: B
   Diff: 2

2) Which of the following is the European country?

   A) Jamaica

   B) Botswana

   C) Mozambique

   D) Zambia

   E) Ukraine

   Answer: E
   Diff: 2

3) Which of the following is landlocked (does not have a sea coast)?

   A) Bulgaria

   B) Jamaica

   C) Mozambique

   D) Zambia

   E) United States

Answer: D
Diff: 2

4) Botswana is identified by the number

   A) 20.　　　B) 21.　　　C) 22.　　　D) 52.　　　E) 53

Answer: D
Diff: 1

5) Bogota is the capital of

   A) Croatia.

   B) Ecuador.

   C) Hungary.

   D) Kazakhstan.

   E) Morocco.

Answer: B
Diff: 1

6) The capital of country #52 is

   A) Lusaka.　　　B) Akmola.　　　C) Ankara.　　　D) Luanda.　　　E) Sofia.

Answer: A
Diff: 1

7) Kingston is the capital of

   A) 22.　　　B) 40.　　　C) 42.　　　D) 57.　　　E) 63.

Answer: D
Diff: 1

8) The capital of country #40 is

    A) Nairobi.

    B) Gaborone.

    C) Maputo.

    D) Bamako.

    E) Ottawa.

Answer: C
Diff: 1

9) Lusaka and Gaborone have which of the following in common? They both

    A) island country capitals.

    B) are in the Caribbean.

    C) have Atlantic Ocean ports.

    D) sit south of the Equator.

    E) belong to the European Union.

Answer: D
Diff: 2

10) Which pair of countries share a border?

    A) Zambia & Botswana

    B) Bulgaria & Ukraine

    C) Jamaica & Botswana

    D) Mozambique & Democratic Republic of the Congo

    E) Bulgaria & Zambia

Answer: A
Diff: 2

Europe

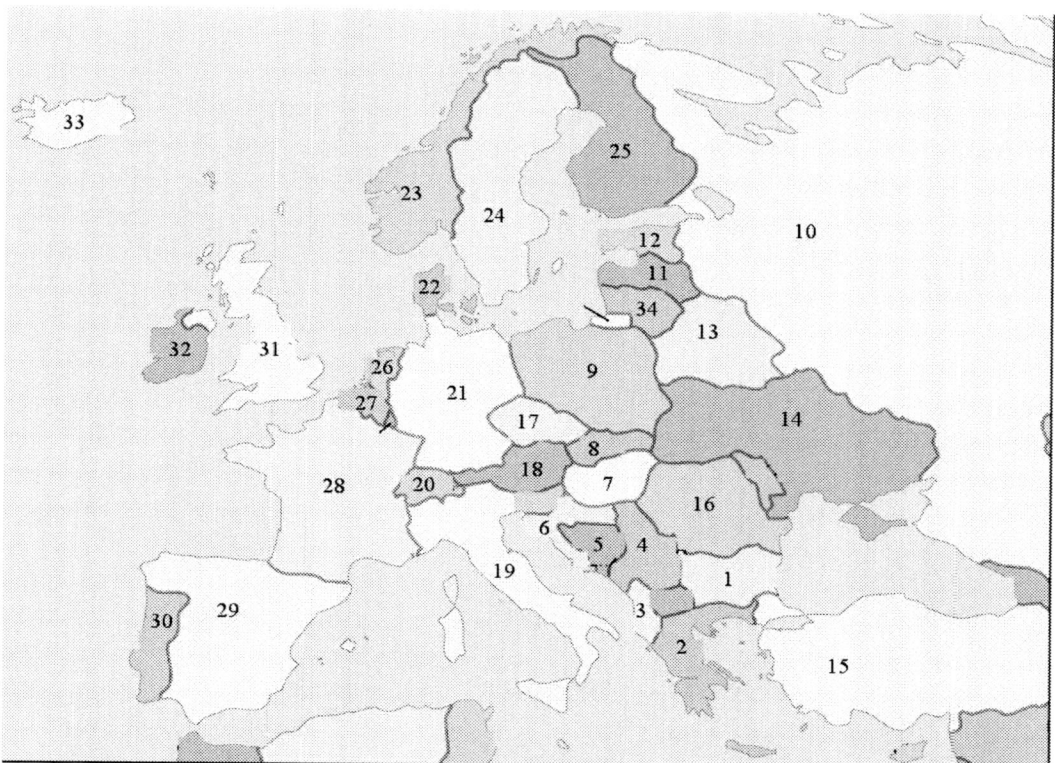

11) Kiev is the capital of the country labeled by number

    A) 16.   B) 14.   C) 12.   D) 8.   E) 6.

Answer: B
Diff: 1

12) Bulgaria is labeled with number

    A) 1.   B) 4.   C) 6.   D) 16.   E) 26.

Answer: A
Diff: 1

13) The capital of country #1 is

    A) Ankara.

    B) Kinshasa.

    C) Sofia.

    D) Lusaka.

    E) Bratislava.

Answer: C
Diff: 1

Chapter 13 Appendix

13.1 Minimal Choice

1) Eckert IV, Bartholomew's Nordic and Mollweide are all examples of

    A) equal area map projections.

    B) earth-orbiting satellites providing satellite imagery.

Answer: A
Diff: 1

2) In a cartogram, _____ is distorted for effect.

    A) area   B) location

Answer: A
Diff: 2

3) The critical factor for data to be meaningful for GIS is that

    A) its specific location in space can be identified.

    B) it can be seen in satellite images.

Answer: A
Diff: 1

4) Isopleth maps rely heavily on

    A) lines.   B) dots.

Answer: A
Diff: 3

5) Topographic maps are examples of

    A) isopleth maps.   B) choropleth maps.

Answer: A
Diff: 3

6) Small-scale maps cover a _____ portion of the Earth's surface on a page.

    A) large   B) small

Answer: A
Diff: 2

7) Representative fractions are _____ that indicate the ratio between linear distance on a map and actual distance on the Earth's surface.

　　A) map scales　　　　　　　　　　　　B) proportional charts

Answer: A
Diff: 2

13.2 Multiple Choice

1) Because of the difficulty of projecting a round, 3-dimensional earth on a 2-dimensional piece of paper, maps of the world typically vary according to

　　A) shapes of the land masses.

　　B) relative sizes of the land masses.

　　C) relative altitude of the land masses.

　　D) shapes and relative sizes of land masses.

　　E) shapes and relative altitudes of lan 1 masses.

Answer: D
Diff: 3

2) The Prime Meridian

　　A) is essentially a latitude line.

　　B) passes through Greenwich, England.

　　C) forms an angle of 0 degrees with earth's equator.

　　D) was established by the Greeks.

Answer: B
Diff: 1

3) The Prime Meridian

　　A) always crosses the equator at an angle of less than 90 degrees.

　　B) does not cross through any part of the United Kingdom.

　　C) is the main reference point for latitude determination.

　　D) runs through both poles.

Answer: D
Diff: 2

4) Contour lines

    A) cannot be used to make an isoline map.

    B) connect points of equal elevation.

    C) were common on maps made before the nineteenth century, but are rarely used now.

    D) are required to make sense of a three–dimensional map.

Answer: B
Diff: 1

5) Chloropleth maps represent data with

    A) tonal shadings.   B) dots.

    C) special symbols.   D) arrows of varying lengths.

Answer: A
Diff: 1

6) Which type of map projection is best for representing cultural, demographic, and economic data?

    A) Peters projection

    B) Robinson projection

    C) Mollweide projection

    D) Dymaxion projection

    E) Mercator projection

Answer: C
Diff: 2

7) The _____ map projection deliberately emphasizes the true areas of countries.

    A) Robinson

    B) Peters

    C) Dymaxion

    D) Mollweide

    E) Mercator

Answer: B
Diff: 2

8) The _____ map projection presents the true shapes of landmasses but distorts their relative sizes.

   A) Mercator

   B) Dymaxion

   C) Mollweide

   D) Robinson

   E) Peters

Answer: A
Diff: 2

13.3 True or False

1) Isoline maps connect data points that have equal value.

Answer: TRUE
Diff: 1

2) The most controversial of the various types of map projections discussed in the text is the Mercator projection.

Answer: FALSE
Diff: 3

3) The Dymaxion projection is based on triangles.

Answer: FALSE
Diff: 2

4) Latitude measures angular distance, while longitude measures linear distance.

Answer: FALSE
Diff: 2

5) Topographic maps contain isolines.

Answer: TRUE
Diff: 1

13.4 Matching

Latitude & longitude: Match the line to its correct name

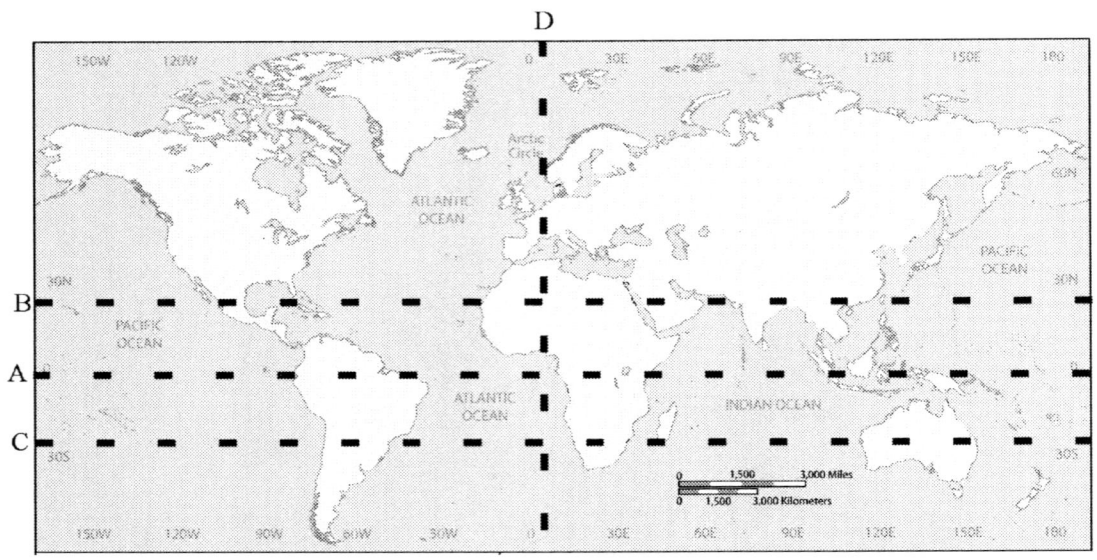

1) The prime meridian
   Diff: 2

2) the equator
   Diff: 2

3) a line of longitude
   Diff: 2

4) Tropic of Capricorn
   Diff: 2

5) Tropic of Cancer
   Diff: 2

A) A

B) B

C) C

D) D

1) D   2) A   3) D   4) C   5) B